Myths, Legends
& Sacred Stories

a visual encyclopedia

Myths, Legends
& Sacred Stories

a visual encyclopedia

Written by Philip Wilkinson

DK Delhi
Senior Editor Sreshtha Bhattacharya
Senior Art Editor Vikas Chauhan
Project Editor Neha Ruth Samuel
Project Art Editors Mansi Agrawal, Heena Sharma
Editors Kathakali Banerjee, Isha Sharma
Assistant Editors Upamanyu Das, Sai Prasanna
Assistant Art Editors Sanya Jain, Tanisha Mandal
Illustrators Surbhi Bahl, Mohd Zishan
Jacket Designer Suhita Dharamjit
Senior DTP Designer Neeraj Bhatia
DTP Designers Pawan Kumar, Vikram Singh
Pre-production Manager Balwant Singh
Production Manager Pankaj Sharma
Managing Editor Kingshuk Ghoshal
Managing Art Editor Govind Mittal

DK London
Senior Editor Pauline Savage
Senior Art Editor Louise Dick
US Editor Megan Douglass
US Executive Editor Lori Cates Hand
Picture Researcher Sarah Smithies
Jacket Design Development Manager Sophia MTT
Producer, Pre-production Robert Dunn
Producer Meskerem Berhane
Managing Editor Lisa Gillespie
Managing Art Editor Owen Peyton Jones
Publisher Andrew Macintyre
Associate Publishing Director Liz Wheeler
Art Director Karen Self
Publishing Director Jonathan Metcalf

First American Edition, 2019
Published in the United States by DK Publishing
1450 Broadway, Suite 801, New York, NY 10018

Copyright © 2019 Dorling Kindersley Limited
DK, a Division of Penguin Random House LLC
19 20 21 22 23 10 9 8 7 6 5 4 3 2 1
001–305059–November/2019

A catalog record for this book is available from the
Library of Congress.
ISBN 978-1-4654-8245-7
ISBN (PLC) 978-1-4654-8629-5

DK books are available at special discounts
when purchased in bulk for sales promotions,
premiums, fund-raising, or educational use. For
details, contact: DK Publishing Special Markets,
1450 Broadway, Suite 801, New York, NY 10018
SpecialSales@dk.com

Printed and bound in China

A WORLD OF IDEAS:
SEE ALL THERE IS TO KNOW

www.dk.com

Contents

ASIA 106

AFRICA 168

THE AMERICAS 194

OCEANIA 216

About this book

From as far back as we know, people have told each other stories. Tales featuring gods and goddesses, heroes and heroines, and magical beings are known as myths. Stories about events that may have happened, or people who may have existed, are often referred to as legends. Some stories deal with the cultural and religious identities of people, and these are considered sacred. All these tales, no matter how fantastical, reflect truths about human existence: they can tell us what life was like for people long ago and what their beliefs are today.

STORIES AROUND THE WORLD

Nearly every civilization, past and present, has a collection of stories. They were originally passed down by word of mouth, whether told while sitting around a fire or by lively songs and dances—in some parts of the world, this is still the case today. Many stories are known to us through ancient written artifacts such as clay tablets and papyrus manuscripts. No matter how they are related, all tales evolve over time, which explains why details vary and deities can have different names.

An ancient manuscript written in Maya picture-writing

THE PURPOSE OF STORIES

Myths and sacred stories have helped people explore difficult questions about their existence: "How was the world formed? Where did humans come from? What happens to us when we die?" They also gave meaning to natural events, such as earthquakes or storms.

The Hindu god Brahma creating the universe after emerging from the god Vishnu on a lotus leaf

6

The fire-breathing monster called the Chimaera from Ancient Greece

A MAGICAL REALM

The world of myths is very different from our own. There are magical beings and supernatural creatures, and events are not always explained logically. At the same time, this world can be very similar to ours, with characters who face the same emotions as we do—love, sadness, or jealousy—and show qualities such as bravery or frustration. This is what makes mythology so fascinating—it is sometimes familiar, sometimes strange.

COMMON THEMES

Myths and sacred stories from one part of the world vary greatly from those of another. However, they do tell similar types of tales, such as the creation of the world, the land of the dead, the origins of traditions, and the struggle between good and evil. Most feature a great many gods, who rule different aspects of life such as the weather or love, as well as characters including tricksters and shape-shifters.

A painted stone depicting worship of the sun god Ra, the supreme deity in Egyptian mythology

AN INSPIRING WORLD

Over the years, myths have inspired great books (*Ulysses* by James Joyce), pieces of music (*The Ring of the Nibelung* by Richard Wagner), and paintings (*Prometheus Bound* by Peter Paul Rubens). Even today, films and computer games continue to draw from the endlessly varied and vibrant world of myths.

An Australian Aboriginal bark painting depicting Lumaluma and the sacred power of Mardayin

EUROPE

From the gods and goddesses of Ancient Greece to the tricksters and monsters of Scandinavia, tales from Europe feature characters who can be unpredictable—sometimes violent, sometimes caring. Though no longer part of active beliefs, the myths describe worlds in which deities have a direct impact on human life, changing the course of everything from love to war.

On this Greek vase, Greek and Trojan soldiers fight over the dead body of the Greek warrior Patroclus. The hero's death was a turning point in the Trojan War, spurring Achilles's return to the fight.

The creation of the universe

The Ancient Greeks had several stories to explain the origins of the universe and of the gods and goddesses. The most well-known myth features two powerful creators, Gaia and Uranus, who make the world and give rise to the first beings.

The Romans adopted most of the deities of Ancient Greece, and gave them different names.

◄ MOTHER EARTH
*The Roman equivalent of the Greek goddess Gaia was Mother Earth (*Terra Mata *in Latin). She is shown here with a child, fruits, and flowers, all of which symbolize her creativity and fertility.*

In the beginning, there was nothing but a vast, dark void called Chaos. Out of this nothingness emerged two creative forces: Gaia, the earth, and Uranus, the sky. When these two forces met, Uranus let rain fall over Gaia's surface. As the water flowed across the land, it formed the great river Okeanos (see p.12), which completely surrounded the earth. Gaia and Uranus then created the hills and mountains.

THE FIRST CREATURES

When the world's natural features were fully formed, Gaia gave birth to many children, the ancestors of the beings that would come to live on Earth. Some of these were the three Cyclopes and the three Hundred-Handed Giants. The Cyclopes were gigantic, one-eyed creatures of enormous strength. They were skilled in the crafts, and forged thunderbolts that sometimes shook the world. Equally terrifying were the Hundred-Handed Giants, which each had one hundred arms and fifty heads.

Uranus felt threatened by the strength and skill of the Cyclopes and the Hundred-Handed Giants and feared an attack by them, so he trapped the creatures in the Underworld (see p.26).

Out of the void emerged **two creative forces: Gaia**, the earth, and **Uranus**, the sky.

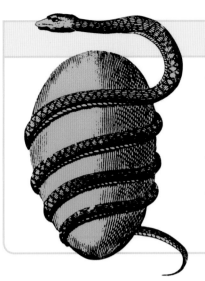

THE PRIMAL EGG

An alternative version of the Greek creation story features a goddess named Eurynome, who took the form of a dove and laid a great egg. A serpent called Ophion wrapped himself around the egg to warm it. When the egg hatched, out came Uranus, Gaia, the mountains and rivers of the earth, the planets, the stars, and everything else that exists.

With the **death of Uranus**, Kronos became **king of the Titans** and the **ruler of the universe**.

Gaia then gave birth to more children, the Titans. These were a group of powerful, supernatural giants who were the very first Greek deities. There were 12 of them: six male Titans—Oceanus (see p.12), Hyperion, Iapetus, Coeus, Crius, and Kronos (see p.12)—and six female Titanesses—Rhea (see p.12), Phoebe, Tethys (see p.12), Theia, Themis (see p.12), and Mnemosyne. The youngest Titan, Kronos, was their leader. Another important Titan was Kronos's brother, Iapetus, whose descendants were the very first humans. The Titanesses gave birth to the next generation of gods and goddesses, with Rhea producing five of the deities who came to be known as the Olympians (see pp.16–17).

THE RULE OF KRONOS

Gaia was upset about the imprisonment of the Cyclopes and the Hundred-Handed Giants, so she persuaded her son Kronos to kill Uranus and to take over his role as the supreme ruler of the universe. Gaia carved a sickle for Kronos to use to kill his father. The Titan then asked his brothers to help him in this task. Hyperion,

▲ **HUNDRED-HANDED GIANTS**
These giants were banished by Uranus to a region of the Underworld called Tartarus (see p.26). There they guarded the souls of those sent to Tartarus after death.

Iapetus, Crius, and Coeus agreed, but Kronos did not manage to convince Oceanus to help.

The four Titans held the powerful Uranus down as Kronos used the sickle to kill their father. However, the old god cursed Kronos with his dying breath, saying that the Titan, too, would be killed by his own sons (see pp.14–15). With the death of Uranus, Kronos became king of the Titans and the ruler of the universe.

CYCLOPES ▶
The three one-eyed Cyclopes were known for their skill as builders, craftworkers, and metalworkers.

11

The Titans and their children

Immortal and powerful, the Titans were the offspring of the primal creators Gaia and Uranus. They were gigantic figures, known for their strength and endurance. There were a total of 12 Titans and Titanesses in the beginning, but some of them gave birth to more of their kind, while others were the parents of Olympian gods.

Kronos

- **Also known as:** Cronus, Saturn (Roman)
- **Shown with:** Wings, sickle, and hourglass

The leader of the first generation of Titans, Kronos was a destructive god. After killing his father Uranus, he became the ruler of the universe during the Golden Age (see p.18). He was also husband to the Titaness Rhea. Kronos was overthrown by his own children in a war between the Olympians and the Titans (see pp.14–15).

Rhea

- **Also known as:** Mother of the gods
- **Shown with:** Crown, lions by her side

This Titaness was worshipped as the protector of women during childbirth and of those with babies or young children. She was also the wife of the Titan Kronos, and according to most accounts, they had six children together—the deities Zeus, Poseidon, Hades, Hera, Hestia, and Demeter (see pp.14–15).

Oceanus

- **Also known as:** Okeanos River
- **Shown with:** Horns on head, oar resting on his shoulder

The Titan Oceanus and his wife, the Titaness Tethys, created countless seas, rivers, streams, springs, and lakes. They also had 3,000 daughters—magical nymphs known as the Oceanids, who lived in the fresh waters, and were particularly associated with springs. Oceanus was worshipped by the Ancient Greeks as the god of the Okeanos River, which was believed to encircle the world.

The idea of scales to measure good or bad actions goes back to Ancient Egyptian times.

Themis

- **Also known as:** Lady Justice
- **Shown with:** Bronze sword, scales of justice

The Titaness Themis was the goddess of fairness, order, and law. She had the power to foretell the future, and was said to watch over public meetings and courts of law. If she was ignored or not respected, Themis would send Nemesis, the goddess of retribution, to punish the wrong-doers.

Helios

- **Also known as:** The sun
- **Shown with:** Golden flying chariot

The sun god Helios was the son of the Titan Hyperion. He took the form of a young man who wore the sun as a crown. To ensure that Earth was lit and warmed by its rays, Helios carried the sun across the sky on his chariot, which was drawn by four swift horses.

The Hesperides

- **Also known as:** Goddesses of Evening, Nymphs of the West, Atlantides
- **Shown with:** Golden apples

The three Hesperides lived in the far west, near the setting sun. Their parentage was not known for certain, but it was said that they were the daughters of the Titan Atlas (see p.15). The Hesperides looked after a garden in which the trees bore golden apples. The hero Hercules stole these apples (see pp.32–33), but the goddess Athena (see pp.24–25) later returned them to the garden.

The Greek word *mouseion* ("temple of the Muses") is the root of the term "museum" in many languages.

The Muses

- **Also known as:** Goddesses of the arts
- **Shown with:** Various, including scrolls, lyre, comic mask, tragic mask, celestial globe

There were nine muses, daughters of Mnemosyne, the Titaness of memory. Each was a goddess and supporter of a creative art or science. The muses were: Calliope (patron of epic poetry), Euterpe (lyric poetry), Erato (love poetry), Thalia (comedy), Melpomene (tragedy), Clio (history), Polyhymnia (sacred poetry), Urania (astronomy), and Terpsichore (dance).

| Calliope | Euterpe | Erato | Thalia | Melpomene | Clio | Polyhymnia | Urania | Terpsichore |

The overthrow of Kronos

When Kronos, king of the Titans, tries to kill his own children, his wife Rhea hatches a plan to save them. One of her offspring, the god Zeus, leads his siblings in a ruthless war against their wicked father. Kronos is eventually defeated, and the gods are finally able to rule the cosmos.

EUROPE

When Kronos's father Uranus was fatally attacked by his sons, with his final breath he foretold that Kronos, too, would die at the hands of his children (see p.11). In order to ensure that this never came to pass, Kronos decided that none of his offspring should live. Whenever his wife, the Titaness Rhea (see p.12),

▲ THE SIXTH CHILD
To save her newborn baby, Rhea gave Kronos a stone wrapped in a cloth, and the Titan swallowed it, believing he had disposed of another child.

had a baby, Kronos swallowed the newborn child. Rhea was so distraught by the time Kronos had swallowed her fifth baby that she decided to take action. When her sixth child, Zeus, was born, Rhea immediately hid him away

on the island of Crete, leaving him in the care of the nymph Amalthea, who raised the child as her own. Rhea gave Kronos a cloth-wrapped stone to swallow instead of the newborn baby.

ZEUS'S REVENGE

When the god Zeus grew up, Amalthea revealed to him that she was not his mother, and told him of his father Kronos and the Titan's evil plan to kill all his children. Zeus was enraged and decided to take his revenge on Kronos. He asked Metis, the Titaness of wisdom and cunning, for help. She gave him a potion for Kronos to drink. Zeus tricked his father into doing so, and the Titan threw up the children he had swallowed. These were the five gods and goddesses—Poseidon, Hades, Demeter, Hestia, and Hera—who had grown up and become strong inside their father's body.

Zeus also discovered that Kronos had imprisoned the Cyclopes and the Hundred-Handed Giants (see pp.10–11) in the Underworld (see p.26). The god freed these creatures and, in return, the Cyclopes, who were expert metalworkers and craftworkers, made powerful weapons for Zeus and his siblings. They gave a thunderbolt to Zeus, a trident to Poseidon, and a helmet to Hades that made the wearer invisible.

DEFEATING THE TITANS

Led by Zeus, the gods and goddesses, the Cyclopes, and the Hundred-Handed Giants waged war against Kronos. Although the king called on his fellow Titans, led by Atlas, to fight

many years, until Zeus finally killed Typhon by hurling a volcano called Mount Etna at his head. Zeus then threw Typhon's remains into Tartarus, to be locked up for eternity.

Once the gods had overcome their enemies, they made their home on Mount Olympus, and came to be known as the Olympians (see pp.16–17). The world was divided between the three brothers: Zeus, the leader of the gods and goddesses, took the sky as his realm, while Poseidon was given the sea, and Hades took over the Underworld. The Olympians now ruled all of creation.

▲ ATLAS IS PUNISHED
Atlas was not locked up in Tartarus at the end of the war. Instead he was condemned to hold the heavens on his shoulders forever.

on his side, Kronos's children defeated them using their magical weapons, and trapped most of them in Tartarus, deep in the Underworld. Gaia, the mother of the Titans, was angered by

the imprisonment of her children. To defeat Zeus, she released Typhon, a monstrous storm giant with a body of snakes. Typhon turned out to be Zeus's greatest foe, and the two fought each other for

The twelve Olympians

The major deities of Greek mythology were known as the "Olympians" because they lived at the top of a huge mountain known as Olympus. From here they ruled the universe and watched over human life. This most powerful generation of deities was both worshipped and feared by the Ancient Greeks.

After the gods and goddesses won their war against the Titans (see pp.14–15), they settled on Mount Olympus, high above the lands below. Zeus became the leader of these deities. They were 12 in number: Aphrodite, Apollo, Ares, Artemis, Athena, Demeter, Hephaestus, Hera, Hermes, Hestia, Poseidon, and Zeus. Although the god Hades was the brother of Zeus and Poseidon, and had fought alongside them in the war with the Titans, he ruled over his own realm, the Underworld (see p.26). This was separate from Mount Olympus, and so he was not considered to be one of the Olympians.

All the deities of Mount Olympus took human form, and many had children with mortals. Many of the

The goddess of the hearth (fireplace), Hestia looked after people's domestic lives. She carries a scepter, and was worshipped in Ancient Greece as the protector of homes.

Aphrodite, the goddess of love and beauty, is shown with a veil, which she often lifted for her admirers. She was married to Hephaestus.

Demeter carries a sheaf of wheat, symbolizing her role as the goddess of fertility and of agriculture, especially the harvest.

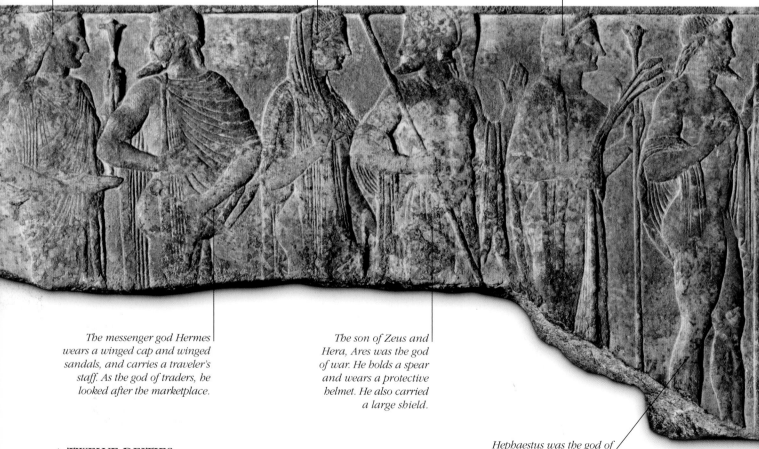

The messenger god Hermes wears a winged cap and winged sandals, and carries a traveler's staff. As the god of traders, he looked after the marketplace.

The son of Zeus and Hera, Ares was the god of war. He holds a spear and wears a protective helmet. He also carried a large shield.

Hephaestus was the god of craftsmanship and fire. His skill in metalworking was unmatched. All the weapons wielded by the Olympians were made in his forge.

▲ TWELVE DEITIES

The Olympians feature on this marble relief carving from a Greek temple, and are depicted with the objects and symbols associated with them.

Olympians—Apollo, Ares, Athena, Artemis, Aphrodite, Hephaestus, and Hermes—were the offspring of Zeus, but the siblings did not always live in harmony with each other. Just like humans, the Olympians were not perfect, and often quarreled or showed signs of jealousy.

GREEK SOCIETY

The Ancient Greeks believed that the Olympians worked together to look after Greek society as a whole, but that they each had their own area of influence, such as love, war, or wisdom. If people needed help from a deity, they would make offerings at their temples. To ensure a calm sea, sailors made sacrifices to Poseidon before going on a voyage, and farmers would pay homage to the fertility goddess Demeter before harvesting their crops. Those who failed to make offerings were believed to face terrible consequences. As a result, the people of Greece held the Olympians in dread as well as awe.

MOUNT OLYMPUS

Although the Ancient Greeks thought of Olympus as the home of the gods, it was only in c. 600 BCE that they agreed that a mountain near the city of Thessaloniki, in modern-day northern Greece, was the Mount Olympus of legend. Still known as Mount Olympus, it is Greece's highest mountain, with 52 peaks. Stefani peak (right) is also known as the "Throne of Zeus."

Hera, the queen of the Olympians, carries a royal, lotus-tipped scepter. As the goddess of women, marriage, family, and childbirth, she was especially worshipped by married women.

The goddess of wisdom and warfare, Athena wears battle armor and is shown with an owl—her symbol.

Artemis, the goddess of the hunt, is always shown with a bow and a quiver of arrows. She was also associated with the moon, and was believed to help women in childbirth.

Apollo was the twin brother of Artemis. He was the god of music, healing, and prophecy, and is shown with a lyre. He was also the patron god of archers.

The mighty Poseidon was god of the sea, but was also responsible for powerful forces such as earthquakes. He is shown with his trident, a three-pronged weapon.

The sky god Zeus was the leader of the Olympians and the most widely worshipped deity of the Greek world. He wields the thunderbolt, his most powerful weapon.

The creation of humankind

The task of creating humans was full of setbacks, according to Greek mythology. It involved a process of trial and error, with both the Titans and the Olympians attempting to create lasting inhabitants for Earth. The Titan Prometheus was finally successful, but in trying to improve the lives of his creations, he made the other gods angry.

When the Titans ruled the world under the leadership of Kronos (see p.12), they wanted to create humans to live on Earth. Their initial efforts resulted in a group of beings who lived a life of comfort in harmony with nature. These people did not have to work, and also did not seem to grow old. Because their lives seemed as precious as gold, these humans came to be known as the Golden Race, and the blissful time in which they lived was called the Golden Age. These humans were mortal, however, so when the Golden Race finally died out, the world was left unpopulated.

◄ THE GOLDEN AGE
Food was plentiful in the Golden Age and no one had to work hard to get it. This abundance is represented by the ears of corn held by Kronos.

ZEUS'S ATTEMPT

Once the Olympians had replaced the Titans as the most powerful beings in the cosmos (see pp.14–15), they tried to create humans with a longer lifespan. These creations were not very intelligent and often argued among themselves. Because they were less noble than the Golden Race, they came to be known as the Silver Race. These beings stayed young for up to a hundred years and could have children, but died quickly once they reached adulthood. This made the humans resentful, and so they refused to worship the

◄ THE BRONZE AGE
The humans in the Bronze Age fought one another for money and power, and ultimately died out.

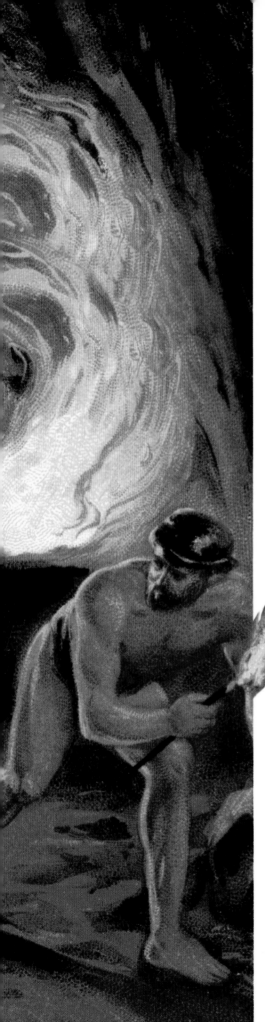

◀ STEALING FIRE
While Hephaestus was busy at his forge, Prometheus sneaked away with fire by hiding it in a hollow stalk of the fennel plant.

gods. Insulted, the Olympians banished the humans to the Underworld (see p.26).

Frustrated by this failure, Zeus himself tried to create humans who would not disappoint the gods, this time making them out of clay. These people came to be known as the Bronze Race, because their armor and everyday tools were made of bronze. Unfortunately, these Bronze Age humans were even more quarrelsome than their predecessors. They waged vicious wars against each other that eventually wiped them out, leaving Earth without humankind once more.

PROMETHEUS'S CREATIONS

Finally, the young Titan Prometheus decided to try his hand at making a lasting human population. Like Zeus, he, too, worked with clay. These beings prospered because Prometheus was willing to help them. He taught them useful skills, such as how to sail a boat and how to make medicines out of herbs. He also taught these humans how to please the deities with animal sacrifices, taking some meat for themselves and offering the rest to the gods. One day, some humans killed a bull for food, but were unsure which parts of the animal to give to the gods. They turned to Prometheus once more for help.

PROMETHEUS'S TRICK

Unfortunately, the Titan was also a trickster and could not resist causing mischief. Crafty Prometheus wrapped the bull's meat in its skin and the animal's bones in its fat, and offered the Olympians a choice between the two. Enticed by the thicker, fattier option, Zeus chose the bones covered in fat, and was enraged when he discovered the deception. He decided to punish humanity by keeping the gift of fire from them.

Prometheus felt responsible for this, and defied Zeus by stealing fire from the forge of the god Hephaestus (see p.20) and giving it to the humans. He then taught the people how to use this fire for cooking, keeping themselves warm, and for metalwork. When Zeus found out, he punished Prometheus by chaining him to a rock on Mount Caucasus and leaving him to be pecked at by a gigantic eagle. Zeus decreed that Prometheus would serve his punishment for eternity. Prometheus lay bound on the rock for centuries, until Zeus allowed him to be freed by the hero Heracles (see pp.30–33), who released the Titan by killing the eagle.

◀ THE PUNISHMENT
Each day, the eagle would peck at Prometheus's liver, an agonizing torture. The liver regrew every night for fresh punishment the next day.

19

Aphrodite and Hephaestus

Myths about Aphrodite, the goddess of love, describe the many times she is unfaithful to her husband Hephaestus, the god of metalworking and craftsmanship. He creates a cunning device to catch his wife and her lover Ares, the god of war, so the other gods can laugh at them.

▲ HEPHAESTUS
Usually shown with a blacksmith's hammer, the god Hephaestus was born with a physical disability: he could not walk upright.

Hephaestus was a metalworker of amazing skill, and could make items that combined the finest craftsmanship with powerful magical abilities, such as the winged helmet and sandals of the messenger god Hermes (see p.28). Hephaestus loved his wife Aphrodite very much and used his skills to create beautiful gifts for her, including dazzling jewelry and a golden chariot pulled by doves. Rather than returning his affection, Aphrodite fell in love with other men. There were many rumors about Aphrodite's affairs, and some of the gods and goddesses laughed at

Hephaestus for staying loyal to his wife. When Hephaestus discovered that she was in love with his brother Ares, the god of war, he hatched a plan to catch the couple. He made a strong net using bronze wire that was so fine it was almost invisible. He also built a framework to hold the net above Aphrodite's bed, with a device that allowed the net to be dropped down.

Hephaestus waited until Aphrodite was with Ares, then released the net as the pair embraced, trapping them in it. Next, he gathered the net up with the couple inside it and summoned the gods and goddesses of Mount Olympus (see pp.16–17) to witness their humiliation. When they saw Ares and Aphrodite caught in the net, they all laughed. Now Aphrodite, rather than her husband, was the figure of mockery.

◄ APHRODITE AND ARES
This marble relief shows Aphrodite and Ares meeting in secret. The war god has set aside his shield upon meeting his lover but still wears his golden helmet.

Pygmalion's statue

The Roman poet Ovid retold an earlier story from the island of Cyprus about Pygmalion, a sculptor who fell in love with one of his statues. The myth tells of the creative and inspirational power of art.

▲ **THE STATUE COMES TO LIFE**
Aphrodite (right) was sympathetic to people in love, and was moved enough to grant desperate Pygmalion's wish.

The sculptor Pygmalion poured all his effort and talent into his art. Over time, his sculptures became more and more lifelike, and everyone who saw them admired their beauty.

One day, Pygmalion began carving a statue of a woman that was more realistic than anything he had made before. The woman, made of white ivory, was so enchantingly beautiful that Pygmalion fell in love with her. The sculptor asked the goddess Aphrodite if there was any way in which he could marry the statue. The goddess of love decided to grant Pygmalion's wish by turning the statue into a real woman and joining the pair in marriage. Later writers named the woman Galatea, which means "she who is milk-white."

Pandora's jar

The Greek writer Hesiod was the first person to tell the tale of Pandora, a woman created by the gods to punish humanity for Prometheus's theft of fire. Pandora's story is one way in which the Ancient Greeks explained the origins of human suffering.

The first humans on Earth had no fire to keep themselves warm or to cook their food. When the Titan Prometheus (see pp.18–19) stole fire from the god Hephaestus in order to help humankind, Zeus was furious and decided to punish the people of Earth.

Zeus asked Hephaestus to create a woman, Pandora, who would carry disease and sorrow to Earth. Zeus gave Pandora a jar filled with these punishments, but he called them "gifts from the gods," so the mortals would be deceived. The gods brought Pandora to Prometheus's brother Epimetheus, who fell in love with this beautiful woman and married her.

Eventually, Pandora's curiosity got the better of her and she opened the jar. Out poured all the diseases and sorrows, which have troubled Earth ever since. Realizing her mistake, Pandora quickly shut the jar, leaving inside the only good thing: the gift of hope. This gave people something to live for when surrounded by misery.

THE JAR OF MISERY ▶
While the older Greek stories mention a pithos *(jar), modern retellings call it "Pandora's box."*

Apollo, the musician

The Olympian Apollo was the god of light, healing, and prophecy. He was also known for his great skill in playing the lyre (a stringed instrument) and came to be associated with music. The Roman poet Ovid recounts a musical contest between Apollo and Marsyas that has terrible consequences for one of the participants.

The god Apollo owned a sacred herd of cattle, which he tended with care. The messenger god Hermes (see p.28) was jealous of Apollo's herd and longed to possess these beautiful animals. One day, Hermes noticed that the cattle were unattended, so he stole them and hid them in a cave on the Greek island of Pylos. Apollo found out where Hermes had hidden his cattle, and went to see the messenger god to demand his property back.

When he reached the cave, Apollo saw Hermes playing a lyre, an instrument the messenger god had created by attaching strings made from cattle intestines to a turtle shell. A fine musician himself, Apollo was so delighted by the sound of the lyre that he let Hermes keep the cattle in exchange for the instrument.

◀ APOLLO AND HIS LYRE
The god Apollo was an expert player of the lyre. He taught Orpheus (see pp.34–35) to play this instrument.

THE CONTEST
Apollo soon mastered the lyre and news of his skill spread far and wide. Marsyas was a satyr (a creature with the torso of a man and the hindquarters of a goat) and a brilliant player of the aulos, a wind instrument with two pipes that he himself had invented. In an act of arrogance, Marsyas challenged Apollo to a musical contest, and the god accepted—

◀ MARSYAS'S PIPES
Marsyas tried to outplay Apollo using an aulos in a musical contest. The aulos was a popular instrument in Ancient Greece.

on the condition that the winner would be able to punish the loser in any way they wished. The satyr was so confident of victory that he agreed right away. Apollo and Marsyas were equally matched in skill, and the crowd that had gathered to witness their contest could not decide on a winner. Apollo then proposed a solution: the decision would be made after both of them had played their instruments while hanging upside-down. Being a stringed instrument, the lyre was easier to play in this position, while Marsyas's aulos was very difficult to blow when upside-down. Apollo was declared the winner, and chose to punish Marsyas for his hubris (see p.40) by tying him to a pine tree and killing him.

Apollo and Marsyas were equally matched and **the crowd could not decide** on a winner.

The Oracle at Delphi

The god of prophecy, Apollo, gave the priestess at Delphi the ability to predict the future. Known as the Oracle, her prophecies were often hard to understand.

▲ **CONSULTING THE ORACLE**
Visitors could meet the Oracle only on certain days, and often had to line up. The priestess delivered her prophecies from a three-legged stool.

Apollo's mother, the Titaness Leto, told the god how she had been harassed by a serpentlike monster called the Python. Apollo tracked it down to the Greek town of Delphi, where it was wreaking havoc. The god cornered the serpent and shot poison-tipped arrows at it until it died. The people of Delphi were overjoyed, and built a temple to Apollo in gratitude. He was pleased by this and blessed the temple's head priestess with the power of prophecy. She came to be known as the Oracle and was visited by many people, who came to consult her about their future. However, as the priestess's speech was often jumbled, her prophecies could be difficult to follow. Despite their confusing nature, the words of the Oracle always came true, often in mysterious ways (see pp.46–47).

Daphne's plight

The story of the nymph Daphne is found in the Roman writer Ovid's book of transformations, the *Metamorphoses*. The tale describes Apollo's love for Daphne and how she comes to take the form of a laurel tree.

Eros, the god of love, was famous for his skill with the bow and arrow, and was known to use his gold-tipped arrows to make people fall in love. When Apollo, the patron of archers, mocked Eros's archery skills, the god of love decided to play a trick on him.

Eros shot Apollo with one of his gold-tipped arrows, and made him fall in love with the nymph Daphne. Eros also shot Daphne with a special lead-tipped arrow, which would make her reject Apollo. The lovestruck god tried to win Daphne's love, but she refused to accept him. As she fled from Apollo, Daphne prayed to Zeus to be transformed into something that would make Apollo lose interest in her, so Zeus changed her into a laurel tree. When Apollo finally came to his senses, he made a wreath of leaves from the laurel tree, and wore it forever afterward as his crown.

◀ **LAUREL TREE**
Branches sprout from Daphne's head and arms in this statue of the nymph's transformation. After Daphne was turned into a laurel, the tree became sacred to Apollo.

Athena's gift

The goddess of war and wisdom, Athena was sympathetic to her human followers and was the protector of warriors, craftworkers, and the people of Athens. This story tells of her unusual birth and how she comes to be Athens's patron goddess.

◄ **ATHENIAN COIN**
The citizens of Athens paid tribute to Athena by placing her symbol, the owl, on some of their coins.

The god Zeus (see pp.14–15) heard a prophecy from the creator goddess Gaia (see pp.10–11) that if his wife Metis (see p.14) gave birth to a son, the child would take away his power. Zeus swallowed Metis before she could give birth to their

◄ **ON THE ATTACK**
Athena fought Enceladus in a war with the giants. In this battle, her shoulders were protected by a garment called the Aegis.

baby. Later, Zeus complained of a painful headache. The god Hephaestus (see p.20) split open Zeus's head, and out sprang the goddess Athena, fully grown and clad in battle armor, ready to take on her role as the goddess of war. She did not challenge her father's supremacy.

Athena competed against the sea god Poseidon (see p.45) for power over Greece's largest city. The gods decreed that the one who gave the people of the city the greatest gift

would win. Poseidon struck the ground with his trident (see p.116), bringing forth a saltwater spring. Wise Athena created the first olive tree, planting it on a nearby hill, where it provided the people with food and firewood. Athena's gift was judged to be greater, and she became the patron goddess of the city. It was named "Athens" in her honor.

Arachne's pride

The tale of the mortal woman Arachne illustrates how the goddess Athena could become angry. It also shows the perils that humans had to face when they did not respect the powerful and vengeful gods.

▲ **ATHENA'S WRATH**
In a fit of jealous rage, Athena struck Arachne and tore up her tapestry.

Arachne was a mortal woman who became famous as the most skilled weaver of her time. While most people said that her gift came from Athena, the protector goddess of weavers and embroiderers, Arachne insisted that her ability was her own.

Athena was angered by Arachne's pride, and challenged the woman to a weaving contest. At the contest, Arachne wove a tapestry depicting

Zeus with his lovers, while Athena made one showing the gods defeating the humans. To Athena's surprise, the mortal woman's weaving was indeed better than her own. The goddess was infuriated, not only because of the unflattering way in which Arachne portrayed her father, but also by the quality of her work—Athena thought that no mere human had the right to weave with more skill than a goddess.

She then attacked Arachne with her own weaving shuttle. Terrified of the goddess's rage, Arachne tried to kill herself, but Athena felt this was too harsh a fate. Instead she transformed her rival into a spider, the creature that is the greatest weaver of all.

▲ FERRYING THE DEAD
Charon the boatman took the dead across the Acheron and Styx rivers. Those who were buried without a coin in their mouth would not be allowed on Charon's boat.

The Underworld

The Ancient Greeks believed that when people died they went to the Underworld. Writers such as Homer and Hesiod described it as a dark place, ruled by the god Hades with his wife Persephone. Few mortals visited the Underworld and returned to Earth, as Hades did not allow it.

The god Hades was known to the Ancient Romans as Pluto. He was also worshipped as a god of wealth.

The Underworld was also known as Hades, after its king. The darkest and most sinister part was a deep pit called Tartarus. The souls of the dead were sent here on their arrival in the Underworld to be judged for their actions on Earth. Wicked souls were sent to the terrible dungeons of Tartarus, where sinners faced gruesome punishments for their misdeeds in life, whether

▶ HADES AND CERBERUS
The god Hades is often depicted with his three-headed hound Cerberus, which guarded the entrance to the Underworld.

these were crimes against their fellow humans or offenses against the gods. The souls of those who had lived ordinary lives were allowed to wander the Asphodel Meadows, a fertile plain filled with pale-gray flowers, where they existed as silent, joyless shadows. The souls of heroes and virtuous humans went to Elysium, which was a place of happiness and hope.

THE RIVERS OF HADES

After death a person's soul crossed the Acheron River ("woe"), which flowed into the larger Styx River ("hatefulness"), on its way to the Underworld.

The waters of the Styx were poisonous to living people, but also had magical powers (see p.51). A boatman called Charon ferried a soul across these rivers in exchange for a fare of one obol coin. This is why, in Ancient Greece, the dead were buried with an obol in their mouth. The other rivers in Hades were the Cocytus ("lamentation"), fiery Phlegethon ("flaming"), and the Lethe ("forgetfulness").

The abduction of Persephone

The goddess Demeter and her daughter Persephone were responsible for the growth of plants and good harvests. Their story tells of how the love of the god Hades for Persephone and her disappearance from Earth brought about the origin of the seasons.

In modern Greece, the pomegranate fruit is a symbol of fertility and good luck.

◄ DEMETER MOURNING
Flowers and ears of corn decorate Demeter's hair, but the blooms fall to the ground to symbolize the loss of her daughter Persephone.

RETURN OF PERSEPHONE

Zeus saw what had happened. He knew that life on Earth would perish without the two goddesses, and so he asked Hades to return Persephone to her mother. However, Persephone had eaten some pomegranate seeds while in the Underworld, so could no longer return permanently to the land of the living. Zeus then asked Hades to share Persephone with Demeter for some months every year. Hades agreed to this, and from then on Persephone spent half the year

on land, helping her mother bring about a plentiful harvest in the spring and summer. She spent the other half in the Underworld, leaving Demeter in mourning, which caused a difficult fall and a harsh winter to cover the land. This is how the changing seasons came to be on Earth.

Demeter kept the farmers' fields rich and fertile by making crops grow and ripen. Her daughter Persephone helped her in these tasks, and so the pair were vital to the well-being of the land and its people.

Hades, the king of the Underworld, fell in love with Persephone. One day, while she was working alone in a field, Hades caught her and carried her to the Underworld. Distraught at the disappearance of her daughter, Demeter searched all over Earth looking for her, leaving the crops to die without her care. The trees also withered, and famine spread across the land.

REUNITED ►
Zeus's son Hermes (see p.28) helps Persephone out of the Underworld, toward the welcoming arms of her mother, Demeter.

Tricksters

Some of the most entertaining characters in mythology are tricksters, who use their wits to tease and trick both deities and humans. Sometimes clever, sometimes foolish, tricksters enjoy causing mischief and disrupting the way things are normally done.

◄ SUSANO-O
This Japanese deity of the sea and storms is thrown out of heaven because of his bad behavior at his sister Amaterasu's court.

◄ HERMES
The Greek messenger god is known to steal items belonging to the other gods, including Poseidon's trident, Apollo's cattle, and Aphrodite's belt.

◄ MOHINI
The only female avatar (form) of the Hindu god Vishnu, Mohini enchants all those she encounters. She helps to keep the amrita, *("nectar of immortality"), out of the hands of the Asuras.*

◄ ANANSI
The spider Anansi appears in many West African myths, cleverly outwitting creatures much stronger than himself.

▼ **MONKEY KING**
Mischievous Monkey is one of the best-loved characters in Chinese mythology, even though he upsets all the gods by causing mayhem in Heaven.

▲ **ERIS**
The Greek goddess of disagreement, Eris is best-known for her part in starting the Trojan War.

▶▶▶ **SEE ALSO** ▶▶▶

■ The Trojan War, pp.48–51
■ Loki and Balder, p.70
■ The adventures of Monkey, pp.136–139
■ Amaterasu and the mirror, pp.142–143
■ The churning of the ocean, pp.152–153
■ The tricks of Anansi, pp.182–183
■ Maui's feats, pp.228–231

▲ **SINBAD**
A hero from the Central Asian stories One Thousand and One Nights, *Sinbad the sailor uses his wits to survive terrible dangers.*

LUGH ▶
The Irish sun god is a master of many skills, which he uses to gain entry to the king's court at Tara.

▼ **LOKI**
This Norse god uses his shape-shifting powers to obstruct those who want to bring order to the universe.

Maui changes into a lizard to trick Hine-nui-i-te-pō, the goddess of death.

▲ **MAUI**
In Oceanian mythology, Maui is a mortal who tries to cheat Hine-nui-i-te-pō, also called the Ancestress of the Night, so that he can live forever.

The labors of Heracles

Heracles was the greatest of all the Greek heroes. After being tricked into committing a terrible crime, Heracles was punished by the gods. He was made to undertake 12 labors, challenges that ranged from killing deadly monsters to embarking on impossible quests. The most well-known stories about these labors were told by the Ancient Greek writers Apollodorus and Euripides.

The courageous and powerful demigod Heracles was the son of Zeus, king of the gods, and Alcmene, the granddaughter of Perseus (see pp.36–37). Zeus's wife Hera was upset when her husband and Alcmene had a child together, and her resentment grew worse as she saw Heracles grow up, get married to Megara, and have children. Filled with hate, the goddess drove Heracles out of his mind, so much so that he killed his wife and children.

Despite the fact that it was really Hera's doing, the gods decided that Heracles should be punished for these crimes, and appointed Eurystheus, king of Mycenae, to decide what form this punishment should take. Eurystheus thought of 12 tasks, or labors, for Heracles, each one seemingly more impossible than the next.

◀ **THE MIGHTY HERO**
Heracles wore the skin of the lion he slew in his first task to remind people of his great strength.

▲ **NEMEAN LION**
This lion's golden fur could not be pierced with weapons. Heracles had to kill the beast with his bare hands.

▲ **LERNAEAN HYDRA**
The blood of this beast was poisonous. Heracles used it to coat his arrowheads to make them more deadly.

▲ **CERYNEIAN HIND**
Heracles had to capture the Ceryneian hind, a deer that ran faster than a speeding arrow.

Heracles cornered the lion in a cave ... killed the animal ... and made its **skin into a cloak**.

BATTLING BEASTS

The first four labors that Eurystheus set Heracles were to kill a series of beasts that had brought misery to the people of Greece. The first task was to slay a lion that had been terrorizing the people of Nemea. Heracles cornered the lion in the cave where it lived, and then he killed the animal, skinned it, and made its skin into a cloak that he wore ever after. Next, Heracles had to slay the Lernaean Hydra, a many-headed creature with poisonous breath that killed those who approached it. Whenever someone attempted to cut off the beast's heads, replacements regrew immediately. To stop the creature from regenerating in this way, Heracles had his nephew Iolaus burn and seal each wound with a flaming torch after Heracles had cut off the head. The plan worked and together the pair managed to slay the monster.

The hero's third labor was to catch a golden-horned hind, a huge deer that had been eating all the crops in the fields around the Greek town of Ceryneia. The creature ran so fast that it took Heracles an entire year to hunt it down and capture it. For his fourth task, Heracles had to defeat a monstrous boar that lived on Mount Erymanthus. He chased the boar across the snow-covered lands around the mountain, until it eventually tired out. Heracles returned to Mycenae with the defeated boar slung over his shoulder. King Eurystheus was so alarmed at the sight of the fearsome creature that he hid in a large chest.

MORE CHALLENGES

The next set of labors were no less demanding, and placed Heracles in many dangerous situations. His fifth task was to clean the stables of King Augeas, which were filled with enormous heaps of horse dung—this was more difficult and humiliating than any of his previous challenges. It was a chore that would have taken a mere mortal an entire lifetime to accomplish, but Heracles knew this labor needed ingenuity as well as superhuman strength. He shifted huge rocks to divert the path of the rivers Alpheus and Peneus so that they ran through the stables, washing away the revolting mess.

HERCULES IN THE SKY

The constellation Hercules is so-called after the Roman form of Heracles's name. It was one of the constellations seen by the Ancient Greek astronomer Ptolemy. Its stars roughly make the shape of the hero kneeling and brandishing his club.

The star pattern in Hercules

▲ **ERYMANTHIAN BOAR**
For his fourth task, the hero caught the Erymanthian boar, an animal that was destroying everything in its path.

▲ **AUGEAN STABLES**
Heracles realized that only the force of moving water would be able to clean the stables quickly, so he diverted the rivers.

▲ **STYMPHALIAN BIRDS**
Bringing down these birds using only a slingshot required skill and endurance.

The sixth labor required Heracles to destroy a flock of flesh-eating birds near Lake Stymphalus. The fierce creatures were difficult to approach, but Heracles used a noisy rattle to frighten them, so that he could shoot them down using a slingshot as they flew into the air. Capturing the Cretan Bull from King Minos of Crete was the seventh labor. Heracles went to Minos's palace and simply asked the king for the bull. Minos granted him permission to take it away if he could catch it. Mighty Heracles went to the fields where the bull had been destroying crops, grabbed the beast by the neck with his bare hands, forced it to the ground, and captured it.

For his eighth labor, Heracles had to retrieve the flesh-eating horses owned by King Diomedes of Thrace. Heracles tamed the mares by feeding them, and seized the opportunity to seal their mouths. The ninth labor was to fulfill a request made by Admete, the daughter of Eurystheus. She desired the Belt of Hippolyta (see p.126), queen of the Amazons

HERO OR GOD?

In Greek mythology, the hero Heracles was a demigod, the child of a god (Zeus) and a mortal (Alcmene). Heracles was worshipped as a deity in some cities in Ancient Greece, but also in Rome. The Romans called him Hercules, and built a temple dedicated to him near the Tiber River in Rome.

(a tribe of women warriors). This belt was special because it was a gift from the war god Ares (see pp.16–17). Hippolyta agreed to give Heracles the belt, but vengeful Hera caused an argument between Heracles's companions and the Amazons. A war broke out between them and Heracles had to retrieve the object by force. The tenth labor was acquiring the cattle of the fearsome giant Geryon, who lived on the island of Erytheia. This involved a long and arduous journey across the Libyan Desert and over the ocean. Helios (see p.13), the sun god, lent Heracles

> Many sporting clubs and teams use the Roman name Hercules as a symbol of their strength and skill.

his golden chariot to cross the ocean to the island. Here, Heracles battled the two-headed dog Orthrus and the three-bodied giant Geryon, before he gathered the cattle to take them back to Eurystheus.

THE FINAL QUESTS

Heracles's last two challenges involved longer and more dangerous journeys. The 11th labor took the hero to Mount Atlas, where he had to steal the golden apples from the Garden of the Hesperides (see p.13), daughters of the Titan Atlas. In the garden he came across Atlas holding the sky on his shoulders (see p.15). Atlas agreed to fetch the apples for Heracles if the hero would take his place for a moment. When Atlas returned with the apples, he would

▲ CRETAN BULL
The hero used his sheer strength to defeat this bull, which he later sacrificed to the goddess Athena.

▲ MARES OF DIOMEDES
To capture the mares, Heracles also had to murder their owner Diomedes, who guarded these beasts.

▲ BELT OF HIPPOLYTA
Obtaining Hippolyta's belt meant a confrontation with the Amazons, some of the most accomplished Greek warriors.

not take back the sky, so Heracles had to trick him into doing so. For his final labor, Eurystheus asked Heracles to bring him the three-headed hound Cerberus, which guarded the gates of the Underworld (see p.26). Once Heracles had entered the land of the dead, he struggled to find a way out. He eventually reached the throne of Hades, the king of the Underworld, who agreed to let Heracles take Cerberus, but only if he could tame the creature with his bare hands. Despite the dog's deadly forked tongue, the hero eventually succeeded. Heracles was allowed to leave the Underworld along with Cerberus and return to Earth. Once he had proved his feat to Eurystheus, the hero returned Cerberus to Hades. After 12 long years, his labors were complete at last.

THE ADVENTURES CONTINUE

Heracles later went on to join Jason and the Argonauts on their quest for the Golden Fleece (see pp.42–43). After returning from that journey, Heracles participated in an archery competition in the city of Oechalia. The king of the city had offered his daughter Iole's hand in marriage to the winner of the competition, but failed to

▲ **HERACLES AND OMPHALE**
While Heracles served Queen Omphale, she made him carry out various tasks such as spinning yarn. She would make him work in front of all her maidens as they looked on in amusement. To show her power over him, Queen Omphale boldly wore his lion skin.

fulfill this promise when Heracles won. Enraged at the king, Heracles killed him and his sons. This meant that the hero had to undergo yet another punishment, this time serving Queen Omphale of Lydia for three years. This "labor," however, was far from severe, as the queen fell in love with Heracles, and the pair eventually married.

▲ **GERYON'S CATTLE**
Hera sent a fly to bite and torment Geryon's cattle, making them more difficult for Heracles to capture.

▲ **GOLDEN APPLES**
Only Heracles was strong enough to hold the sky up in place of Atlas while the Titan gathered the golden apples for him.

▲ **CERBERUS**
For his final labor, Heracles captured the vicious creature called Cerberus, which was a seemingly impossible task.

Orpheus and Eurydice

The story of the musician Orpheus and his wife, the nymph Eurydice, centers on Orpheus's music, which had the power to charm gods, humans, and even trees. Orpheus's tale also describes his journey to the Underworld to try to bring Eurydice back to life. This Greek myth has been retold not only by ancient authors, but also in books, films, and operas ever since.

The classical Greek lyre was a harplike instrument.

Whenever Orpheus sang or played his lyre, the beautiful melodies enthralled more than just people: rivers changed their courses and trees uprooted themselves to get closer to the wonderful music. It was believed that Orpheus had inherited his remarkable musical ability from his mother, the muse Calliope (see p.13). Apollo, the god of music and art (see p.22), had given Orpheus his lyre and also taught him to play the instrument.

Orpheus's wife was the nymph Eurydice, whom he loved dearly. One day, while in the woods with her sisters, Eurydice was bitten by a snake and died. Plunged into sadness, Orpheus spent his days playing songs so mournful that they made even the gods and nymphs weep. The gods recommended that Orpheus visit the Underworld to bring Eurydice back. No mortal had visited the Underworld and returned— the demigod Hercules had done so (see p.33), but Orpheus did not have his superhuman strength. However, Orpheus did have his musical talent, and thought he could use this.

IN THE UNDERWORLD

Charon ferried Orpheus across the River Styx (see p.26). When Orpheus arrived at the court of Hades and Persephone (see pp.26–27), king and queen of the Underworld, he played his lyre for them, impressing Hades with his music. Orpheus asked Hades if Eurydice could be restored to life, and the king granted the request, but on one condition: when Orpheus led his wife out of the Underworld, he was not to look back at her.

Orpheus guided his wife through the dark realm, walking slightly ahead of her so that he would not see her. However, he did not trust Hades, and risked glancing back to check if Eurydice was still following him. As soon as he did this, Hades snatched Eurydice back, condemning her to remain in the land of the dead forever. Orpheus had to continue out of the Underworld on his own.

LAMENTING HIS FATE

Devastated by his mistake, Orpheus wandered the Earth playing his lyre and singing sorrowful songs.

▲ ORPHEUS AND HIS LYRE
Orpheus's music could help people in danger. It lulled a dragon to sleep so that Jason could steal the Golden Fleece (see p.42).

POETS OF LESBOS

The Greek island of Lesbos had a shrine to Orpheus. From c. 700 BCE, this island was home to several poets, including Sappho, the greatest female poet in Ancient Greece. Their poems were sung to music played on the lyre, a style known as "lyric poetry."

Ancient Greek female poet from Lesbos

... when Orpheus led his wife out of the Underworld, **he was not to look back at her**.

He retreated to a cave where he could live alone. Orpheus did, though, attract many followers of Apollo, who were impressed by his music.

However, a group of nymphs who had known and loved Eurydice remained angry that Orpheus had failed to rescue her from the Underworld. In their fury the nymphs attacked him, tearing his body apart and throwing his head, still singing, into the sea. Orpheus's head washed up on the shores of the island of Lesbos, where his mother Calliope built a shrine around it to inspire future generations of musicians and poets on this island.

Many people considered the lyre a divine musical instrument. It was also played by the god Apollo.

▼ **ORPHEUS LEADS EURYDICE**
The musician held his wife's hand as he led her through the rocky land of the Underworld, which was full of dangerous creatures such as snakes.

Perseus and Medusa

One of the greatest heroes of Greek mythology, Perseus was a demigod—the child of the mortal woman Danaë and the god Zeus. He is most famous for slaying monsters such as the terrifying Gorgon called Medusa.

EUROPE

There once was a king of the Greek city of Argos called Acrisius. When he visited the Oracle at Delphi (see p.23), the priestess predicted that Acrisius would be killed by his daughter's son. Fearful for his life, Acrisius locked his daughter Danaë and her young son Perseus in a chest and threw it into the sea. The chest floated to the island of Seriphos, where the pair were rescued by a fisherman named Dictys, who was the brother of Polydectes, the island's king. Dictys took Danaë and Perseus in and gave them a home.

Perseus grew up to be a man known for his courage and strength. One day, at a meal attended by Perseus and other young men, King Polydectes asked his guests what gifts they could give him. Most offered their best horses, but Perseus boasted that he could present Polydectes with the head of the Gorgon Medusa, a monster who could turn anyone who looked her in the eyes into stone. Polydectes had fallen in love with Danaë and wanted to marry her. The king was certain Perseus would oppose this, and saw this near-impossible task as a chance to be rid of him.

A HERO IN THE MAKING

Anxious to keep his promise, Perseus appealed to the gods for help. Hermes (see p.28) loaned the hero his winged sandals so that Perseus could travel swiftly to Medusa's lair. Hephaestus (see p.20) provided Perseus with a razor-sharp, diamond-edged sword

MEDUSA THE GORGON ▶
Once human, Medusa was cursed by Athena, who turned her into a terrifying monster with snakes instead of hair.

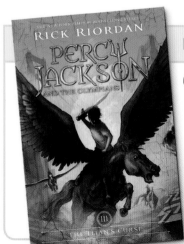

MODERN RETELLINGS: PERCY JACKSON

Created by Rick Riordan, the *Percy Jackson and the Olympians* book series features a character called Percy, who is a demigod and son of Poseidon. While his name recalls the Greek hero Perseus and his exploits, the character has adventures that are based on the stories of numerous Ancient Greek heroes, such as Orpheus (see pp.34–35) and Theseus (see pp.38–39).

called a harpe (see p.116), and Athena lent Perseus her metal shield (see p.117), which Perseus polished so that it was as shiny as a mirror. As he approached Medusa, Perseus held up the mirrorlike shield so he could see her without meeting her gaze, and sliced off the Gorgon's head with one stroke of the harpe. Then he put the head in a bag to carry back with him.

When Perseus returned to Seriphos, he discovered that Polydectes wanted to marry his mother. Seeing the king's proposal as an insult to his father Zeus, Perseus angrily showed Polydectes the Gorgon's head, which turned the king to stone.

PROPHECY FULFILLED

When Perseus heard of the Oracle's prophecy to his grandfather Acrisius, he decided to stay away from Argos. Many years later, he traveled to the kingdom of Thessaly, where the king was holding funeral games to honor his dead father. Perseus was keen to compete in the discus event, but when he threw the discus, it went astray, hitting and killing one of the spectators. The victim was Acrisius, which fulfilled the Oracle's prophecy.

▲ GREEK GAMES
Discus-throwing was a popular athletic event in Ancient Greece and featured in the early Olympic games.

37

Theseus and the Minotaur

Theseus was one of the great mythical heroes of Athens. He is famous for his daring exploits, most notably the killing of a monster called the Minotaur. In spite of this great triumph, Theseus's story ends on a sad note, as tragedy befalls his family on his journey home.

Although archaeologists have never found a labyrinth, Cretan palaces were built very like a maze.

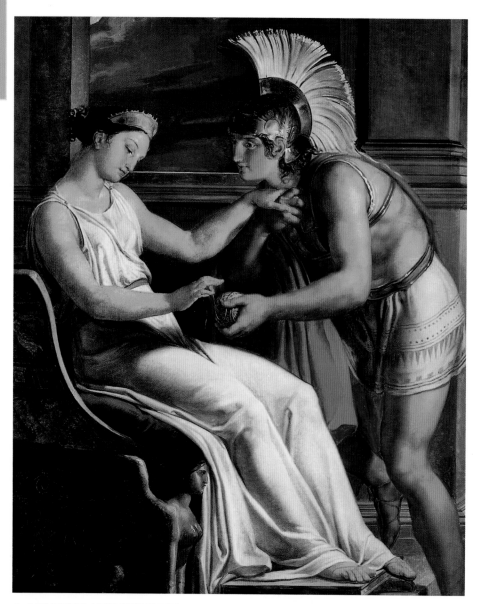

▲ ARIADNE AND THESEUS
Ariadne did not want Theseus to be killed by the Minotaur, so she begged the inventor Daedalus (see p.41) for help. He suggested she use a ball of thread to navigate through the maze, so she gave Theseus a yarn she had spun.

King Minos of Crete kept a flesh-eating, bull-like creature called the Minotaur imprisoned in the middle of a vast labyrinth (maze). Having won a war against Athens, Minos forced its king, Aegeus, to send 14 of the finest young people of Athens every year as food for the Minotaur.

> Theseus **promised his father** that if he succeeded ... he would return flying **white sails** ...

JOURNEY TO CRETE

Theseus was the son of King Aegeus, and he vowed to kill the Minotaur to put an end to this ritual sacrifice of Athenian youths. He decided to go to Crete as one of the chosen 14 and set sail from Athens on a ship with black sails. Theseus promised his father that if he succeeded in putting the monster to death, he would return flying white sails—a signal that everything had gone well.

When Theseus arrived in Crete and heard of the labyrinth, he realized it was almost impossible for a person to find their way in and out of it without getting lost. Even if he was able to reach the center, the beast would almost certainly devour him. However, when King Minos's daughter Ariadne saw Theseus, she fell in love with him and decided to help. She gave Theseus a ball of thread to mark his path through the labyrinth, so he could retrace his steps and get out again.

▲ THE LABYRINTH
Built by the skillful inventor Daedalus, the labyrinth was a prison with a single opening, designed to confuse anyone who entered it.

THE BEAST

Theseus entered the dark and gloomy labyrinth, unwinding the thread behind him. When he finally reached the center and came face to face with the Minotaur, he drew the sword his father had given him and fought the monster. After a gruesome battle, Theseus killed it.

Theseus then swiftly made his way back through the labyrinth, following Ariadne's thread as he went, and successfully emerged into the daylight. Eager to return home, he dashed to his ship, taking Ariadne with him.

A TRAGIC END

In their rush to get away, neither Theseus nor his crew remembered to hoist the white sails. King Aegeus had been waiting anxiously on a cliff top outside Athens for his son's return. When he caught sight of the ship with black sails, he was convinced that the Minotaur had killed Theseus. Overcome with grief, Aegeus threw himself into the sea, where he drowned. Although Theseus would be remembered forever as the great hero of Athens, his father never knew of his son's victory.

BULL-LEAPING

Wall paintings (above) in the palaces of Crete depict athletes jumping over the backs of bulls. Archaeologists think that bull-leaping was an ancient religious ritual performed as worship of the animal. This might mean that the Minotaur story arose from the real-life reverence of bulls.

EUROPE

THE BEAST IS KILLED ▶
Despite being a creature of unusual strength, the Minotaur could not defeat Theseus. The young hero eventually overpowered the monster and killed it.

Bellerophon and Pegasus

The story of Bellerophon follows his heroic exploits as he kills the monster Chimaera. Later, however, he is punished for his hubris (arrogance).

HUBRIS

In Greek myth, a mortal's hubris (arrogance) was always punished by the gods. For example, Helios's son Phaethon tried to drive his father's chariot across the sky and was killed when Zeus shot it down with his thunderbolt.

When Bellerophon was a young man, he was sent to the Greek city of Argos. The king of Argos, Proetus, believed Bellerophon had tried to steal his wife. He therefore banished him to the kingdom of Lycia as a punishment. Proetus wrote a letter to Iobates, king of Lycia, asking him to kill Bellerophon, but Iobates did not want to murder a guest—a crime that would anger the Erinyes (see pp.58–59). Instead, he asked Bellerophon to get rid of the terrifying Chimaera (see p.149)—a fire-breathing monster that was part lion, part goat, and part snake—that was destroying Lycia. Iobates expected Bellerophon to die in the attempt, but the goddess Athena (see pp.24–25) helped the youth by giving him the magical winged horse Pegasus. By flying above the monster, Bellerophon avoided the Chimaera's deadly breath and was able to kill it. Iobates was grateful, and in time even befriended Bellerophon.

A TRAGIC END

Bellerophon was so proud of killing the Chimaera that he became arrogant and overambitious. He rode Pegasus into the sky to visit Mount Olympus, home of the gods, where no mortal had ever been. Angry at his vanity, Zeus made Pegasus throw off Bellerophon, who tumbled to the ground and died.

◀ FIGHTING THE CHIMAERA
The fire-breathing Chimaera tried to attack Bellerophon, but Pegasus's power of flight kept them out of reach of the flames.

The fall of Icarus

Retold by Roman writers such as Ovid and Pliny, the tale of the legendary inventor Daedalus and his son Icarus comes from Ancient Greece. Set on the Greek island of Crete, it contrasts the overconfidence of Icarus with the care and wisdom of his father.

Daedalus worked for King Minos of Crete as a craftsman and inventor. He created all kinds of devices, from the potter's wheel to the labyrinth, or maze, in which Minos kept a fearsome monster called the Minotaur. When Theseus killed the Minotaur and escaped the labyrinth (see pp.38–39), Minos was furious with its inventor and shut Daedalus and his son Icarus in a tower in the middle of the sea. Frustrated at his imprisonment, Daedalus planned their escape. He realized that although they could not open the locked door, they would be able to escape through the window—if they could fly. The ingenious inventor made pairs of wings for himself and young Icarus, using a wooden framework, to which he attached feathers using wax. The wings fit well and looked like they would work. However, Daedalus instructed Icarus to not fly too high, in case the heat of the sun melted the wax, removing the feathers. He also told his son to not fly too low, because the waves from the sea below might splash water on to the feathers, adding weight and bringing him down.

A DISASTROUS FLIGHT

Icarus took off and, to his joy, found the wings worked perfectly. He was so pleased with his ability to fly that he ignored his father's warnings and climbed higher. The heat from the sun melted the wax and the feathers came apart just as Daedalus had predicted, causing helpless Icarus to fall to his death in the sea.

Daedalus witnessed this tragic incident as he flew, and although he reached safety when he landed on the island of Sicily, he was devastated by his son's death.

ICARUS TUMBLES ▶
While Icarus (right) fell tumbling through the clouds, Daedalus (above) frantically searched the skies for his son. To his father's dismay, Icarus plunged into the sea below.

Jason and the Argonauts

The tale of Jason and his travels with his companions is one of the best-known quest myths. In this adventure, full of monsters and dangers, the Argonauts have to use all their strength, bravery, and cunning to bring back the precious Golden Fleece in order for Jason to reclaim his throne.

King Aeson, Jason's father, ruled the kingdom of Iolcus in Greece. When Jason was only a child, his uncle Pelias captured Aeson and made himself king. In time, when Jason was old enough, he demanded his kingdom back. Pelias said that Jason could be king only if he found and brought back the Golden Fleece. This valuable sign of kingship was fiercely protected by King Aeëtes of Colchis, and Pelias did not expect Jason to succeed.

▲ PELIAS AND JASON
Pelias thought retrieving the Golden Fleece was an impossible task, but Jason accepted the challenge.

The journey to Colchis would be difficult, but Jason persuaded many of Greece's greatest heroes—such as Hercules (see pp.30–33) and Orpheus (see pp.34–35)—to travel with him. He also had the shipbuilder Argus make him a special ship called the *Argo*. Parts of this ship were built from an oak tree sacred to the god Zeus, which gave it extra strength.

A PERILOUS JOURNEY

Jason and his band of famous warriors, known collectively as the "Argonauts," set sail for Colchis. They faced many hazards on their voyage. On one of their stopovers, the Argonaut Hylas was pulled into a well by some water nymphs. Distressed by this, Hercules abandoned Jason's quest in order to rescue his friend. On another stop, they were challenged to a boxing match by King Amycus, a renowned fighter who often killed his opponents. The Argonauts put forward their best boxer, Polydeuces, who defeated and killed the king. The Argonauts also rescued a blind man called Phineus, who was being attacked by the Harpies (see p.148), fearsome birdlike monsters. Grateful for their assistance, Phineus helped the *Argo*'s crew in return. He used his gift of prophecy to foresee dangers that lay ahead and to find ways to avoid them. Phineus revealed to the Argonauts the secret of how to slip through the Clashing Rocks, a pair of cliffs on either side of a narrow channel that moved together, smashing vessels as they tried to pass through.

CHALLENGES AT COLCHIS

Jason's troubles did not end when the Argonauts reached Colchis. King Aeëtes had set a fierce dragon to protect the Golden Fleece, which hung from a tree. Luckily for Jason, the king's daughter, the sorceress Medea (see p.190), had fallen in love with him and came to his aid. Medea had the idea of asking the musician

Orpheus to lull the dragon to sleep with his music. While the dragon slept, Jason stole the Fleece and set out for Iolcus. The journey back home was equally dangerous for the Argonauts. They had to sail past another monster, Scylla (see p.148), and avoid being sucked into a powerful whirlpool called Charybdis. After overcoming several other obstacles, the *Argo* was finally on its way back to Iolcus for Jason to claim his kingdom.

THE GOLDEN FLEECE

The Golden Fleece was the fleece of a winged, golden-wooled sheep. Scholars think that the idea for this may have come from the practice of sifting for gold in rivers, where a sheep's fleece was used to trap the tiny particles.

AT THE CLASHING ROCKS
Jason released a dove to fly ahead. The rocks closed to crush the bird, but it escaped. As the cliffs parted, the Argonauts rowed quickly through.

Greek sea deities

The Mediterranean Sea was important to the Ancient Greeks, because they relied on it for transportation, and for the food it provided through fishing. Their mythology included many sea deities who would protect worshippers, but could raise storms in the path of those who offended them.

Scenes depicting sea gods in their realms were popular in Ancient Greek mosaic art.

Pontus

- **Also known as:** The Sea
- **Shown with:** Horns that are crab claws; seaweed

Pontus was the primal sea god who existed before the gods of Mount Olympus were born. He was a son of Gaia (see pp.10–11). Pontus was the father of all the creatures that lived in the oceans.

Often portrayed as a giant head rising out of the sea, Pontus has a watery beard.

Poseidon's chariot is pulled by fish-tailed horses called Hippocampi.

Proteus

- **Also known as:** The Old Man of the Sea
- **Shown with:** Herdsman's staff

Proteus was a helper to the supreme god of the oceans, Poseidon, and tended to Poseidon's flocks of sea creatures.

Proteus's character was changeable, reflecting the shifting nature of the weather and tides. He was known for his ability to shape-shift and to foretell the future.

Poseidon

- **Also known as:** God of the Sea; Neptune (Roman)
- **Shown with:** Trident; sometimes with fish-tailed horses or dolphins

One of the most powerful deities among the Olympians (see pp.16–17), Poseidon was the ruler of the sea. While he protected his worshippers from storms and shipwrecks, if angered, Poseidon would unleash earthquakes or storms, which could destroy ships, drown people, and flood the coasts.

Poseidon uses his trident to stir up storms.

Triton is Poseidon's son.

Triton

- **Also known as:** Messenger of the Sea
- **Depicted with:** Conch-shaped shell

A fish-tailed sea god, Triton was the son of Poseidon and the sea goddess Amphitrite. He acted as Poseidon's messenger, and was known by the conch-shaped shell he carried, blowing it to transmit messages underwater. Knowledgeable about tides and currents, Triton sometimes helped sailors navigate their way to safety.

Triton is a merman, shown with one or two fish tails.

Leucothea

- **Also known as:** Goddess of the Sea Spray, The White Goddess
- **Depicted with:** Shawl

Leucothea was once the mortal princess Ino, daughter of King Cadmus of Thebes. When her husband was driven mad by the goddess Hera, Ino took one of her sons and jumped off a cliff into the sea to escape him. The gods took pity, and transformed her into Leucothea, the goddess of sea spray who aided sailors in distress.

The tragedy of Oedipus

The story of the Greek hero Oedipus shows how fate can never be avoided. The myth features the Oracle at Delphi, a priestess who could predict the future, and highlights the danger of misinterpreting her prophecies. This dramatic tale is the subject of two famous plays by the Ancient Greek playwright Sophocles, and has been retold many times.

King Laius and Queen Jocasta of the Greek kingdom of Thebes were told by the Oracle at Delphi (see p.23) that their son would kill his father and marry his mother. Filled with terror by the prophecy, they abandoned the infant on a mountainside. However, a shepherd found the baby and took him to Polybus, the king of the neighboring kingdom of Corinth. Polybus and his queen, Merope, named the child Oedipus and brought him up as if he were their own son.

As a young man, Oedipus was accused of not being his father's son, but Polybus and Merope denied this. Oedipus visited the Oracle at Delphi, hoping to learn the truth of his parentage. The priestess, however, told him the same thing that she had told Laius and Jocasta: Oedipus was fated to kill his father and marry his mother. Confused at this revelation, Oedipus believed that the Oracle was referring to Polybus and Merope, whom he loved dearly. Hoping to avoid this terrible prophecy, Oedipus left the city of Corinth.

> Oedipus approached **the Sphinx** and was **able to answer its riddle**. In frustration, the beast **killed itself**.

OEDIPUS IN THEBES

On the journey, Oedipus met a chariot-driver at a crossroads. When the stranger rudely ordered Oedipus to get out of his way, the pair fought bitterly, and Oedipus ended up killing the chariot-driver. Oedipus continued on his travels and eventually arrived at the road that led to Thebes. Here he heard that the King of Thebes, Laius, had not returned from a journey, and that a monster called the Sphinx had been tormenting his people. The Sphinx would pose a riddle to passersby and devour those who were unable to answer it. Oedipus approached the Sphinx and was able to answer its riddle. In frustration, the beast killed itself.

This success brought Oedipus fame, and in the absence of Laius, he was given Queen Jocasta's hand in marriage and was crowned king. The pair lived happily for many

Oedipus answers the sphinx's riddle.

The wings of a sphinx were said to resemble those of an eagle.

◄ **THE SPHINX**
This mythical animal occurs in different forms across many cultures. The Greek form has a human head, a lion's body, and bird's wings.

years, until Thebes was struck with a terrible plague. To find a solution to the devastation, Oedipus sent a messenger to the Oracle at Delphi, who said that Laius had been killed, and the plague would end only when his murderer was found. Oedipus cursed the culprit and vowed to find him.

PROPHECY

Tiresias   Oedipus

The Ancient Greeks believed that oracles and sibyls had the power of prophecy (the ability to predict the future), although they often made predictions using vague words. The prophet Tiresias plays an important part in Oedipus's story.

THE ORACLE'S PROPHECY

Weeks later, Oedipus was no closer to finding Laius's killer. He met a blind prophet named Tiresias, who revealed that the chariot-driver Oedipus had killed at the crossroads many years ago was actually his real father, Laius. He added that Oedipus's wife Jocasta, was in fact his mother.

When Jocasta learned that Oedipus was the child she had abandoned so many years ago, and that the Oracle's prophecy had come true, she took her own life. Driven out of his mind by the events that had unfolded, Oedipus took one of Jocasta's dress pins and stabbed himself in the eyes, making himself blind. He then left his kingdom and spent his life wandering, comforted only by his faithful daughter Antigone. She acted as a guide for the blind Oedipus until he reached Colonus, a town close to Athens. The hero Theseus

▲ THE BLINDING OF OEDIPUS
When Oedipus blinded himself, it was seen as a tragic metaphor for the fact that he had been blind to the truth about his parents.

(see pp.38–39), by now the king of Athens, welcomed Oedipus and told him he would be looked after in the city. Oedipus never overcame his distress, but died peacefully before embarking on his final journey: to the Underworld (see p.26).

◀ ANTIGONE LEADS OEDIPUS
Oedipus's daughter Antigone was the only person to take pity on her father. Her name means "worthy of her parents."

47

The Trojan War

The *Iliad,* an epic poem by the Ancient Greek writer Homer, describes the final part of the war waged by the Greeks against the coastal city of Troy. The war ends after ten long years with the destruction of Troy. While some episodes in this tale feature gods and goddesses, others may be based on things that actually happened.

The events that led to the war between the Greeks and the people of Troy began with an incident on Mount Ida, where the goddesses Hera, Athena, and Aphrodite had an argument. Eris, the goddess of conflict (see p.29), had given them a golden apple inscribed with the words "for the fairest," but the three goddesses could not agree on who was the most beautiful. To solve the problem, Zeus asked the Trojan prince Paris to decide who should be awarded the apple. Each goddess tried to bribe Paris with the offer of a gift: Hera promised political power, Athena offered wisdom and success in battle, and Aphrodite assured him the love of Helen, the most beautiful woman in the world.

Helen

Helen was the wife of Menelaus, the king of the Greek state of Sparta. Paris chose Aphrodite's gift and gave her the golden apple, hoping to meet Helen in the future.

Years later, when Paris was in Sparta on a diplomatic mission, he saw Helen and instantly fell in love with her. As promised by Aphrodite, Helen also fell in love with Paris and escaped with him to Troy. Infuriated by this, Menelaus asked his brother Agamemnon, the king of Argos, for help. Under Agamemnon's command, the Greeks gathered a large army and a fleet of hundreds of ships, and set sail for Troy to bring Helen back.

A CATALOG OF HEROES

While the Greeks were led by King Agamemnon, the Trojan leaders were great generals such as Prince Hector of Troy. The opponents each had thousands of soldiers, with Achilles and Odysseus of Ithaca (see pp.54–57) for the Greeks and renowned warriors including Prince Paris and Aeneas (see pp.60–61) for the Trojans. Both sides also had the support of

◄ **THE "MASK OF AGAMEMNON"**
Found at the Ancient Greek site of Mycenae, this gold mask was once believed to depict the face of King Agamemnon.

gods: Hera and Athena, still offended by Paris's decision, supported the Greeks; Aphrodite, Apollo, and Poseidon favored Troy.

REBELLION IN THE RANKS

The Greeks attacked the city of Troy and the two sides fought for nine years with no overall victory. Much of the fighting was on the beach, outside the massive walls that protected Troy from its enemies, but the war also ranged more widely across the surrounding lands. At one point in the war, the Greeks raided a Trojan temple of the god Apollo, and Agamemnon abducted one of its priestesses. Apollo was angered by this and inflicted a plague upon the

Greek army. After nine days of suffering, the Greeks, led by Achilles, decided to end their misery by asking Agamemnon to release the Trojan priestess. Agamemnon reluctantly agreed but took Achilles's mistress for himself instead. In retaliation, Achilles withdrew his troops—warriors called

the Myrmidons—from the war. The Myrmidons were some of the bravest and best-equipped of all the Greek soldiers, and their leader was one of the greatest of all the Greek heroes. Without them, the Greeks began to lose ground, and it looked as though Troy would win the war.

To try to change their fortunes, Patroclus, who was Achilles's closest friend, went to the hero and begged him to return to the fight. When Achilles remained unwilling, Patroclus persuaded Achilles to let him lead the Myrmidons instead, disguised in Achilles's magical, impenetrable armor (see p.99). With the return of the Myrmidons, the Greek soldiers

... the **Greeks began to lose ground**, and it looked as though **Troy would win** the war.

The magical armor of Achilles meant that blows from swords, spears, and arrows had no effect.

GIFTS OF ACHILLES ▶

The Greek hero Achilles was given three magical gifts by his father, Peleus—his armor, his spear, and his chariot horses.

fought more fiercely, and the newly united Greek army seemed to be winning again, until the god Apollo stripped Patroclus of his armor, and the Trojan commander Hector killed him.

Devastated by the death of his friend, Achilles returned to the battlefield to seek revenge, vowing to kill Hector. The two warriors met in battle outside the city walls, each demonstrating fearsome strength and skill. Unfortunately for Troy, Achilles succeeded in putting Hector to death. Achilles showed no respect for his opponent when he dragged Hector's body across the battleground behind his chariot. Later, when Achilles refused to hand Hector's body over to the Trojans, he was visited by the Trojan king, Priam, who pleaded for the return of his dead son. In the end, Achilles agreed, and Priam was able to give Hector a proper burial.

▲ **THE DEATH OF PRIAM**
Showing no mercy for an old man, the Greeks ruthlessly killed Priam in the temple of Zeus.

A WOODEN GIFT

The Trojan army had suffered major losses and seemed to be losing their good fortune, but they refused to give up their city. The massive walls around Troy were almost impossible to breach, and no matter how many blows the Greeks delivered, it seemed that they would never take over the city and win the war. The turning point came when the goddess Athena guided the ingenious and cunning Greek hero Odysseus toward an idea for invading and defeating Troy. Odysseus suggested building a huge, hollow wooden statue of a horse and giving it to the Trojans as an offering to Athena. Hidden inside, however, would be a number of soldiers.

The Greeks built the horse and left it outside Troy's walls, with a message saying that they were returning home as they had been unable to take the city, and that this was their parting gift. They then returned to their ships,

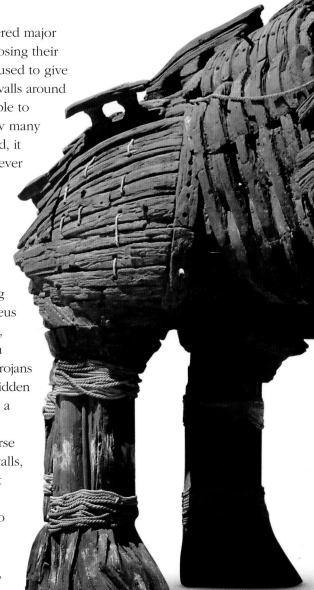

MODERN TROJAN HORSES

The phrase "Trojan horse" is now used for something harmful that is hidden inside an innocent disguise. A well-known example is a damaging computer program embedded in something that looks like a piece of genuine software. It is designed to trick people into installing it on their computer, which allows others to remotely gain access to important data stored there.

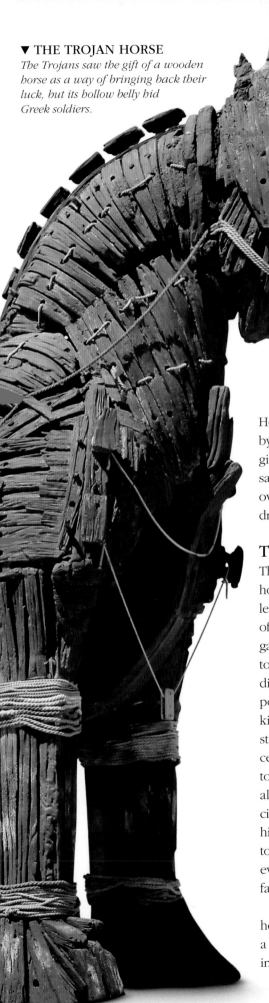

▼ THE TROJAN HORSE
The Trojans saw the gift of a wooden horse as a way of bringing back their luck, but its hollow belly hid Greek soldiers.

Ruins found in Hisarlik, in modern Turkey, are believed to be those of the ancient city of Troy.

pretending to prepare to sail away. A Trojan priest called Laocoön was suspicious of the gift, fearing that it was some kind of trick. However, his concerns were ignored by the other Trojans, who pulled the giant horse into the city. When they saw the Greeks retreating, they were overjoyed and spent the evening drinking in celebration of their victory.

THE FALL OF TROY
The Greek soldiers hidden inside the horse waited until nightfall before letting themselves out. Under the cover of darkness, they crept toward the city gates and opened them wide, signaling to the rest of the Greek army in the distance. Hordes of Greek soldiers poured into Troy, plundering and killing as they went. The Trojans, still drunk from the evening's celebrations, were in no state to resist the invasion, which allowed the Greeks to take over the city easily. As Troy burned around him, King Priam, fearful for his life, took refuge at the altar of Zeus, but even the gods could not change his fate, and he was killed.

Although Achilles seemed invincible, he had one weak spot. When he was a baby, his mother had dipped him in the magical River Styx (see p.26) in order to try to make him immortal. Unfortunately, she had held him by the back of his heel while dipping him in the river upside down, leaving this as the only vulnerable part of his body. The heel is where Paris attacked Achilles, killing him.

The massacre of the Trojans continued throughout the night and into the next day. When the dust settled, both sides had lost innumerable soldiers, but in the end it was the Greeks who had won the war.

▲ ACHILLES'S HEEL
Guided by Apollo, Paris shot a poisoned arrow right through Achilles's heel, which killed him.

51

Underworld deities

Most mythologies have an Underworld, usually a dark and unpleasant realm in which the souls of people dwell after death. These places are ruled by some of the most fearsome gods and goddesses, many of whom are evil or vengeful, although some are protectors and helpers of the souls of the dead.

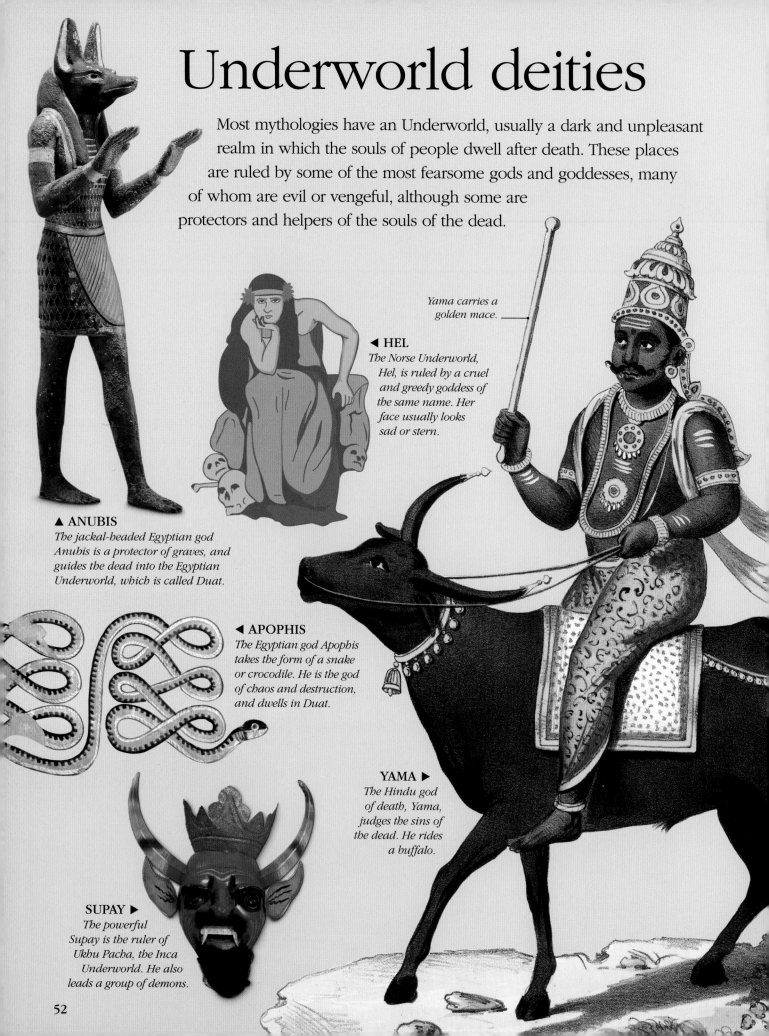

◄ **HEL**
The Norse Underworld, Hel, is ruled by a cruel and greedy goddess of the same name. Her face usually looks sad or stern.

Yama carries a golden mace.

▲ **ANUBIS**
The jackal-headed Egyptian god Anubis is a protector of graves, and guides the dead into the Egyptian Underworld, which is called Duat.

◄ **APOPHIS**
The Egyptian god Apophis takes the form of a snake or crocodile. He is the god of chaos and destruction, and dwells in Duat.

YAMA ►
The Hindu god of death, Yama, judges the sins of the dead. He rides a buffalo.

SUPAY ►
The powerful Supay is the ruler of Ukhu Pacha, the Inca Underworld. He also leads a group of demons.

◀ IZANAMI
Japanese creator deity Izanami is fatally burned when she gives birth to the fire god Kagutsuchi. Soon after, she goes to the Underworld and becomes its goddess.

SEE ALSO
- The Underworld, p.26
- The world tree, pp.66–67
- Inanna in the Underworld, pp.110–111
- Izanagi and Izanami, pp.140–141
- The Great War, pp.164–167
- The Egyptian afterlife, pp.178–179
- The Feathered Serpent, pp.196–199

The god wears a string of eyeballs.

◀ MICTLANTECUHTLI
This gruesome god is the king of Mictlan, the Aztec Underworld. He is depicted with blood smeared on his face.

ERESHKIGAL ▶
The Sumerian queen of the dead is Ereshkigal, who rules a vast realm beneath a range of mountains.

▲ AMMUT
The monstrous Egyptian goddess Ammut ("the devourer of the dead") eats the hearts of the sinners who arrive in Duat.

HADES ▶
In Greek mythology, Hades is the name of both the Underworld and its ruler. The god Hades is strict, but rarely cruel.

Hades has a fierce three-headed dog called Cerberus.

Baron Samedi greets dead people after their burial.

BARON SAMEDI ▶
In the Vodou religion of Haiti in the Caribbean, Baron Samedi is the loa *("spirit") of the dead. He is also a bringer of life, with the power to cure any disease.*

Odysseus journeys home

King of the Greek island of Ithaca, Odysseus was known for his cunning and wisdom. He fought on the side of the Greeks in the Trojan War, a conflict between the Greeks and the people of the city of Troy that lasted ten years. His most famous story is told in Homer's epic poem the *Odyssey*, which describes his journey back home from the war, and features stormy seas, monsters, and twists of fate.

After the war with Troy (see pp.48–51), Odysseus longed to be reunited with his wife Penelope and his son Telemachus, who had been a boy when Odysseus left for the war. He set sail for home with a small fleet of ships, but the journey back to Ithaca turned out to be long and perilous.

Odysseus's first stop was the island of the lotus-eaters, which was overgrown with a mysterious lotus plant. The fruit and flowers of this plant were so delicious that those who ate them stopped caring about anything else but eating more. Some of Odysseus's crew ate the fruit and stopped

LAESTRYGONIAN GIANTS ▶
On one stop, flesh-eating giants killed and ate many of Odysseus's men, and even destroyed their ships. Odysseus saved his ship by hiding it in a cave near the shore.

wanting to get home, but Odysseus made these reluctant sailors return to their ships and forbade the rest of the crew from eating the lotus.

At the next stop, Odysseus and his men encountered the Cyclopes (see pp.10–11), one-eyed giants who devoured human flesh. One of the Cyclopes, Polyphemus, imprisoned the travelers in a cave, and began to eat them one by one. Odysseus planned an escape. He

introduced himself to Polyphemus as Outis, which means "no one" in Greek. He then tricked the giant into getting drunk, before blinding him with a red-hot stick from a fire. When Polyphemus shouted, "Outis (no one) is killing me," the other giants were confused by the misleading name and did not come to his aid. Odysseus and his remaining companions were able to get away.

BATTLING THE WINDS

Although they had survived these early obstacles, the Greeks were constantly harassed by violent winds and storms that delayed their voyage. When their ships reached an island ruled by Aeolus, the god of the winds, Odysseus thought his luck would turn. Aeolus gave him a leather bag containing all the winds except one, which he set free to blow the ships back to Ithaca.

However, when they were within sight of Ithaca, some of the sailors grew curious, and opened the bag to look inside it. All the winds escaped the bag and a fierce storm raged all around them, blowing them back to the island of Aeolus. The god of the winds turned them away this time, because he assumed that the gods were angry with Odysseus. The rough winds blew Odysseus's ships to another island, which was home to a group of giants called the Laestrygonians. These beasts attacked the Greek ships, destroying all but one. Odysseus used this to make his escape, but could only take some of his sailors.

LURED AWAY

Odysseus's troubles were far from over, however. The next port for this band of travelers was the island of Aeaea. This island was the home of Circe (see p.191), a witch who had the power to transform people into animals. Circe invited the Greeks to a banquet, and as they ate, she

▲ CIRCE
Known for her vast knowledge of magical herbs and potions, the enchantress Circe could transform her enemies into dogs, lions, or, as with Odysseus's men, pigs.

▼ POLYPHEMUS ATTACKS THE SHIP
As Odysseus escaped, he taunted the giant by revealing his true identity. Polyphemus tried to take his revenge by destroying Odysseus's ship, but the Greeks managed to escape.

began to turn them into pigs. Seeing this, Odysseus immediately swallowed a magical herb that had been given to him by the god Hermes. This prevented him from being transformed. When Circe saw that Odysseus had the power to repel her magic, she turned his men back into humans.

Circe advised Odysseus to visit the Underworld (see p.26), and consult the prophet Tiresias (see p.47) about what the future held for him and whether he would be able to get home. The Greek hero became one of the very few mortals to make the journey to the Underworld and return safely.

In the Underworld, Tiresias foresaw that Odysseus would be shipwrecked on the way home, and that if he survived, he would only reach Ithaca in another's ship. He also told Odysseus that his house was overrun by men who ate his food and courted his wife.

The Romans called Odysseus "Ulysses" and considered him a villain not a hero.

▲ THE UNENDING TAPESTRY
Penelope kept her suitors at bay by saying she would pick a husband when she had finished weaving a tapestry. She would then secretly undo her work each night, which meant that the tapestry was never finished.

The words of Tiresias made Odysseus worry about his kingdom and the safety of his family. He returned to his ship more determined than ever to reach home. Little did he know that more perils awaited him.

The Greek ship had to sail past the island of the Sirens, creatures that were half bird and half woman. They sang beautiful songs that enchanted sailors, causing them

ANCIENT GREEK SHIPS

The Ancient Greeks lived mostly near the coast and on islands, so they relied heavily on ships for transportation and became excellent ship-builders. Their vessels had vast sails, and strong oars to guide the ships in the right direction in poor wind.

Modern reconstruction of an Ancient Greek ship from c.300 BCE

> The **words of Tiresias** made Odysseus worry about his kingdom and **the safety of his family**.

to crash their ships on the island's rocky coast. Odysseus commanded his sailors to block their ears, and had them tie him to the mast of the ship, so that he could hear the songs of the Sirens without endangering the ship.

After escaping the Sirens, the travelers had to make their way between Scylla (see p.148), a six-headed monster, and Charybdis, a powerful whirlpool. This brought Odysseus's ship to the island of the goddess Calypso, who fell in love with the Greek king and wanted him to stay with her. Calypso was so persuasive that Odysseus remained with her for seven years. In the end, his longing for his wife and son overcame Calypso's hold over him, and he and his men resumed their journey.

THE SHIPWRECK

Odysseus and his companions struggled with more unpredictable winds. During a terrible storm, their ship was hurled against rocks and destroyed. Odysseus survived the shipwreck and washed up on an island ruled by Alcinous, the king of the Phaeacians. The king's daughter Nausicaa found Odysseus on the beach, and took him to the palace where she clothed and fed him. Nausicaa fell in love with Odysseus, but he insisted on returning home. Alcinous provided Odysseus with a new ship, and a tired and aged Odysseus finally arrived back in Ithaca. Yet Odysseus's difficulties were not yet over. As Tiresias had predicted, in Odysseus's absence his house had been taken over by a group of men, who were vying to become king by marrying his wife Penelope.

PENELOPE'S SUITORS

Although Odysseus should have come back from the war years ago and most people thought he must be dead, Penelope believed that her husband would return. She tried various tricks to keep her suitors away. When Odysseus's father died, Penelope began weaving a funerary tapestry for him. She told her suitors that she would pick a husband only after this work had been completed. However, she never

▼ **A KING IN DISGUISE**
On his return to Ithaca, Odysseus visited his palace disguised a beggar, so that he could see what Penelope's suitors were up to, and plan their defeat.

▶ ODYSSEUS'S REVENGE
With the help of Telemachus, Odysseus killed all the suitors as punishment for trying to steal his wife and kingdom.

intended to finish this tapestry, and hoped that the men would tire of waiting and leave. Unfortunately, her plan was eventually found out and she was forced to make a decision on a new husband. Penelope declared that she would marry the man who could string Odysseus's powerful bow, knowing that her suitors would fail to do so.

Odysseus himself decided to compete. He disguised himself as an old, ragged beggar, revealing his identity to his son Telemachus, but nobody else. At the contest, Odysseus was the only one who

succeeded in stringing the bow. Penelope was overjoyed when she realized the winner was none other than her husband Odysseus. With the help of Telemachus, Odysseus then killed all the suitors, and was finally reunited with his wife and his son.

EUROPE

> Penelope declared that **she would marry** the man **who could string Odysseus's bow.**

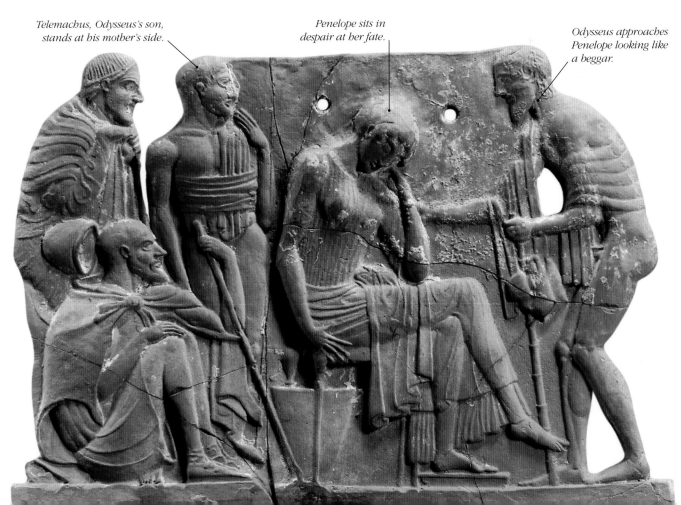

Telemachus, Odysseus's son, stands at his mother's side.

Penelope sits in despair at her fate.

Odysseus approaches Penelope looking like a beggar.

The trial of Orestes

Three plays by the great Ancient Greek playwright Aeschylus, known collectively as the *Oresteia*, follow the tragic hero Orestes as he sets out to avenge the murder of his father. The stories illustrate how, in Ancient Greece, a court trial came to be seen as a better way to seek justice than pursuing personal revenge.

EUROPE

Agamemnon, the king of the Greek city-state of Argos, was about to set sail for the war against Troy (see pp.48–51), but his large fleet of ships was held up because the winds were blowing in the wrong direction. The Greeks believed that Artemis, the goddess of the hunt, was making the winds unfavorable because Agamemnon had killed a deer, an animal that was sacred to her. A prophet told Agamemnon that the only way to remedy this was to kill his daughter Iphigenia as a sacrifice to Artemis. Reluctant at first, the king eventually did as he was advised, and soon the winds changed, allowing the Greeks to set sail for Troy.

A QUEEN'S BETRAYAL

The Trojan War kept Agamemnon away from his kingdom for nearly a decade. During this time, his queen Clytemnestra was unfaithful to him with Aegisthus, who was Agamemnon's cousin and a rival for the throne of Argos. She was also bitterly angry about the death of her daughter Iphigenia and plotted her revenge against Agamemnon.

When he returned home from Troy, Agamemnon was unaware that Aegisthus was living in his house. With the help of her lover, Clytemnestra killed Agamemnon. The wicked Aegisthus then made himself king, and ruled Argos with Clytemnestra.

A TERRIBLE CRIME

Agamemnon's son Orestes was away from Argos when his father was killed. When Orestes returned home many years later, he learned of Agamemnon's murder. The god Apollo (see p.22) encouraged Orestes to avenge his father's death by killing those responsible for it. Orestes disguised himself and sneaked into the palace, where he murdered Aegisthus and Clytemnestra.

THE ERINYES

As Clytemnestra lay dying, she cursed Orestes to be pursued to the point of madness by the Erinyes, three fearsome goddesses of vengeance. Apollo took pity on Orestes and sent him to Delphi, the site of the god's temple (see p.23). At Delphi, Apollo

> Athena renamed the Erinyes as the Eumenides ("kindly ones") to pacify them.

KILLING THE KING

The act of killing a king is a common theme in many myths. Although this crime is often committed for political power or revenge, as in this story, it is sometimes caused unknowingly, as with Oedipus (see pp.46–47). People thought that the murder of a king brought misfortune upon the land, and required purification of the culprit by the gods for order to be restored.

The killing of Agamemnon

▲ SEIZED BY THE ERINYES
Also known as the Furies, the Erinyes relentlessly chased Orestes, torturing him until he went mad.

purified Orestes, and he was healed of his madness. However, the Erinyes continued to hound Orestes until he prayed to the goddess Athena (see pp.24–25) for help.

Athena responded by setting up a trial for Orestes in Athens, where he would face judgement for the murders he had committed. The judges in the trial could not agree on a verdict, but

Athena, who oversaw the court, intervened and declared that Orestes should not be too harshly punished, and should go free. She decreed that, from then on, justice should be decided by trial within a court of law.

ORESTES IS PURIFIED ▶
The purification ritual involved the sacrifice of a pig. Apollo held a piglet over Orestes's head to cleanse him of his sins.

59

◄ FLEEING TROY

Anchises was 80 years old and frail by the end of the Trojan War. His son Aeneas had to carry him as they escaped the burning ruins of Troy.

Aeneas's destiny

The Ancient Roman poet Virgil explained the mythical origins of the city of Rome in his epic poem, the *Aeneid*. The story begins after the Trojan War has ended, and follows the defeated Trojan prince Aeneas as he leads a group of survivors in their quest to find a new home.

Aeneas was the son of Anchises, the brother of King Priam of Troy. After their defeat by the Greeks in the Trojan War (see pp.48–51), Aeneas, Anchises, and the other surviving Trojans were forced to flee Troy. Setting sail from the city, they traveled across the Mediterranean Sea. When they reached the island of Delos, Aeneas made sacrifices to the god Apollo, who told the Trojans to go to the island of Crete.

While in Crete, Aeneas had a vision in which the gods told him to go to Italy, where he would play a part in establishing a great new city. On the journey there, Aeneas and his fellow Trojans stopped off in Sicily. Unfortunately, Aeneas's aged father had been weakened by his travels and died, which deeply upset the Trojan prince.

DIDO OF CARTHAGE

A storm then blew Aeneas's ships away from Italy to the city of Carthage, where he met its great queen, Dido. The two fell in love, and Aeneas briefly forgot his vision and the instructions from the gods. However, Jupiter, king of the gods (the Roman equivalent of the Greek Zeus), sent his messenger Mercury (known as Hermes to the Greeks) to remind Aeneas

of his destiny. Realizing his mistake, Aeneas left Carthage immediately, without even saying goodbye to Dido. The Carthaginian queen watched heartbroken as Aeneas's ships departed from her shores. Feeling that life was no longer worth living, she killed herself.

Dido drapes a garland of flowers around Aeneas.

IN THE UNDERWORLD

Aeneas returned to Sicily, where he honored the first anniversary of his father's death by organizing funeral games. Aeneas still missed his father and so he went to the settlement of Cumae, which was home to a sibyl—a priestess of Apollo who had the power of prophecy. The Sibyl of Cumae led Aeneas to the Underworld (see p.26), where he was able to meet Anchises again.

During their time together, Aeneas's father foretold the establishment of the city of Rome and showed his son a vision of the spirits of the great people who would be born there. Aeneas also met the spirit of Dido in the Underworld, realizing for the first time that the queen he had deserted was dead.

SAILING TO LATIUM

Upon his return from the Underworld, Aeneas led his Trojan followers back to their ships and they sailed to a place called Latium, at the mouth of the Tiber River in Italy. Here, the Trojans were warmly welcomed by the local king, Latinus. Aeneas was convinced that this was the place where they should build their new city. He also hoped to marry Latinus's daughter, Lavinia, to create an alliance with the king.

However, the woman's mother Amata had promised Lavinia's hand in marriage to Turnus, the king of the Rutuli tribe.

The sibyl records her predictions in a book.

◄ THE SIBYL OF CUMAE
As well as delivering prophecies, sibyls also acted as bridges between the worlds of the living and the dead. Aeneas sought out the Sibyl of Cumae because he knew that she would be able to lead him into the Underworld and bring him back safely.

EUROPE

The Romans believed their great leader Julius Caesar was a descendant of Aeneas.

A dispute arose between Aeneas and Turnus for Lavinia's hand in marriage and for control of the lands of Latium. The goddess Juno (known as Hera to the Greeks) took Turnus's side and provoked a war between the Trojans and the Rutulians. The conflict was eventually won by the Trojans, after Aeneas defeated and killed Turnus in hand-to-hand combat. This left the Trojan prince free to marry Lavinia and inherit the lands of her father. Aeneas and his fellow Trojans lived in harmony with the people of Latium and Rutuli, and, in time, they all came together to form the settlement by the Tiber River that would one day be known as Rome.

ROMULUS AND REMUS

Many years after Aeneas had united the people of Troy, Latium, and Rutuli, the story goes that two of his descendants—the twins Romulus and Remus—were abandoned at birth. They were suckled by a she-wolf, and later raised by a shepherd. When they grew up, they established the city of Rome, fulfilling the prophecy given to Aeneas.

◄ AENEAS AND DIDO
The prince and the queen fell deeply in love with one another, but their happiness was cut short when the gods reminded Aeneas of his duty.

Aeneas **had a vision** in which the gods told him that he would **play a part** in establishing a **great new city**.

Vesta, the domestic goddess

The Ancient Romans worshipped Vesta, the goddess of the hearth (fireplace), because they regarded the hearth as the most important place in their homes. This story tells how the goddess is so dedicated to her task of looking after the warmth and light in Roman households that she refuses to marry.

▲ VESTA
The Roman equivalent of the Greek goddess Hestia, Vesta was usually shown clothed in fine robes and carrying a scepter.

Vesta was the protector of the hearth and home, and she wanted to stay unmarried so that she could focus on her duties. She begged her brother Jupiter (the Roman equivalent of the Greek Zeus) to allow her to remain single, and he agreed. However, Vesta was very beautiful, and many were attracted to her, including Priapus, the god of fertility.

The mother goddess, Cybele, decided to throw a party one night and invited many immortals, including Vesta and her admirers. Vesta ate and drank until she was so full and tired that she fell asleep. Priapus saw the sleeping goddess and planned to carry her away. Fortunately, a donkey belonging to Silenus the satyr (a creature that is part man, part goat) was standing nearby. It brayed loudly as Priapus approached, waking Vesta from her slumbers. As the other gods and goddesses came running in alarm, Priapus fled in shame.

Vesta was safe, and able to continue in her important role as guardian of Roman homes.

Vesta **begged her brother** Jupiter **to allow her to remain single**, and **he agreed**.

ROMAN HOUSEHOLD DEITIES

In addition to Vesta, the Ancient Romans worshipped two groups of gods, the Lares and the Penates, as special guardians of their households. Families usually kept small shrines to them in their homes, and would give offerings in return for protection from thieves. The Penates also looked after the family's larder and food supply.

At the Temple of Vesta in Rome, women celebrated the Vestalia festival to honor the goddess.

The spring deity

The Roman goddess Flora looked after flowering plants and crops, and was also associated with the season of spring. Her story is one of happiness and good fortune.

The goddess Flora helped plants and trees on Earth to bloom and bear fruit. She was also a meadow nymph and made her home in the fields. It was said that everyone who visited the countryside became happy and contented just like her.

One day, the god of the west wind, Favonius (the Roman equivalent of the Greek Zephyrus), blew in Flora's direction. Favonius caught sight of Flora and was enchanted by her. After watching her for a while, the god began to follow Flora, hoping to win her affections. The shy nymph was startled at first and tried to run away, but Favonius continued to pursue her until he caught up with her. All ended well, as Flora fell in love with Favonius when she saw him. The couple soon married and lived happily together. Their combined powers of bringing fertile soil and good weather gave Earth abundant harvests.

▲ **TAPESTRY OF FLORA**
Flora wears flowers and foliage in her hair as she walks among spring flowers in this tapestry.

Pomona's orchard

The Roman deity Pomona was the goddess of fruit trees and orchards. A tale from Roman poet Ovid's *Metamorphoses* describes how the god Vertumnus tries to win Pomona's hand in marriage.

▲ **THE GODDESS OF PLENTY**
Pomona is one of the few Roman goddesses who does not have a Greek counterpart. She represented abundance and was always shown carrying flowers and fruit.

Pomona spent her days tending to the fruit trees to ensure a plentiful harvest. Her work kept her so busy that she rarely had time for anything else—including love. To focus on her important tasks, she did not allow any male suitors to enter her orchard.

One of Pomona's admirers was Vertumnus, the god of seasons. In order to be allowed into the orchard, he disguised himself as an old woman. He praised the fruit trees and Pomona's beauty, and told her to marry the honest and faithful Vertumnus. The old woman then related the tragic story of Iphis and Anaxerete. He told Pomona how Iphis was in love with the noble woman Anaxerete, and killed himself after he was scorned by her. In the end, Anaxerete herself turned to stone when she saw Iphis's dead body.

The old woman then revealed herself to be Vertumnus and asked for Pomona's hand. Moved by the story of Iphis's love for Anaxerete, Pomona agreed to marry her admirer, and together they presided over the flourishing of the land.

The creation of the cosmos

The creation story of the Norse, people who lived in present-day Scandinavia from c.800 CE to c.1300 CE, tells of how the world is formed between two regions of extreme heat and cold. It also describes the first beings to emerge from the ice—the ancestors of the Norse creator gods—as well as the origin of the first man and woman.

In the beginning, there was nothing but a barren, frozen emptiness called Ginnungagap. Over time, two realms gradually formed on either side of this space. In the south was Muspelheim, a place of heat and fire, and in the north was Niflheim, an icy world. The cold air blowing from Niflheim and the warm breeze that flowed from Muspelheim met in the frosty expanse of Ginnungagap that lay between them, causing it to thaw.

THE FIRST GIANTS

The first life forms emerged out of the melting ice in Ginnungagap: an enormous cow called Audhumla

ODIN, VILI, AND VE ▲
The three brothers played an important part in creating the world. Led by Odin, these Norse deities were the first of the Aesir.

and a monstrous frost giant called Ymir. Audhumla fed Ymir with her milk, and licked the ice around her to quench her thirst. As she did so, the ice continued to melt, freeing a giant being named Búri. Ymir's body produced more frost giants, until many of them roamed through Niflheim. Bor, the son of Búri, married one of them—a giantess named Bestla. Their three children—Odin, Vili, and Ve—became the first of the Norse gods.

THE CREATION OF THE WORLD

The three gods and the giants were always fighting. Eventually, Odin, Vili, and Ve combined their strength to slay the frost giant Ymir. A river of blood flowed from Ymir's dead body and drowned almost all the remaining frost giants, except for Ymir's grandson Bergelmir, who survived the flood along with his wife. The couple later established a second generation of frost giants in the distant realm of Jötunheim (see pp.66–67).

From Ymir's body, Odin, Vili, and Ve made Earth: Ymir's bones became the mountains, his blood the rivers and seas, and his skull the sky. The three creator gods then built for themselves a fortress in the sky, high up in the clouds, and named it Asgard (see pp.66–67). These gods, as well as their children, were known as the Aesir (see pp.66–67), or sky gods.

THE FIRST HUMANS

One day, the three Aesir creators were walking along a beach when they came across two trees, an ash and an elm. The gods decided to use the trees to create new beings. From the ash tree they formed Ask, the first man, and from the elm they made Embla, the first woman.

At first the new creations had no life, so each of the gods gave them a gift. Odin breathed into them the breath of life, Vili gave them thoughts and feelings, and Ve blessed them with

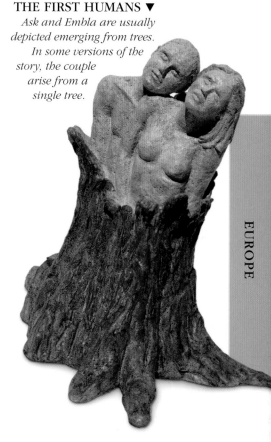

THE FIRST HUMANS ▼
Ask and Embla are usually depicted emerging from trees. In some versions of the story, the couple arise from a single tree.

EUROPE

the senses of sight and hearing. The gods then created a home for the first humans at the center of the Norse cosmos, and called it Midgard (see p.67). Ask and Embla married and settled in Midgard, and became the ancestors of humankind.

The Norse word for "god" means "pillar" or "vital force," things that held the cosmos together.

◄ THE FIRST CREATURES
For a long time, Audhumla, Ymir, and Búri (left to right) were the only beings that lived on the barren, frozen landscape of Ginnungagap.

65

The world tree

In Norse mythology, an enormous ash tree called Yggdrasil holds up the entire universe. The tree supports nine realms (lands) where different kinds of beings live. Old Norse texts such as the *Poetic Edda* and *Prose Edda* have different descriptions of where the nine realms are located, so it is difficult to confirm their exact positions on the tree.

The entire Norse Universe, from the highest realm to Hel, the Underworld, was built around the "world tree" known as Yggdrasil. The tree held up the nine realms that made up the cosmos, and was home to all: animals, giants, gods, and humans, as well as the souls of the dead.

The most powerful gods and goddesses, known as the Aesir, lived in a realm called Asgard, which was

Yggdrasil has influenced the setting of modern fantasy novels, comics, and even video games.

The stags fed on Yggdrasil's leaves and small branches, keeping the tree pruned.

Bifröst allowed the souls of dead heroes to reach Valhalla (the magnificent hall of the god Odin), which was their resting place in Asgard.

The frost giants lived in the frozen mountains of the wintery land of Jötunheim.

The land of Vanaheim was home to a group of gods and goddesses known as the Vanir.

Dwarves, also known as dark elves, lived in a region called Svartalfheim. They were expert metalworkers and craftsmen.

The fiery world of Muspelheim near the bottom of the tree was inhabited by the fire giants.

▼ HEIMDALL
The god Heimdall stood at the end of Bifröst, guarding the entrance to Asgard. He held his horn Gjallarhorn ready to sound the alarm if Asgard was attacked.

YGGDRASIL ▶
There are many different depictions of Yggdrasil, depending on the source of information. This is an artist's impression of one version of the world tree.

Hraesvelg the eagle made the wind by flapping its wings.

Ratatosk the squirrel often carried rude messages from Nidhogg to Hraesvelg.

The fortified land of Asgard, home to the powerful Aesir, was the highest realm on the world tree.

A place of light and glory, the realm called Alfheim was home to noble beings known as the light elves.

The land of humans, Midgard, was located right in the middle of the world tree.

Jörmungand was large enough to surround the central realms and still grasp its own tail.

Niflheim was an icy cold realm, except for where warm water spouted from the hot spring Hvergelmir.

A cunning serpent called Nidhogg lived among Yggdrasil's roots.

The Underworld was where the souls of evil men and women went after death. It was the realm of Queen Hel (see p.52).

▲ MIMIR'S WELL
The head of the frost giant Mimir could be found among the roots of Yggdrasil. Nearby was a well, the waters of which were a source of wisdom (see p.68).

EUROPE

held up in the sky by the branches of the tree. Asgard was connected to Midgard, the realm of the humans, by a rainbow bridge called Bifröst. Only the gods and goddesses, as well as the souls of heroes who had died in battle, were allowed to use this bridge.

Near Midgard were the realms of Vanaheim, Jötunheim, Alfheim, and Svartalfheim. A vast ocean surrounded these lands, and was home to the monstrous serpent Jörmungand.

In the roots of the tree were three further realms: Muspelheim, a world of fire; Niflheim, which was icy cold; and the Underworld, home of the dead.

Like any tree, Yggdrasil was inhabited by animals and birds. A serpent called Nidhogg gnawed at the roots of the tree. The serpent's enemy was a large eagle named Hraesvelg, which lived at the top of the tree. Four stags called Dáinn, Dvalinn, Duneyrr, and Durathrór lived among the branches of Yggdrasil, while a squirrel called Ratatosk ran up and down the tree.

The well-being of the cosmos depended entirely on the health of Yggdrasil. When the tree shook, it signaled the start of Ragnarök, the end of the universe (see p.71).

Odin's wisdom

One of the strongest and bravest of all the Norse gods, Odin is also wise. As the leader of the Aesir, he never stops seeking knowledge, but has to make sacrifices in order to gain wisdom.

Odin, the god of war, was a fierce and noble warrior. However, he also sought wisdom. Odin had dreamt of his death and the destruction of the world in Ragnarök (see p.71), and wished to find a way to avoid it.

Beneath the roots of the world tree Yggdrasil (see pp.66–67) there were three magical wells. One was called Mimir's Well. Here sat the head of the wise god Mimir. This well's water gave any drinker knowledge, but demanded a sacrifice in return. Odin took out one of his eyes as payment for a sip of the water, and became wise, but he still did not gain all the knowledge he sought.

Odin yearned for the knowledge of the magical runes (see right), which sprang from the Well of Urd under Yggdrasil. For this, Odin was prepared to make a second sacrifice. He strung himself upside down from Yggdrasil's trunk and then pierced himself with a spear, offering his whole body to this well.

After nine days and nights, the water gave up its greatest secret to Odin: the knowledge of the runes for making magic spells. Odin had now become the god of wisdom.

▲ **ODIN'S WOLVES AND RAVENS**
Odin had two hungry wolves, Freki and Geri, and two ravens, Hugin and Munin. The ravens flew around gathering news for Odin from all over the cosmos.

RUNES

In one version of the myth, Odin is believed to have created the first Norse alphabet, which took the form of runes. Formed mainly of straight and diagonal lines, runes were easy to carve on stone. Some runic inscriptions were even believed to have magical powers.

Thor's hammer

Odin's son Thor controls the thunder and wields his great power through a huge and magical hammer. The story of what happens when Thor's hammer is stolen shows how, at times, strength is not enough on its own, and may need to be combined with cunning.

The thunder god Thor carried a great hammer called Mjölnir. It was made for him by dwarves, whose skills gave the weapon supernatural strength and power. Thor used the mighty hammer to crush his enemies, and the weapon never missed its target, always returning to Thor no matter how far it was thrown. Thor could also use the hammer in traditional blessing ceremonies, performed on those he favored. Many gods and giants were jealous of Thor for Mjölnir.

LOKI'S PLAN

One giant, Thrym, wanted Thor's hammer so badly that he stole it, and said he would return it only if he were able to marry Freyja, the goddess of love (see p.223). However, the goddess refused to marry the giant, so Thor decided to retrieve his hammer another way. He asked the trickster god Loki (see p.29) for help.

Loki came up with a clever plan. He dressed Thor up as the goddess Freyja and sent him to Jötunheim, the realm of the frost giants, to pretend to marry Thrym. It was customary for the owner of the hammer to bless the bride at the wedding feast, so when the time came for this ritual, Thrym

picked up Mjölnir. Then Thor, still in disguise, grabbed his hammer and killed the frost giant. He proceeded to destroy the entire feasting hall as well. A triumphant Thor later returned to Asgard, reunited with his hammer once again.

The Vikings wore charms shaped like Thor's hammer for protection.

◄ MIGHTY THOR
Thor is often depicted fighting the giants, the enemies of the Aesir gods, as in this 19th-century painting.

Loki and Balder

The Norse trickster god Loki loved playing amusing pranks, but sometimes his mischievous actions took a more serious turn. On one occasion, the god Balder becomes the target of Loki's trickery—with tragic consequences.

Balder was the son of the god Odin (see p.68) and his wife, Frigg (see p.126), the most powerful of the Norse goddesses. Loved by all the gods, Balder was the origin of all that was good in the world. One night, he had a terrifying dream that he would die. When he told his mother about this, the goddess became distressed at the thought of losing her son. Anxious to protect Balder, she made every living thing in the world promise to not harm him. However, in her haste, Frigg overlooked the mistletoe, a small and harmless plant.

LOKI'S TRICK

The gods, now convinced that nothing could hurt Balder, used him as a target when they practiced shooting arrows. Determined to make mischief, crafty Loki tricked Frigg into revealing that she had not asked the mistletoe not to harm Balder. Loki took immediate advantage of Frigg's mistake. He sharpened a branch of mistletoe into an arrow, and gave it

▲ DEATH OF BALDER
In this depiction of Balder's death, blind Höd pierces his brother with a spear of mistletoe rather than an arrow, with Loki helping to guide the spear.

to Balder's brother, the blind god Höd. When Höd shot at Balder during practice, the arrow, guided by Loki, went straight through Balder's body and killed the young god. The trickster god's actions would eventually cause the devastating battle of Ragnarök (see opposite). Enraged by his prank, the gods tied Loki up under a poisonous snake that dripped venom onto his face. He remains there in agony, but one day will break free.

> Balder's name may mean "white one" or "shining one" as he was the fairest of all beings.

MISTLETOE

Mistletoe grows on other trees, taking nutrients from them. Because it remains green all winter while its host may look lifeless, mistletoe was often thought to have magical properties. In some northern European cultures, it was used in religious rituals and even in medicine.

Ragnarök

The story of Ragnarök, or "The Fate of the Gods," is an unusual tale in Norse mythology, because it predicts the future: how the world will end. This ominous event will see the gods, goddesses, giants, and humans wiped out in an epic battle.

The death of Balder (see opposite), erased the source of beauty and goodness from the world. At the time of Ragnarök, violence and evil will begin to spread through the universe, and humans will fight one another. The warmth of the sun will fade, leaving Earth bitterly cold and dark.

In the middle of this chaos, Loki will break free from his tethers (see opposite). Accompanied by the fearsome wolf Fenrir, the giant serpent Jörmungand, and Hel (see p.52), the queen of the Underworld, Loki will lead a force of frost giants (see pp.66–67) and monsters in a war against the gods. At the same time, a group of fire giants from Muspelheim march across Bifröst, the rainbow bridge (see pp.66–67). Seeing all of this unfold, Heimdall sounds the Gjallarhorn (see p.99) to warn the gods of their approach.

FIGHTING TO THE DEATH

The gods will go to war with their enemies even though they know the outcome of Ragnarök has been foretold (see p.68). Odin (see p.68) leads his band of warriors in an attack against the ferocious Fenrir, but the wolf's enormous jaws will swallow them all. Wielding his mighty hammer, Thor (see p.69) fights and kills the serpent Jörmungand, but dies from its venomous bite. In another fight, Loki and Heimdall will be locked in fierce combat, until they both die. Soon, almost every living creature in the world will join the fighting. At the end of the battle, only a handful of gods

will be left and all else will be wiped out. The remains of the world will then sink beneath the sea, and from it, another lush, green one will emerge. A man named Lif and a woman named Lifthrasir will appear from the branches of Yggdrasil, and start a family, eventually repopulating Earth. The gods who had survived will then arise from the Underworld, and a new cosmos will be created.

▼ **FENRIR AND ODIN**
Large and fierce, Fenrir towers above Odin as the god charges at the wolf on his horse, Sleipnir.

The Ring saga

This famous Norse myth tells of the misfortunes that happen to those who come to possess the cursed treasure of the dwarf Andvari. The main part of the story follows the fate of the hero Sigurd, and describes how he is ruined by wearing a gold ring from Andvari's hoard.

Armed with the reconstructed sword, Sigurd kills the dragon Fafnir by slicing through the beast's scaly body.

The sword is tested on the smith's anvil, but the blade breaks into two parts.

The smith Regin (left) forges the sword, while Sigurd works the bellows to blow air over the fire and keep it hot.

◀ FORGING THE SWORD
The making of Sigurd's sword is shown (bottom to top) on this carved wooden panel, which formed part of the doorway to a church in Setesdal, Norway.

The dwarf-king Hreidmar had three sons: a blacksmith named Regin, a shape-shifting fisherman called Otr, and the fierce Fafnir. One day, the gods Odin (see p.68), Loki (see p.70), and Hoenir killed Otr when he was in his otter-form, then skinned and ate him. Hreidmar angrily demanded compensation for the death of his son, asking the gods to give him enough gold to fill Otr's skin. To fulfill this demand, Loki stole the treasure of the rich dwarf Andvari, and gave this to Hreidmar. What Loki did not know, however, was that Andvari had placed a curse on his hoard of gold rings, brooches, and necklaces that would bring bad luck to whoever possessed it.

The first to suffer from the curse was Hreidmar. He was killed by his son Fafnir, who took the precious gold items for himself. Fafnir, in turn, was transformed into a dragon by the curse and spent his days viciously defending his ill-gotten gains.

▲ FAFNIR
Transforming into a dragon made Fafnir into a force of evil, but it also gave his blood magical properties.

THE PLOT AGAINST FAFNIR
When Regin heard of his father's murder, he decided to avenge his death and take the treasure for himself. Regin had raised a boy named Sigurd, after the death of the child's father, King Sigmund. He told Sigurd stories of the gold that was guarded by the dragon Fafnir, hoping to entice him into going after the monster. Regin asked Sigurd to bring the dragon's heart so the blacksmith could eat it. He also made a special sword for Sigurd to kill the dragon.

Armed with his new weapon, Sigurd successfully killed Fafnir. While cooking the heart for Regin over a fire, Sigurd licked his finger, accidentally tasting the dragon's blood. Sigurd instantly became aware that Regin plotted to kill him and keep the treasure for himself, so in a flash, Sigurd cut off Regin's head. With the last of Hreidmar's sons now dead, the treasure was Sigurd's to claim. The young hero took the

THE GERMANIC TALE

Written in c. 1200 CE, the German epic poem *Nibelungenlied* (*The Song of the Nibelungs*) is based on the tale of Sigurd, which was well-known in medieval Germany. In it, the characters have German names: Sigurd is called Siegfried, and Brynhild is named Brünhild.

treasure and even placed a gold ring on his finger. Little did he know that he, too, was now doomed.

THE FORGOTTEN PROMISE

Sigurd loved Brynhild, and they agreed to get married. He gave Brynhild his gold ring as a symbol of his love and went on his way, promising to return before long. Soon he reached the kingdom of King Gjuki and his wicked wife Grimhild, and became a friend of their sons Gunnar and Guthorm. Grimhild tricked Sigurd into drinking a magic potion that made him

forget his beloved Brynhild, and he now promised to marry Grimhild's daughter, Gudrun.

Grimhild then arranged a marriage between Brynhild and her son Gunnar. However, Brynhild refused the match, saying she would only accept a man who could cross the wall of fire that surrounded her castle. Brynhild thought only her beloved Sigurd would be able to do this. Spellbound by the magic potion, Sigurd shape-shifted into Gunnar to attempt the feat. He succeeded in his task, which tricked Brynhild into marrying the real Gunnar.

Eventually, Brynhild found out that she had been fooled by Sigurd, and in a fit of rage had him killed. Ultimately, his death only caused her more pain and, inconsolable, Brynhild killed herself. The cursed treasure of Andvari had brought an untimely end to their love story.

This panel, from the other side of the church doorway, shows (bottom to top) how Sigurd tasted the dragon's blood, and realized that Regin planned to kill him.

Sigurd kills Regin with a blow of his sword.

Sigurd's horse Grani carries a chest, which Sigurd had filled with treasure from Fafnir's lair.

The Norse and German tales were adapted into four operas by the German composer Richard Wagner.

Sigurd and Regin roast Fafnir's heart over a fire, as Sigurd tastes the dragon's blood on his thumb.

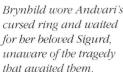

▶ **BRYNHILD**
Brynhild wore Andvari's cursed ring and waited for her beloved Sigurd, unaware of the tragedy that awaited them.

The impossible quest

The national epic of Finland, the *Kalevala*, brings together a number of different traditional tales. It contains stories about the rivalry between Finland and another country, the Land of the North, or Pohjola. Central to the poem are the adventures of three Finnish heroes, Väinämöinen, his brother Ilmarinen, and the trickster Lemminkäinen.

The hero Väinämöinen was the son of Luonnotar, a female nature spirit who lived in the ocean. Väinämöinen spent so long in his mother's womb that he was born as an old man, but what he lacked in youthful energy, he made up for in determination. Väinämöinen swam across the ocean until he reached a new land, which he made his home. This land would come to be known as Finland. Väinämöinen wanted to marry Aino, the sister of the giant Joukahainen, but Aino would not have him as a husband because he was too old. Heartbroken, Väinämöinen decided to go to the land of Pohjola in the north to find himself a bride.

A STRING OF TASKS

Väinämöinen arrived in Pohjola after an arduous journey, and met its ruler Louhi, who had magical powers. She promised Väinämöinen her daughter's hand in marriage, but only if he could build a sampo, a magical object that could produce salt, flour, and gold. No one had ever built a sampo, and Väinämöinen did not know how it could be done, but he decided to try. In the meantime, he met Louhi's daughter, the Maid of the North, and proposed marriage to her. To his surprise, she agreed to marry him even if he failed to fulfill her mother's demand for a sampo. The Maid did, however, set down further conditions and near-impossible tasks for Väinämöinen to complete before the wedding could take place. The challenges included peeling a stone, knotting an egg, splitting a hair with a blunt knife, and making a boat out of a weaving shuttle. Queen Louhi made things even more difficult for him by sending spirits who constantly distracted him from these tasks. Frustrated by this, Väinämöinen asked his brother, the master craftsman Ilmarinen, to help him out by making the sampo for him. In fact, Ilmarinen was the only person in Finland who had the skill to create such a device, and after much hard work, he finally managed to forge the magical sampo. However, Louhi still refused Väinämöinen's requests to marry her daughter, and asked him to perform yet more tasks, such as ploughing a field full of vipers. Amazingly, Väinämöinen managed to pass all the tests. Louhi now reminded him that her daughter

Finnish scholar Elias Lönnrot put together various folk poems and stories to make the epic poem *Kalevala*.

Väinämöinen plays the kantele by plucking its strings.

◀ VÄINÄMÖINEN
In some versions of the myth, Väinämöinen is a godlike figure, while in others he is a mortal hero. In both cases he possesses musical skill and great wisdom.

was promised to the man who had actually built the sampo, so Väinämöinen was prevented yet again from marrying the woman he desired. The Maid of the North became Ilmarinen's bride.

> ... after much **hard work**, he finally managed to **forge the magical sampo**.

THE PLOT AGAINST POHJOLA

Ilmarinen's marriage to Louhi's daughter did not last long, however. The Maid of the North had previously ill-treated Kullervo, a powerful magician whom she had made her slave. When she damaged Kullervo's magical knife, he placed a curse on her that made her cattle attack and kill her. Ilmarinen now asked for Louhi's other daughter in marriage, but Louhi refused. Angry Ilmarinen decided to leave Pohjola and return with Väinämöinen to Finland. The sampo remained in the Land of the North.

Ilmarinen and Väinämöinen grew resentful about what had happened: not only had the land of Pohjola deprived them of married life, but its people now had all the food and riches provided by the sampo. Väinämöinen and Ilmarinen eventually decided to return to

▲ FORGING THE SAMPO
No one knows exactly how a sampo worked or what it looked like. The myth only tells us that crafting this mysterious object required magical skills and may have involved metalworking.

► THE SWAN OF TUONELA
Lemminkäinen found it impossible to kill the great swan after he had heard its mournful yet beautiful song.

Pohjola with several followers to steal the sampo and bring it to Finland. On this quest, the brothers were also joined by the trickster Lemminkäinen, who himself had reason to seek revenge against the people of Pohjola. Lemminkäinen, too, had traveled to the North in search of a bride and been given impossible tasks to do. One of these had involved

traveling to Tuonela, the Underworld, to kill a swan that swam on the dark waters there. His visit to the treacherous Underworld had brought him to the brink of death, and Lemminkäinen had only survived this ordeal because his mother had been able to revive him.

THEFT OF THE SAMPO

During the long sea voyage to the North, the three travelers caught a large fish. Väinämöinen made a

Furious at the **loss of the sampo**, the queen ... used her **magical powers** to create **a violent storm**.

harplike musical instrument, called a kantele (see p.99), from a bone of the fish. The aged hero Väinämöinen was a skilled musician, and his voice, accompanied by the music of the kantele, had the power not only to charm listeners but to lull them into a deep sleep. When the trio arrived at Pohjola, Väinämöinen played his magical kantele, and Louhi and her attendants fell into a slumber. The three quickly loaded the sampo onto their boat and sailed away.

Their escape seemed certain until the heroes could no longer resist celebrating their victory. This was their undoing, as their loud cheering woke up Louhi and her people. Furious at the loss of the sampo, the queen attacked their boat to retrieve it. Then she used her magical powers to create a violent storm. The boat tossed and turned, throwing the sampo into the ocean, where the object was smashed into dozens of pieces.

Väinämöinen fished as many of the fragments out of the water as he could, but some of them fell to the very bottom of the ocean, where they carried on producing the salt of the ocean water. The brothers knew it was impossible to rebuild the sampo—this magical source of wealth was gone for ever. Väinämöinen distributed the

fragments he had salvaged among the people of Finland, in the hope that even the broken parts would bring his country some good fortune.

Near the end of his life, Väinämöinen found his strength declining. He laid his kantele to one side, launched his boat once more, and sailed away across the water and up a sunbeam toward the sky. Here he dwells, and some say that one day he will return to help the people of Finland when they need him most.

◀ **DEFENSE OF THE SAMPO**
When Louhi attacked the boat, she took the form of a large, terrifying bird. The three heroes and their followers successfully fought her off.

FINNISH CULTURE

Finland was ruled by Russia from 1809 to 1917. The Finnish people used the arts—including painting and music portraying the land's traditional myths—to keep the Finnish identity, language, and culture alive. The *Kalevala*, first published in 1835, was a key part of this movement.

Väinämöinen

Elias Lönnrot

Beowulf

Written in c.975–1010 CE in the Anglo-Saxon (Old English) language, the epic poem *Beowulf* tells the story of a great warrior-king who has to overcome terrifying monsters and save the kingdom of Denmark, before rescuing his own people. The poem, whose author is unknown, probably comes from older folk tales. It explains how bravery and loyalty are qualities that are worthy of reward.

Beowulf was a warrior-prince and hero of the Geats, a tribe in southern Sweden. When he traveled to Denmark to visit King Hrothgar, the Danish king told Beowulf about Grendel, a fearsome monster who had recently broken into the royal hall at night and killed some of his soldiers as they slept. Beowulf volunteered to kill the monster, and kept watch in the hall that night. When Grendel returned to the hall, Beowulf fought and killed the monster with his bare hands.

GRENDEL'S MOTHER

Hrothgar's troubles, however, were far from over. Angered by her son's death, Grendel's monstrous mother emerged from her lair at the bottom of a deep lake and entered the hall, killing more of Hrothgar's soldiers in revenge. Determined to put an end to the bloodshed, Beowulf set out for her lair. He dived into the murky depths of the lake and engaged the monster in a fierce fight. Beowulf found it difficult to wound her because she had tough, scaly skin that could not be easily pierced by a sword. Eventually, however, Beowulf stole a sharp sword from Grendel's mother's

◄ GRENDEL
The poem describes Grendel as having skin as thick and hard as steel, and hands with razor-sharp claws.

armory, and drove it through the beast, killing her. Amazed by Beowulf's success, a grateful Hrothgar honored the young warrior with many gifts. Beowulf returned to his own people in triumph, and eventually became their king.

THE FINAL BATTLE

Fifty years later, when King Beowulf was an old man, his people were faced with a terrifying threat. A fire-breathing dragon was attacking the Geats and destroying the land because someone had stolen a precious cup from its

horde of treasure. Beowulf and a group of his bravest warriors pursued the dragon and cornered it, but their swords were not strong enough to defeat the beast.

Most of the warriors gave up in despair, until only Beowulf and a steadfast soldier named Wiglaf remained in the fight. While Beowulf attacked the dragon with his sword, Wiglaf was able to get close and deliver a swift blow to the creature's belly with his knife. The pair managed to kill the dragon, but Beowulf was gravely injured in the struggle. Old and weakened, the warrior-king lay down to die, with Wiglaf, overcome with grief, by his side. With his dying breath, Beowulf proclaimed faithful Wiglaf as his successor, passing on his armor and weapons to the new king.

FACING THE DRAGON ►
The dragon's fiery breath made it hard for Beowulf and his warriors to approach it.

VIKING MEAD HALLS

Viking leaders lived in large one-room halls, where they held lavish feasts for their followers. King Hrothgar's hall in *Beowulf* would have been a building similar to this modern replica in Sweden. These feasting halls had wooden walls, roofs of wood or thatch, and few windows.

The Good God

In Irish mythology, the Daghda was king of a tribe of magical beings and a leader of great power. Although known for his magical abilities and superhuman strength, he could also be a comedic figure, whose exploits sometimes ended in laughter.

The Tuatha Dé Danann were godlike beings who came from an Otherworld to live in Ireland. Their king was the Daghda ("the Good God" in Irish). To wield his power, he used two prized possessions. The first was a "cauldron of plenty": a large, bottomless pot that never ran out of food and allowed him to feed everyone who came to his table. The second was a magical club that could kill with one end and restore life with the other. The Daghda was stronger still when he combined forces with the Morrígan, goddess of war, with whom he was in love.

A LOT OF PORRIDGE

Although the Daghda was a fearsome warrior, on one occasion he realized that his forces were not ready to fight the Fomhoire, another supernatural tribe, so he went to the enemy camp

▲ THE MORRÍGAN
This goddess could predict the outcome of a battle. She would take the form of a crow on the battlefield, ready to foretell who the victor would be.

to request a truce. The Fomhoire accepted this offer but tried to trick the Daghda. At the feast held to celebrate the peace between the two sides, the Fomhoire presented the Daghda with enough porridge to feed an army. This made the god very happy, as this was his favorite food. They then warned the Daghda that he would have to finish all the porridge by himself or face death. To the Fomhoire's amazement, the Daghda managed to eat all the porridge before falling asleep, sending them into fits of laughter. The Daghda's love of porridge had kept him alive and saved his army from war.

◄ THE HAPPY WARRIOR
The Daghda was a cheerful leader. He happily wields his magical club in this wood carving.

The Young Son

Aengus, the Irish god of love, was the son of the Daghda and the river goddess Boann. He was often called "the Young Son" because he took the form of a handsome young man while on quests to help young lovers. Some of Aengus's most well-known adventures feature his shape-shifting abilities.

The god Aengus would change his form to help those who struggled to find love. One day, he came to the aid of Gráinne, a woman who had been promised in marriage to the great military leader Finn (see p.86)—though she was really in love with Diarmud, one of Finn's officers. The two young lovers ran away together but were chased by Finn and his warriors. Aengus changed his appearance to look like Diarmud, distracting the pursuers and giving the lovers time to escape.

A GOD IN LOVE

Aengus also had to change shape to woo his own beloved, a shape-shifter called Caer Ibormeith. This young woman could take the form of a swan and only appeared in human form for a single day each year. Aengus was, of course, able to recognize her when she was human, but when she took the form of a swan, he could not distinguish her from any of the other birds.

AENGUS'S PALACE

Brú (or Brug) na Bóinne, meaning "palace of Boyne," was said to have been the home of Aengus. It features in various Irish myths and is located at the bend of the Boyne River in eastern Ireland. The site contains many prehistoric tombs, some of which are almost 5,000 years old.

The only way to know her was to transform into a swan himself. Once he had done so, Aengus was able to follow Caer, who accepted him as her partner by flying next to him while she sang a magical song. The couple then flew off to Aengus's palace, Brú na Bóinne, and lived together happily.

▼ **FINDING LOVE**
Aengus had fallen in love with Caer in a dream. He would be allowed to marry her if he could identify her in swan form.

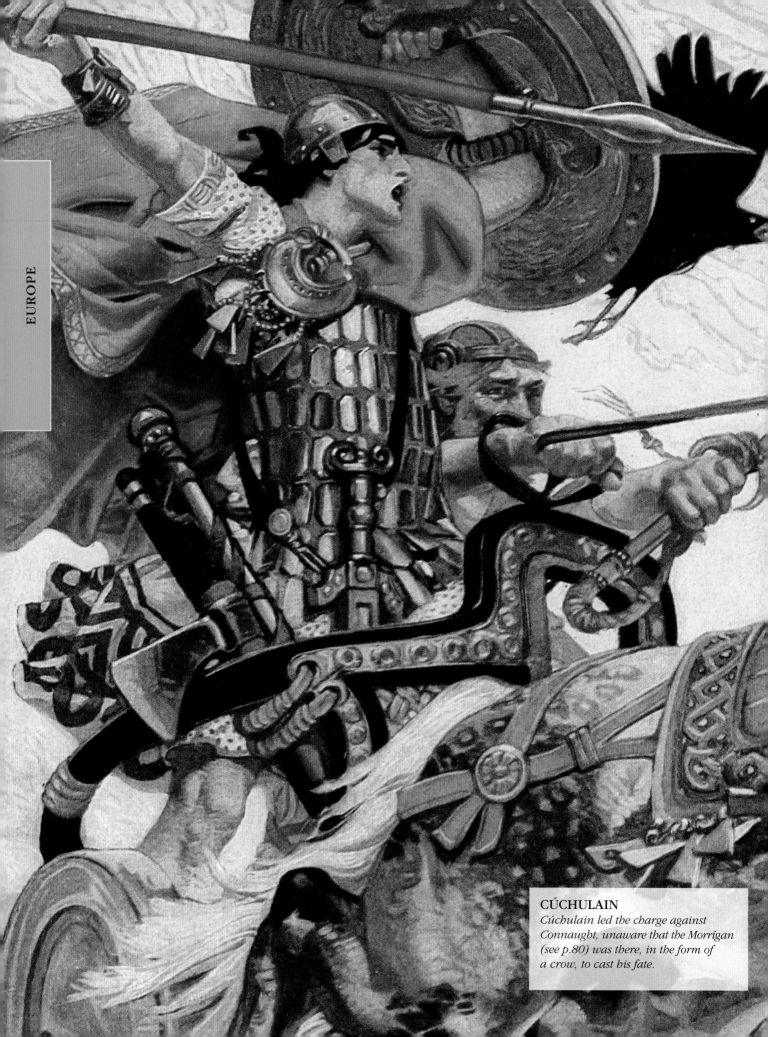

CÚCHULAIN
Cúchulain led the charge against Connaught, unaware that the Morrígan (see p.80) was there, in the form of a crow, to cast his fate.

Cúchulain's fate

Born of a mortal woman and the Irish sun god Lugh, the demigod Cúchulain was the greatest warrior in the Irish kingdom of Ulster. His most remarkable triumphs were in the wars between Ulster and the kingdom of Connaught.

Even as a boy, Cúchulain was quite extraordinary. He could swim like a fish at an early age, and by the time he was a young man, he had become famous for his feats of strength. Never were his qualities more needed than during a conflict with the forces of Connaught.

Queen Medb of Connaught wanted the Brown Bull of Cooley—one of Ulster's most prized beasts—and sent her warriors to capture it. Ulster's fighters had been cursed to fall ill whenever they engaged in battle. Cúchulain, however, was immune to this curse because he was the son of a god, and he took on Connaught's warriors single-handedly. In the heat of battle, Queen Medb sent in the powerful warrior Ferdiad. Cúchulain had seen omens that suggested his death was imminent: the wine in a glass turned to blood, and he witnessed a girl washing bloodstained clothes and weapons, which he identified as his own. In spite of these daunting visions, Cúchulain fought bravely and killed Ferdiad. Unfortunately, a spear then pierced Cúchulain's body. He propped himself up next to an upright stone and died standing, a hero till the very end.

Deirdre's sorrows

The doomed love of Deirdre and Naoise is one of the saddest stories in Irish mythology. It has been retold countless times and is the subject of several plays.

Deirdre was the daughter of Feidhlimidh, a poet in the court of King Conchobar of Ulster. From a young age, it was clear that she would grow into an impressive woman. Realizing this, Conchobar kept Deirdre away from men, secretly hoping to marry her himself when she was old enough. When she was still young, Deirdre saw a calf being skinned and its blood spilling out on the snow. A raven then swooped down to eat the bloodstained snow. Deirdre was so transfixed by these colors that she decided to marry a man who had hair as dark as the raven's feathers, skin as white as snow, and cheeks as red as blood. When Deirdre grew up, she met Naoise, one of the king's knights, and realized he matched this description perfectly. The pair fell in love and ran away to Scotland to escape King Conchobar. Still longing for Deirdre, Conchobar tricked the couple into returning to Ulster, and ruthlessly had Naoise put to death. The king then tried to persuade Deirdre to marry him, but she stayed faithful to the memory of Naoise. Rejecting the king, she took her own life by jumping off a cliff, and came to be known as "Deirdre of the Sorrows."

◄ THE GREAT ESCAPE
Deirdre and Naoise crossed the stormy sea to Scotland to escape.

THE TÁIN WALL
The life of Cúchulain is the theme of a colorful mosaic mural in Dublin, Ireland. This scene shows the mythical Irish hero (far right) fighting Ferdiad, a warrior in Queen Medb's Connaught army.

Finn MacCumhaill

Many Ancient Irish stories feature the hero Finn MacCumhaill. He possessed strength and bravery, and the ability to see into the future. Finn's power was so great that some said he was really the sun god, Lugh.

◄ BRAVE WARRIOR
After defeating Aillén, Finn was regarded as a hero by the Irish people.

Finn's original name was Demhne, and as a young man he studied with a poet called Finn the Seer, a man who could see into the future. The poet had spent many years trying to catch the Salmon of Knowledge, a fish said to possess all the world's knowledge and wisdom. One day while out fishing, Finn the Seer finally caught the salmon. He asked Demhne to cook it for him—but on no account was he to eat it himself. Demhne obeyed, but he burned his thumb while cooking the fish and, without thinking, licked it. When he told Finn what he had done, the poet said that this showed Demhne was fated to eat the salmon, and from that day the young man would be called Finn after his teacher.

When he ate the fish, young Finn became wise and summoned the knowledge of the salmon simply by licking his thumb. He also gained the power of prophecy.

THE WICKED MUSICIAN

Finn defended the Irish people from many dreadful enemies, including supernatural ones. One such daring feat was his encounter with Aillén, a fire-breathing musician. Every year, Aillén would put the king's guards to sleep with his music before burning down the palace at Tara. Many warriors tried to defeat him, but none succeeded. Finn took a magical poisoned spear and kept himself awake as he waited for Aillén by breathing in the poison vapor. When Aillén appeared, Finn killed him with the weapon, thereby saving the palace from destruction.

> Finn summoned the **knowledge of the salmon** simply by **licking his thumb.**

THE SALMON OF KNOWLEDGE ▶
Finn the Seer had waited seven years to catch the Salmon of Knowledge. This giant sculpture of the fish stands by the Lagan River in Belfast, Northern Ireland.

The Land of the Young

As well as being a famous poet, Oisín, the son of Finn, was a warrior and adventurer. The best-known story about him explores his visit to the Land of the Young, a mythical Otherworld that is home to supernatural or magical beings.

Ancient Irish people believed that their burial mounds were entrances to the Land of the Young.

Oisín was a brave defender of the Irish people, just like his father Finn. Once when out hunting, Oisín saw a woman riding a white horse and fell in love with her. She was called Niamh Chinn Óir ("Niamh of the Golden Hair" in Irish), and was the queen of the Land of the Young, a realm also known as Tír na nÓg. Niamh accepted Oisín as her husband and asked him to accompany her to the Land of the Young, where no one aged or fell ill. There, they lived happily for many years.

RETURNING HOME

Eventually, Oisín became homesick and decided to return home. Niamh offered him her white horse and told Oisín to not dismount from the horse even after he had reached Ireland. When Oisín arrived, his homeland seemed to have changed a lot—none of the people he once knew were alive. While he was there, he saw some men trying to lift a large rock. Forgetting Niamh's warning, Oisín got down from his horse to help. As soon as his feet touched the ground, he turned into a very old man. Oisín realized that many more years had passed in Ireland than in the Land of the Young, and that he could never go back there again as he was too old. Instantly, Oisín aged further and died.

◄ OISÍN AND NIAMH
The couple rode Niamh's white horse, which could travel over water and land, to the magical Land of the Young.

Pwyll and Rhiannon

Tales of the Welsh prince Pwyll focus on his monster-defying heroism, and describe how he overcame personal troubles to marry his love Rhiannon and, later, to find their lost son.

EUROPE

Prince Pwyll of the Welsh kingdom of Dyfed was in love with Rhiannon, but her parents would not allow them to marry because they had chosen a man called Gwawl to be her husband. However, Pwyll and Rhiannon wed in secret. This enraged her parents, who refused to accept the match. When Rhiannon gave birth to the couple's first son, her parents stole the newborn baby and hid him, accusing Rhiannon of killing her own child.

Unfortunately for Rhiannon, Pwyll believed these false claims and punished Rhiannon by making her kneel on all fours like a horse and offer rides to people.

LOST AND FOUND

A while later, Pwyll left to visit a wealthy neighbor whose young horses had been going missing in mysterious circumstances. Waiting at night by the stable, he discovered that a monster was stealing the foals. The brave prince fought

◄ THE GODDESS EPONA
Since Rhiannon's story involves horses and horselike behavior, the heroine is often associated with Epona, the goddess of horses and mules.

the monster, causing it to turn tail and flee. Inside the stable, Pwyll found his baby son lying in the straw. Overjoyed, he took the child home to Rhiannon. She forgave Pwyll's mistreatment of her, and the couple decided to name their son Pryderi, meaning "care."

◄ PWYLL WOOS RHIANNON
The brave prince of Dyfed was impressed by the intelligent and strong-willed Rhiannon, who went against all odds to marry him.

Pryderi vanishes

When Pwyll and Rhiannon's son Pryderi is a young man, he travels from Wales to England with his friend Manawydan. There they face a mysterious series of misfortunes that seem random at first, but turn out to have a common cause.

After a drought had reduced the kingdom of Dyfed to a barren wasteland, Pryderi and his friend Manawydan traveled to England to seek work. They found jobs in various places, but were let go each time because the local craftsmen became jealous of their great skill. Dejected, they returned to Dyfed.

THE MABINOGION

The stories involving Pwyll, Rhiannon, Pryderi, Brân, Lleu (see overleaf), and many others are collected in *The Mabinogion*, a book of magical medieval Welsh tales, written in c. 1100 CE. It has been translated from its original Welsh several times.

Lady Charlotte Guest's translation (1838–1845)

One day, while hunting for food, the friends pursued a wild boar to a large fort. Curious Pryderi went inside, where he found a large golden bowl. When he touched it, he found himself stuck to the floor and unable to speak, as if under a spell. When Pryderi did not return, Manawydan informed his mother Rhiannon about her son's disappearance. Concerned, Rhiannon went to the fort in search of him, but a thick fog rolled down, covering the building and making her vanish completely.

THE CURSE IS LIFTED

Meanwhile, Manawydan had been trying to grow corn for food, but his crops were dying. When he told a bishop of his troubles, the clergyman revealed that he and Pryderi were the victims of a magical curse, cast by a man named Llwyd, a friend of Gwawl—whom Rhiannon had rejected long ago. This curse was the cause of all the troubles they had faced, including their misfortunes in England. The bishop lifted the curse, and Pryderi and Rhiannon were found alive and well.

▲ THE GOLDEN BOWL
Bowls and cauldrons appear frequently in Welsh myths. Used in religious ceremonies, these vessels were often said to have magical powers.

Pryderi may be an early version of Sir Perceval (see p.93) from the Arthurian legends.

Brân's head

The story of the hero Brân tells of his courage in war and how he is able to protect the people of Ancient Britain even after his death.

The giant Brân was a mighty hero known for his superhuman strength. His sister Branwen was married to Matholwch, the King of Ireland, who treated her poorly. To avenge Branwen, Brân declared war on Ireland.

However, the Irish army greatly outnumbered Brân's soldiers. Not only that, the Irish had another advantage in the form of a magic cauldron that could bring their dead soldiers back to life. Brân's strength and sheer bravery helped the British defeat their enemy, against all the odds. Unfortunately, only seven of Brân's men were left alive, and the hero himself was close to death after being hit with a poisoned spear. To his followers' astonishment, the dying Brân told them to cut off his head, take it back to Britain, and bury it in London.

The soldiers were even more amazed to find that Brân's severed head carried on speaking words of encouragement to them all the way back to Britain. After its burial, Brân's magical head worked as a talisman to protect Britain by repelling invaders.

For the people of Ancient Britain, the human head was a symbol of divine status.

ENJOYING THEIR SUCCESS ▶
Brân's soldiers celebrated their unlikely victory over the Irish with a lavish banquet, with the severed head of their leader looking on.

Lleu's struggles

Among the many magical tales of *The Mabinogion* is the story of the Welsh hero Lleu Llaw Gyffes, who was able to overcome curses and grave danger with the help of his uncle, the magician Gwydion, and another sorcerer named Math.

When Lleu was born, his mother Arianrhod thought he looked like an ugly, shapeless lump, and cursed him never to have a human wife.

When Lleu grew up, his uncle Gwydion and the magician Math took pity on him and decided to help the young man. They used their magical powers to create a beautiful woman from the flowers of the oak tree, broom, and meadowsweet. They named her Blodeuwedd, meaning "flower-faced," and gave her to Lleu to be his wife. For a while, Lleu and Blodeuwedd were happy together. Unfortunately for Lleu, Blodeuwedd met another man—a nobleman called Gronw Pebr—and fell in love with him. Blodeuwedd and Gronw plotted to kill Lleu so they could marry. Gronw attacked Lleu with a spear, but thanks again to Gwydion's magic, Lleu changed into an eagle and flew away just as the spear hit him.

When Lleu was safe, Gwydion transformed him back into human

▲ THE PUNISHMENT
As a nighttime hunter, the owl Blodeuwedd was the natural enemy of other birds, who would attack her if she was seen during the day.

form. To avenge the attack on him, Lleu then killed Gronw. Blodeuwedd was punished by Gwydion, who turned her into an owl so that she would never see the light of day again.

The sword in the stone

The heroic deeds of King Arthur and his knights feature in some of the most exciting legends from Britain and France. This famous story reveals how Arthur becomes the king of Britain by triumphing in an unusual contest, and later establishes his renowned order of brave and chivalrous knights.

▲ MERLIN
Some versions of the story say that the wizard Merlin knew Prince Arthur as a child, and became his teacher and friend.

The British king Uther Pendragon had a son named Arthur, but Arthur's mother, Queen Igraine of Cornwall, was not married to King Uther. This meant that, according to the law of the time, Arthur would not automatically inherit the kingdom when his father died.

A DIFFICULT TEST

Uther wanted to give Arthur a chance to become king when he grew up, so Uther announced a competition. Nearby was a large stone, which had a sword embedded deep inside it, with only the handle sticking out. It seemed impossible to remove the sword, but Uther proclaimed that whoever could do so would become the next king. He later died while Arthur was still young.

Over the years, many knights from all over Uther's kingdom tried to extract the weapon, but none succeeded. However, when Arthur tugged at the sword, it slid easily from the stone, making him the true heir to the kingdom of Britain.

▲ ARTHUR RISES TO THE CHALLENGE
Only the rightful successor to the throne would be able to pull the sword from the stone. Onlookers were astonished when the young Arthur easily accomplished this incredible feat.

THE ROUND TABLE ▲
*The table's round shape
ensured that all the knights who
sat around it had equal status.*

The sword **slid easily** from the stone, **making Arthur the true heir** to the kingdom of Britain.

ARTHUR THE KING

In due course, Arthur became king of Britain and married Lady Guinevere (see p.126), who was said to be descended from a noble Roman family. Arthur ruled wisely and well. He governed his kingdom with the help of the wizard Merlin (see p.191), his valued teacher and advisor, and a group of brave and chivalrous knights. A round table was built in King Arthur's castle at Camelot, and was used by King Arthur to discuss various matters of importance with his order of knights. This group would come to be called the Knights of the Round Table, and included

important figures such as Sir Perceval, Sir Galahad (see p.94), and Sir Lancelot (see p.95).

Arthur's sword remained his trusted weapon until it was damaged in a duel. Then one day, a mysterious figure with magical powers, called the Lady of the Lake, presented Arthur with a new sword, the celebrated Excalibur.

EXCALIBUR

Some versions of the Arthurian legends say that it was the sword in the stone that was named Excalibur (see p.116). Most stories place great importance on the king's weapon, with some giving it magical powers.

The quest for the Grail

Symbolizing good fortune, eternal youth, and wisdom, the mythical object known as the Grail has fascinated people for centuries. Legend has it that only those with a pure heart can obtain the Grail. Many legendary knights from the court of King Arthur spent their entire lives searching for it—but only one was successful.

To the GLORY of
Lieut. Antony Phillip
Corps of Guides killed
at Wlucha Jawar

Hundreds of years before the reign of King Arthur (see pp.92–93), a mysterious object called the Grail had been transported to Britain from a distant land and placed in the care of a person known only as the "Fisher King." Although it had not been seen in many years, the people of Britain felt that the land prospered due to the Grail's presence.

After a long period of plentiful food and increasing wealth, Britain suddenly became barren. King Arthur and his knights wanted to use the Grail to restore the land to its former state, but did not know what it looked like or where it was.

One day, Galahad, son of Sir Lancelot (see opposite), arrived at Camelot, King Arthur's court. Galahad was known across the land for his bravery and nobility. In recognition of this, he was knighted and given a place at the Round Table. As the knights sat around the table, an image of the Grail suddenly appeared in front of them. Arthur's knights took this as a sign that the task of finding the Grail was theirs alone, and set off on this quest. They spread themselves far and wide and searched for many years, but even the bravest and most capable knights returned to Camelot empty-handed.

Sir Galahad, however, did not give up. He traveled across the land until he reached a near-deserted castle. This was home to a man who spent all day fishing by the river. The man revealed himself to be the Fisher King and took Sir Galahad to where he kept the Grail in his castle. He then handed over the precious object so that it could be taken to Camelot.

King Arthur and the knights were overjoyed at Galahad's success and realized that it was his pure heart that made him worthy of finding the Grail. With the Grail now in their possession, the land of Britain prospered once again.

Although it is usually shown as a cup, some also describe the Grail as a plate, a bowl, or even a stone.

◀ SIR GALAHAD
Galahad carried a white shield with a red cross, as in this stained glass window. In some versions of the story, it was given to him by monks at an abbey.

Sir Lancelot's betrayal

The story of Sir Lancelot, King Arthur's most trusted knight, tells of how a single error in judgement by a near-perfect knight leads to treason and tragedy, bringing about the ruin of a whole kingdom.

◀ THE RESCUE
When Guinevere was kidnapped by the wicked Maleagant, Lancelot rescued her and carried her to safety on his horse.

and Lancelot spread among the knights and nobles. Arthur's son Mordred wanted to become king and saw this scandal as an opportunity to weaken Arthur and his faithful Knights of the Round Table. Mordred told his father about Guinevere and Lancelot's affair, which made Arthur furious. He declared war on Lancelot, and his knights were quickly divided between those who favored Lancelot and those who chose to back their king.

Lancelot fled to France. Arthur set off in pursuit, and in the king's absence, Mordred took over the throne of Britain. The knights who had stayed behind to protect the land were shocked by Mordred's treason, and united against him. Hearing of the trouble in Camelot, Arthur returned home. Along with his loyal knights, Arthur fought and killed Mordred, saving his kingdom. However, the king was wounded in the struggle and died soon afterward.

When the news of Arthur's death reached Lancelot, the knight was distraught over the destruction his actions had caused. He joined a monastery and repented his sins, becoming a priest toward the end of his life.

Sir Lancelot was one of the bravest knights in the court of King Arthur (see pp.92–93). He was the king's closest friend and had fought by Arthur's side in many battles. He was also the only knight to have defeated the king in a jousting match. One day, a man called Maleagant attacked Queen Guinevere, Arthur's wife. Lancelot fought him off and rescued Guinevere. The incident made the knight and queen grow close, and they fell in love. Soon rumors of the relationship between the Queen

JOUSTING

Jousting was a game of staged combat played by knights in the Late Middle Ages (c. 1250–1500 CE). Knights on horseback would try to knock down one another with their lances as a way of practicing for battle, while also entertaining spectators.

Mordred wanted to become king and saw this scandal as an opportunity to weaken Arthur.

FIGHTING TO SURVIVE
Robin had to fight off several heavily armed royal guards as he rode away from Nottingham to Sherwood Forest.

The adventures of Robin Hood

The legend of Robin Hood, which developed in England from c.1250 to 1500 CE, tells of a group of outlaws living in a forest. It describes their leader, Robin, as a man who hates injustice, and values courage and loyalty. His heroic exploits have been retold through the ages in many forms, such as poems, plays, and films.

▲ SHERWOOD FOREST
According to local legend, the ancient tree in Sherwood Forest known as the Major Oak was the shelter for Robin's outlaws.

Robin Hood was a nobleman and an excellent archer who lived in the town of Nottingham in England. He was unjustly accused and sentenced to prison for a crime he had not committed. Angry at his unfair treatment, he escaped the city and hid in Sherwood Forest, a private hunting ground belonging to King Richard.

Robin gathered around him a band of outlaw followers who all had their own reasons for living in the forest. They included a giant of a man called "Little John," the brave fighter Will Scarlet, and the minstrel (entertainer) Allan-A-Dale. Also seeking refuge there was a woman called Maid Marian, who had run away to avoid marrying a man she did not love. These outlaws hunted the king's animals for food and robbed wealthy people who traveled through the forest. However, they did not always keep the stolen money for themselves, often giving it to the poor. Robin Hood and his band of "Merry Men," as they came to be known, became famous for their good deeds.

ROBIN AND MARIAN ▶
In some versions of the tale, Marian marries Robin, in others she leaves the forest to become a nun.

THE WICKED SHERIFF

Robin's greatest enemy was the Sheriff of Nottingham, who had tried to capture the outlaw many times. Robin, however, took great pleasure in getting the better of him. One day, the sheriff announced an archery contest, knowing full well that Robin would come to the event to show off his archery skills. Robin and his followers competed in disguise, but were recognized when Robin won the contest. The sheriff tried to have them captured, but the outlaws escaped and took refuge in the castle of Sir Richard, a knight who owed Robin a favor.

Frustrated at this failure, the sheriff told King Richard about Robin's activities. The king issued an order for Robin and Sir Richard to be captured. When the sheriff arrived at the castle, Robin was out hunting, but the sheriff was able to seize Sir Richard. When Robin heard of his friend's capture, he and his men attacked the prison, rescued Sir Richard, and killed the sheriff.

CATCHING THE OUTLAW

The king demanded that Robin be brought to justice for the sheriff's murder. No one was able to capture Robin, so the king disguised himself and some of his guards as monks, and the group made their way to Sherwood. Here, they met the outlaws, and the king tricked Robin into giving them shelter. Once they were in the outlaws' camp, the king revealed his identity and his guards surrounded Robin, who surrendered himself to the king. Richard was so impressed with Robin's loyalty that, instead of taking him prisoner, he asked him to become a royal courtier.

Robin left the forest for a while to serve the king, and even married Maid Marian. However, he preferred the life of an outlaw, and eventually returned to Sherwood, where he spent the rest of his days.

> More than 50 films have been made based on the legend of Robin Hood and his "Merry Men."

Mythical objects

Myths and legends are full of magical objects, from instruments that make enchanting music to armor that protects the wearer from the heaviest blow. Deities and heroes often use these objects to enhance their power.

◀ MERLIN'S STAFF

In British and French legend, Merlin is described as a wise man, prophet, or wizard. He is sometimes shown with a wooden staff, often the tool of wizards.

Daikoku-ten sits on bales of rice, symbolizing plentiful food.

◀ UCHIDE NO KOZUCHI

The Japanese god of wealth, Daikoku-ten, carries a magic mallet. Known as Uchide no kozuchi, it can tap out anything the user desires.

SEVEN-LEAGUE BOOTS ▶

European myths tell of a pair of boots originally worn by a giant. The wearer's stride increases magically over time. In some tales, people wearing these boots can cover 21 miles (34 km)— seven leagues—in one step.

◀ MAUI'S FISHHOOK

The god Maui, who features in tales from Polynesia and Hawaii, possesses a magical fishhook that can catch any creature or object in the sea.

SEE ALSO

- The Trojan War, pp.48–51
- Ragnarök, p.71
- The impossible quest, pp.74–77
- The sword in the stone, pp.92–93
- Ra's creation, p.170
- Maui's feats, pp.228–231

◀ BENBEN STONE

The top stone of an Egyptian pyramid, called a Benben stone, is named after and symbolizes the primeval rock that the sun god Ra stood on to create the world.

▼ VÄINÄMÖINEN'S KANTELE

This stringed instrument from Finnish mythology was first made from the backbone of a fish. It creates music that enchants listeners and makes them fall into a deep sleep.

◀ KHNUM'S POTTER WHEEL

In one Egyptian myth, the creator god Khnum makes humans out of clay from the Nile River, molding them on his potter's wheel.

▼ GJALLARHORN

When Asgard is attacked during the last battle of Ragnarök, the Norse god Heimdall will blow the horn called Gjallarhorn to warn the gods. This signals the end of the world.

The horn sounds so loudly it can be heard all over the cosmos.

ARMOR OF ACHILLES ▶

The armor of the Greek hero Achilles is made of bronze and it cannot be pierced by any weapon. It protects its wearer, such as Achilles's friend Patroclus when he fights in the Trojan War.

Bába Yagá the witch

Many Russian myths feature a wicked witch named Bába Yagá. Few can escape the witch, but one who does manage to outwit her is a girl named Mariassa.

The skulls on the garden fence lit up as lanterns at night.

▲ **BÁBA YAGÁ'S HOUSE**
The witch's house could chase people at her command. The windows acted as eyes for the house and the door lock was said to be made of teeth.

Bába Yagá could seem innocent, but the old woman caught and devoured children, and turned people to stone by looking at them. Her garden fence was decorated with human skulls and her house stood on enormous chicken legs. She lived with a black cat and a monstrous dog, which both guarded her hut. Bába Yagá used a huge grinding vessel, or mortar, to fly in the sky, pushing herself along with the grinding tool, or pestle. The pestle worked as an oar cutting through the air, creating storms as the witch flew.

◄ **CATCHING CHILDREN**
Sitting in her magic mortar deep in the forest, Bába Yagá waited to trap young children.

ESCAPING THE WITCH

There was once a young girl called Mariassa, whose wicked stepmother wanted to be rid of her. She sent her to Bába Yagá to borrow a needle and thread, knowing she was unlikely to return. On the way, the girl called on her aunt, who warned her that she should avoid the sharp teeth of the witch's dog, and told her how to talk to Bába Yagá's cat to seek help. When Bába Yagá tried to grab Mariassa, the girl asked the cat for a way out. It told her to run away with a towel and a comb. As she ran, Mariassa heard Bába Yagá following her, so she threw down the towel, which turned into a river, and the comb, which became a forest. This trapped the witch, letting Mariassa escape.

Tales of Bába Yagá were first printed in 1755 in a book by Russian writer Mikhail Lomonosov.

Bába Yagá's **garden fence** was **decorated** with **human skulls ...**

Vasilisa's escape

The story of the girl Vasilisa tells of how she manages to triumph over the witch Bába Yagá, using some magic tricks from her mother and her own quick wits.

A girl named Vasilisa lived with her elderly parents in a village. When she was young, her mother fell ill. Before she died, she gave Vasilisa a magic doll that would offer wise advice if she gave it good food to eat. In time, Vasilisa's father remarried, but his new wife and daughters were jealous of Vasilisa because of her beauty. They made her do all the hard and dirty housework. However, with instructions from the doll, Vasilisa easily managed to complete the difficult chores.

THE WITCH'S TRAP

One day, when Vasilisa's father was away, her stepmother sent her to Bába Yagá to get some firewood.

The wicked witch trapped the girl and made a servant of her. Bába Yagá delighted in giving the girl absurd and impossible tasks, such as separating out a mixture of tiny poppy seeds and peas. Vasilisa managed to accomplish every task by following her doll's advice, but

The name Vasilisa is derived from the Greek word *basilissa,* a title similar to "queen."

▲ VASILISA AND HER DOLL
Vasilisa lived in a traditional wooden house in the Russian countryside. She had only her magic doll for company.

could see no way of escaping her tormentor. The doll then told her to run away quietly in the middle of the night when the witch was asleep. As Vasilisa tiptoed out of the house, she took with her one of the glowing skulls from Bába Yagá's fence. When Vasilisa returned home with the skull, she held it in front of her stepmother and stepsisters. Its glowing eyes shone on them, turning them to ashes.

CINDERELLA

Many folk tales across different cultures feature children who are ill-treated or rejected by a newcomer in the family, such as a wicked stepmother. A famous European story is the tale of Cinderella, who is treated as a servant by her stepsisters and stepmother. However, like Vasilisa, Cinderella triumphs over injustice in the end.

IN THE DUNGEON
After discovering an old man in the dungeon, Ivan offered him water from the container placed near him.

The death of Koschei

An evil character called Koschei features in numerous Slavic folk tales (from eastern Europe and Russia). The most well-known story about Koschei tells of his death at the hands of the warrior queen Márya Morévna.

Spread originally by word of mouth, the tales of Koschei began to be written down in the 1800s.

A prince called Ivan was riding through the countryside when he came across a field littered with hundreds of dead bodies. He learned that this was the battlefield where the warrior-queen Márya Morévna had defeated the army of Koschei, whom she had captured. Koschei was known all over Russia as a notorious murderer and kidnapper. People were relieved that Koschei had been defeated, but feared that he would return, as he was known as "the immortal."

IVAN DISCOVERS KOSCHEI

Soon after, Ivan met the warrior-queen herself, and they fell in love and got married. When Márya had to depart for war again, she left Ivan at her palace, warning him never to open a particular locked dungeon. However, Ivan was curious and opened the dungeon, where he found a thin, pale old man chained to the wall. This man was Koschei, although Ivan did not realize it. Koschei asked for water, and when Ivan gave him a drink, the villain overpowered Ivan and broke free. Koschei then fled from

◀ **WARRIOR QUEEN**
Queen Márya Morévna is usually shown armed with a sword, the weapon of royal and noble warriors.

the palace on a powerful horse, taking Ivan with him.

MÁRYA'S PURSUIT

When Márya returned, she discovered what had happened and rushed to rescue Ivan. When she reached the pair, Koschei—who was expecting Márya—cut her into pieces and escaped again, leaving her still alive but unable to follow. The queen's three brothers came to her aid and pieced her body back together. Revived, Márya went to the witch Bába Yagá (see pp.100–101) and asked to borrow the fastest horse in

her stable. Bába Yagá gave Márya the weakest-looking animal, but when the queen climbed on the horse, it transformed into a young and powerful stallion.

Márya rode off in pursuit of Koschei and Ivan. After a long chase, she could finally see them in the distance, but her horse still could not catch up. Luck was on her side, however, when Koschei's horse stumbled over a large stone, throwing both captor and prisoner to the ground. Before Koschei could get to his feet, Márya plunged her sword into his body, killing him. She then burned the body to ensure the evil Koschei was not the immortal being people thought he was. Brave Queen Márya and Prince Ivan were reunited at last.

WOMEN WARRIORS

Female warriors such as Márya Morévna are depicted in myths from many cultures. From the Amazons of Ancient Greece to the Valkyries (right) of Norse mythology, these powerful women led armies into battle and also defended the weak against vicious villains.

Ivan and the Firebird

This is a Slavic folk tale (from eastern Europe and Russia) of a wonderful multicolored bird that brings trouble to those who try to catch it. The one exception is a humble stable boy called Ivan, whose capture of the Firebird changes his life.

There was once a king who had an amazing orchard full of trees that produced golden apples. He was proud of his orchard, and noticed when someone began stealing his prized fruit every night. The king ordered the stable boy Ivan to guard the orchard and catch the thief. Ivan discovered that the culprit was the magnificent Firebird, a magical creature with glowing feathers the color of fire. The king then told Ivan to follow the bird and capture it.

AN UNLIKELY COMPANION

Along the way, Ivan met a wolf, who showed him how to trick the bird by getting it drunk using food soaked in beer. The drunken bird was slow and sleepy, so Ivan could easily catch it. When Ivan returned to the palace with the Firebird, the king shut it in a cage. Pleased with Ivan's work, he sent him on another quest—to seek out Yelena, the princess the king wished to marry.

When Ivan found Yelena, the two fell in love. It seemed unlikely that Yelena would be allowed to marry Ivan when she was meant to become the king's bride, but the wolf, who was a shape-shifter, helped Ivan again. The animal transformed itself into a princess and went to the king, who fell in love with her. The pair got married, but as they were about to kiss, she changed back into the wolf, and the king died instantly of shock. Yelena and Ivan were now free to marry, and Ivan was crowned the new king. He was grateful to the Firebird, because his success in catching it had transformed his life, so he set the creature free—not minding the fact that golden apples occasionally went missing from the orchard.

◀ A THIEF IN THE ORCHARD
When Ivan discovered the Firebird stealing the golden apples from the orchard, he tried to catch it, but only managed to grab a single, dazzling feather.

Rusalka and the prince

Many Slavic countries have folk tales involving rusalkas, or water nymphs—magical creatures that resemble humans but can live underwater. A famous story features a water nymph known as Rusalka, and describes the misfortunes that come her way when she falls in love with a human.

RUSALKA ▶
The water nymph rarely emerged from the lake, but could not resist peeking through the water lilies, just to catch a glimpse of the prince.

T he water nymph Rusalka lived in a lake with many other nymphs and male water sprites. These beings were immortal, but would only live forever if they spent their entire life beneath the water of the lake. One day a prince came to the lake and saw Rusalka, and the two fell in love. A witch told Rusalka that she would lose her immortality and her power of speech if she went to live on land with the prince. The wicked old woman also warned her that if the love between them ended, the prince would be doomed. Nevertheless, Rusalka chose to follow the prince onto land and the two were soon married.

DOOMED LOVE

A great banquet was held at the prince's palace to celebrate the wedding. While he was feasting, the prince was captivated by the beauty of a princess from another country, and his love for Rusalka started to fade. Rusalka realized she could no longer be happy with the prince and decided to return to her lake. Now that Rusalka was no longer immortal, she knew she would die if she tried to live underwater. She sought out the witch for advice, who told Rusalka to kill the prince to regain her immortality.

Horrified, Rusalka refused to do this as she still loved the prince. In fact, when he arrived at the lake in search of his bride, she could not resist kissing him. To her dismay, the prince died because of the kiss, fulfilling the prediction that he would be doomed if their love failed. A heartbroken Rusalka was then left to spend the rest of her life in the lake.

MODERN RETELLINGS: *THE LITTLE MERMAID*

Danish writer Hans Christian Andersen wrote a story called *The Little Mermaid,* which closely resembles the Slavic myth about Rusalka. In fact, this tale was so popular that there is a statue of the mermaid in Denmark's capital, Copenhagen. Anderson's version of the myth was later made into a Disney animated film, featuring a mermaid named Ariel.

ASIA

The myths of China, Japan, and the Indian subcontinent form the basis for religions that are widely practiced today. They feature deities and rulers of heavenly kingdoms, believed to be the ancestors of real human leaders, as well as immortals and sages who still influence people's ideas and beliefs. Stories from other parts of the region are some of the oldest known to humankind.

Multi-headed Ravana, the Asura (demon) king of Lanka, is seen fighting the Devas (gods) in this miniature painting by the artist Sahibdin in 1652 CE.

The birth of gods

The story *Enuma Elish* is the creation myth of the city states that developed from c. 2000 BCE in Mesopotamia. This was the land between the Tigris and Euphrates rivers in modern-day Iraq. One part of this epic describes the origins of the gods.

▲ BOUNDARY STONE
This stone once marked a land boundary in Babylon. It shows the symbols of several deities, such as Ea (the turtle), Shamash (the sun), and Ishtar (the star).

The peaceful cosmos at the beginning of time contained two seas: the fresh water and the salt water. Apsu was the god of the fresh water and Tiamat was the goddess of the salt water. When Apsu and Tiamat met, their waters mixed, giving rise to several generations of gods. The greatest among these were Anu, the god of the heavens, and Ea, the god of knowledge.

Apsu and Tiamat did not like the noise made by the younger gods and longed for the time when the cosmos was peaceful. Apsu therefore decided to destroy the younger gods, although Tiamat did not want to wipe out the descendants they had created. When Ea saw that their father was intent on murder, he intervened and killed Apsu, declaring himself the ruler of all the waters.

In time, Ea and the goddess Damkina had a son, Marduk. Ea built an underground chamber in which he raised Marduk, who grew to be a mighty god, filled with more strength and wisdom than his parents.

Marduk creates Babylon

One of the greatest of all the cities of Mesopotamia was Babylon. *Enuma Elish* tells us how this city was established not by a human king, but by a god.

When Marduk, the son of Ea and Damkina, was young, he was granted control of four winds by Anu, the god of the heavens. When he played with these winds, he caused storms in the salt-water sea ruled by the goddess Tiamat. This infuriated Tiamat, who had been angered by the younger gods in the past for the death of her husband Apsu. She gathered an army of demons under the leadership of the god Kingu, and commanded them to declare war on Marduk. Many

of the other gods wanted peace and asked Tiamat to end the conflict, but she would not listen. Marduk was more warlike, and offered to fight Tiamat if the other gods made him their leader. The gods agreed, and Marduk used the four winds to kill Tiamat and cut her to pieces.

Marduk used fragments of Tiamat's body to create the heavens and the mountains of Mesopotamia. Tiamat's tears became the Tigris and Euphrates rivers. To remain unchallenged,

Marduk then destroyed Kingu, and used the blood of the slain god to create the first human, Lullu. He then built the great city of Babylon for Lullu and his descendents.

HEADING INTO BATTLE ▶
Marduk set off on his war chariot to fight the goddess Tiamat. Using the four winds, the young god whipped up a terrible storm and then formed a lightning bolt to deal Tiamat a fatal blow.

Inanna in the Underworld

The goddess Inanna was one of the most widely worshipped deities of the Sumerians of Mesopotamia (in modern-day Iraq). She was linked with love, war, and power. This is the tale of her terrifying journey to the Underworld and the bargain she makes for her release. It also describes how there came to be changing seasons on Earth.

Sometimes shy and obedient, often ambitious and warlike, Inanna's complex nature meant that many gods were attracted to her. These included Enkimdu, the god of agriculture, and Dumuzi, the god of fertility, who was a shepherd. While Inanna preferred Enkimdu because he appeared more prosperous, her brother Utu wanted her to marry Dumuzi because his sheep provided wool, milk, and cheese for the people on Earth. Eventually, Utu persuaded Inanna to marry the shepherd, and the couple ruled over the great city of Uruk (see p.113) together.

Inanna was at times linked with the planet Venus, known as the morning or evening star.

◀ INANNA
The goddess was worshipped in several cultures, and had other names. In Babylon and Assyria she was Ishtar, while the people in the region surrounding the Mediterranean knew her as Astarte.

▲ MESOPOTAMIAN JEWELRY
Wealthy women in Mesopotamia wore fine jewelry, such as this headdress of gold leaves and beads dating from c. 2500 BCE. Inanna had to remove her ornaments when she traveled through the Underworld.

A DANGEROUS QUEST

Inanna had a sister, Ereshkigal (see p.53), whom she loved very much. While Inanna was the goddess of light, Ereshkigal was the goddess of darkness, and lived in the gloomy realm of the Underworld. Inanna missed her sister greatly, and decided to visit her. She knew that going to this dark place would be dangerous, so she told her maid, Ninshubur, to ask the gods for help if she did not return within three days.

When Inanna descended into the Underworld, her journey was even more treacherous than she had expected. Demons made the goddess part with her personal items, including her precious jewelry, until she had absolutely nothing left. When she finally met her sister Ereshkigal and hugged her,

returned to Earth, Inanna learned that Dumuzi had become the sole ruler of her kingdom in her absence. The goddess resented her husband for this betrayal, and so decided that he should be the one to replace her in the Underworld. As Dumuzi was about to obey, his sister Geshtinanna intervened. She volunteered to take Dumuzi's place in the Underworld for half the year, allowing him to return

The **demons drained** the **goddess of life** to **trap** her in the **Underworld.**

the demons thought Inanna was going to carry Ereshkigal off to Earth. They grabbed the goddess of light, and drained her of life to trap her in the Underworld.

When Inanna did not return home after three days, Ninshubur begged the gods for help. The trickster god Enki came to their aid. He knew that it was unlikely that any living thing could return safely from the land of the dead, so he made two beings to send to the Underworld to rescue her. They had no internal organs or power of thought, both essential for a creature to be truly alive.

THE COST OF FREEDOM

Enki's creatures were able to revive Inanna and free her, but there was a catch: the demons would not allow her to leave the Underworld unless Inanna promised to send someone else to take her place. When she

to Earth and avoid a permanent sentence in the darkness. From then on, Dumuzi stayed on Earth for six months to bring spring and fertility to the land, leaving for the Underworld once the crops were harvested. His journeying back and forth brought with it the changing seasons on Earth.

▼ REVIVING INANNA
Enki gave his creations the water of immortality, which they used to revive Inanna. She could now return to Earth.

▲ INANNA AND DUMUZI
The pair are often shown in Mesopotamian carvings as a loving couple holding hands, about to embrace.

Gilgamesh the tyrant

The legendary wicked King Gilgamesh of Mesopotamia (in modern-day Iraq) is the subject of the oldest epic poem to survive from ancient times. *The Epic of Gilgamesh* may be about 4,000 years old, and is one of the earliest surviving works of literature. It explores the themes of power, cruelty, heroism, and friendship, as well as the quest for everlasting life.

The mighty Gilgamesh was the king of the Mesopotamian city of Uruk. He was a cruel ruler who enslaved his people. Tormented by him, the people prayed to the gods for their freedom.

The gods responded by sending Enkidu, a wild man of enormous strength, to curb Gilgamesh's power. When the ruthless Gilgamesh met Enkidu, he tried to distract the wild man by finding him a wife. At the wedding feast, Enkidu saw Gilgamesh flirting with his bride. He felt angry and insulted, so he challenged Gilgamesh to a fight and the pair wrestled for hours. Neither could beat the other, as they were evenly matched in strength. In the end, they called it a draw and became friends.

◀ ENKIDU
The wild man Enkidu was usually portrayed with animal features, such as horns and hoofed feet.

BRAVE HERO ▶
This statue, from the throne room of a Mesopotamian palace, shows a fearless hero overpowering a lion. It is thought to depict Gilgamesh.

DOUBLE TROUBLE

Things became even worse for the people of Uruk, because they now had two powerful tyrants making everyday life miserable. Taking pity on the people, the gods sent a fearsome monster called Humbaba to subdue Gilgamesh and Enkidu, but the pair fought and killed it. Then the gods asked the love goddess Inanna (see pp.110–111) to calm Gilgamesh, hoping she could persuade him to change his ways, but he refused to listen to her.

FINDING THE EPIC

Archaeologists found the text of *The Epic of Gilgamesh* in Assyria (part of Mesopotamia). It was written on clay tablets—mostly broken and incomplete. Some of these were inscribed in c. 1800 BCE, but the story probably goes back further still.

HUMBABA ▶
This clay mask portrays the terrifying face of Humbaba. The monster could kill its opponents with a gruesome bite or with its fiery breath.

Finally, the gods sent the Bull of Heaven—the strongest and most warlike creature of all—to put an end to the tyrannical king's power. However, Gilgamesh and his friend were able to kill the bull. The deadly duo seemed invincible, and the gods realized that the only way to end their tyranny was to kill Enkidu.

QUEST FOR IMMORTALITY

Gilgamesh was deeply upset by the loss of his only friend. He began to worry about his own mortality, knowing that he, too, would die one day. Gilgamesh had heard of an old man, Utnapishtim, who was immortal. Long ago, the gods were angry at the sins of humanity and wiped out the people in a great flood. Only wise Utnapishtim survived, as the gods had helped him build a boat to save himself and the animals. Impressed by his virtue, the gods made Utnapishtim immortal.

When Gilgamesh met Utnapishtim and sought his help to attain immortality, the old man told the king to accept his fate. Gilgamesh seemed unhappy with this answer, so the wise man told Gilgamesh that he could stay young forever if he found and ate a magical herb growing at the bottom of a lake in the Underworld. Gilgamesh traveled to the Underworld and uprooted the plant, but on his way back, a snake stole the herb. Realizing that there was nothing he could do to escape death, Gilgamesh finally accepted his destiny. He returned to his kingdom and spent the rest of his days striving to be a good ruler.

Floods appear in the stories of many cultures, and are usually a punishment from the gods.

◀ REMAINS OF URUK
The ancient city of Uruk was situated in the area near the Euphrates River in modern-day Iraq. At its peak, Uruk was inhabited by almost 50,000 people.

Baal's rise to power

Clay tablets discovered at the site of the ancient city of Ugarit in modern-day Syria and dating from c.1200 BCE reveal stories about the city's gods and goddesses. Many of the myths recorded on these tablets relate to the sky god Baal and his struggle with his brother for power.

Baal wore a tall, conical headdress.

ASIA

This statue of Baal is made of bronze, with gold covering some parts, such as the arm ring.

BAAL ▲
Baal is usually depicted with his arm raised in a threatening gesture as seen in this statue of the god from c. 1400 BCE.

The god Baal was the son of the mother goddess Athirat and El, the supreme god of Ugarit. He was the brother of the sea god Yamm and the war goddess Anat. Although El was immortal, he grew old over time, and Baal's power and influence grew. He became El's equal and controlled the rain, thunder, and lightning.

THE TWO BROTHERS

Baal's rise to power as the sky god drew the envy of Yamm, who decided to challenge Baal for supremacy. Yamm went to their father El and demanded that the supreme god surrender all of Baal's personal treasure. After seizing the valuables, Yamm also captured his brother and forced Baal to serve him.

Baal was able to fight back. The skilled craftsman Kothar wa-Hasis made a pair of clubs (see p.117) with magical powers for the sky god. Baal struck his brother with the first club, but it caused no harm. A blow from the second club, however, injured Yamm and brought the sea god to his knees. Now that Yamm was weakened, Baal tore his body into pieces and scattered them far and wide.

THE PALACE OF BAAL

Having defeated his powerful brother, Baal was now the greatest among El's children. Despite this, he did not have a magnificent palace like the other gods

> Baal's **rise to power** as the sky god **drew the envy of Yamm** …

of Ugarit. He complained to his sister Anat, who went to their parents and demanded a palace suitable for a god of Baal's importance. Their mother Athirat was unwilling, so Baal devised a plan to persuade her. He asked Kothar wa-Hasis to make the most exquisite furniture and ornaments, which caught Athirat's attention. The goddess then gave in, saying that such beautiful items deserved a fitting home. Baal was able to build a palace like no other, and rejoiced in his new home.

El's headdress has bull-like horns.

▶ EL THE SUPREME
Like many other gods of Ugarit, El wore a horned helmet, showing that his strength was similar to that of a bull.

The fearsome Anat

The goddess Anat was responsible for the fertility of the land in Ugarit, but she also had a violent side. Priests used stories about her love of brutality as a way of explaining religious rituals such as sacrifices, which they believed would pacify her and bring about plentiful harvests.

The goddess Anat made the land fertile and presided over the growth of crops, but she also had a warlike streak. As a fertility goddess, Anat had only agricultural tools at her disposal, but she was fond of all kinds of weaponry. Once, she stole the bow and arrows of a mortal warrior named Ahat, enraging her brother, the sky god Baal. He was so angry with Anat that he stopped the rains until she returned the stolen items.

On other occasions, Anat massacred the entire population of two of Ugarit's neighboring cities, and once invited an army to dine at her palace, before chopping off the heads of the soldiers using her scythe. The people eventually forgave her, because they believed these deaths were sacrifices that had to be made in order to make the land more fertile.

TO THE UNDERWORLD

Anat's fearsome nature was called upon when Baal challenged Mot, the god of death, to a duel. Arriving at the doors of the sky god's palace, Mot swallowed Baal whole and took him to the Underworld. In Baal's absence, the rains ceased, causing a terrible drought on Earth.

Anat was distraught at her brother's capture and pitied the parched land, so she decided to travel to the Underworld to rescue Baal. When she reached Mot's palace, she attacked the god of death with her weapons and tools. Anat then burned Mot and ground him to pieces with her millstone, setting Baal free. Baal's return to Earth allowed the rains to begin again, ensuring that crops could grow once more.

UGARIT, A TRADING CITY

Located on the west coast of what is now Syria, Ugarit was a major city from c. 1800 BCE. It profited from trade with Egypt and the countries surrounding the Mediterranean, before being destroyed in c. 1200 BCE, probably by invaders who arrived by sea.

Mythical weapons

Many deities and mortals in myth and legend have incredible
strength, but sometimes what makes them truly
unbeatable is their weapon. Ranging from magical
swords to powerful tridents, these supernatural weapons can protect the
user, cause injuries to enemies, or make things appear out of thin air.

**THOR'S
MJÖLNIR ▶**
*The Norse sky god
Thor uses a hammer
called Mjölnir to
defeat his enemies. Blows
from this hammer are so
loud that they sound
like thunder.*

**◀ NEPTUNE'S
TRIDENT**
*The sea god
Neptune (the Roman
equivalent of the
Greek Poseidon),
makes water appear
from the ground
by striking it with
his trident. This
three-pronged
weapon can even stir
up storms in the sea.*

▲ ARTHUR'S SWORD
*Excalibur, the sword of King Arthur
of Britain, has many magical
powers. It prevents the king from
bleeding to death when wounded,
and even blinds his enemies.*

◀ PERSEUS'S HARPE
*The Greek god Zeus gives a sword
called a harpe to the hero Perseus.
This razor-sharp weapon has a
sickle-shaped projection. Perseus
uses it to kill the Gorgon Medusa.*

◀ SHIVA'S BOW
*This weapon is so powerful that
no human is strong enough to
lift or string it. In the Hindu epic
Ramayana, the hero Rama not only
strings the bow to win Sita's hand
in marriage but also breaks it.*

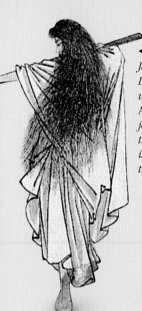

◀ **AMENONUHOKO**
*Japan's creator gods
Izanagi and Izanami
use a spear called
Amenonuhoko ("heavenly
jeweled spear") to churn
the sea and create an
island, which becomes
their home.*

≫ **SEE ALSO** ≫

- Athena's gift, pp.24–25
- Perseus and Medusa, pp.36–37
- Thor's hammer, p.69
- The sword in the stone, pp.92–93
- Baal's rise to power, p.114
- Pan Gu creates the universe, p.128
- Izanagi and Izanami, pp.140–141
- Rama's journey, pp.158–161

▼ **HUITZILOPOCHTLI'S FIRE SERPENT**
*The Aztec war god Huitzilopochtli uses a fire
serpent, Xiuhcóatl, as his weapon. It helps him
fight against his siblings.*

▲ **VISHNU'S SUDARSHANA
CHAKRA**
*The Hindu god Vishnu uses this
spinning disk to destroy evil
Asuras (demons), sometimes
by cutting off their heads.*

*After the Gorgon
Medusa is killed,
her head is placed
on the shield to
increase its power.*

▲ **ATHENA'S SHIELD**
*A shield called the Aegis is one
of the most prized possessions
of the Greek goddess Athena.*

▲ **BAAL'S CLUBS**
*A divine craftsman gives the
Ugarit thunder god Baal a
pair of magical clubs, which
could strike an enemy down
from a great distance.*

PAN GU'S AX ▶
*The Chinese primal god
Pan Gu uses his enormous
ax to separate the elements at
the beginning of creation,
helping him make the world.*

FEASTERS
The Hittites would welcome the spring with elaborate feasts to celebrate Teshub's victory over the serpent Illuyanka.

The triumph of Teshub

Teshub was a weather god of the Hittite people, who lived in Anatolia (in modern-day Turkey) from c.1600 BCE. Weather deities were important to the Hittites because droughts were common in the region. They believed that the actions of these gods dictated the weather on Earth.

◀ TESHUB
The god is usually shown holding a triple bolt and an ax, symbolic of his strength and ability to cause storms.

The storm god Teshub was also the god of war—a dual role that gave him great power. Nevertheless, even with all this might, Teshub could not defeat a dragonlike, fire-breathing serpent called Illuyanka.

His many unsuccessful attempts to defeat Illuyanka made Teshub furious, so he decided to ask the other gods for help. His daughter Inara and the mortal man Hupasiya, whom she loved, came up with a plan. They announced a great feast and invited Illuyanka and his family. The guests were served enormous amounts of delicious food, wine, and beer, which they could not resist. The serpents gorged on the food and drank countless jars of beer, which made them all very sleepy. It also made them fat, so they could not fit through the holes that led to their nests underground.

Hupasiya caught the drowsy Illuyanka and tied him up, so that Teshub could finally put the terrifying serpent to death.

Wrong and Right

Among the Hittites, who were mainly farmers, oxen were seen as both useful creatures and symbols of power and wealth. The story about a dispute between two Hittite brothers, Wrong and Right, illustrates the importance of these animals.

◀ TERRA-COTTA OXEN
In Hittite culture, oxen were a sacred symbol of Teshub (above). They were represented in various art forms, such as terra-cotta pottery.

There was once a man called Appu, who had all the wealth he could want but no children. Appu prayed to the sun god for help and soon had two sons, whom he named Wrong and Right. When Appu died, the two brothers inherited their father's farm and two oxen, and lived in harmony. After a while, Wrong wanted to live apart from his brother, and asked for the property to be split. Right agreed, and the brothers divided up the farm and took an ox each. However, Wrong cheated: he took the stronger of the two animals, which could plow more land and pull heavier loads. When Right found out, he was angry. He complained to the sun god, who made Right's beast larger and stronger than his brother's. In the end, Wrong's trickery did not serve him well, and Right prospered because of the sun god's favor.

The struggle against evil

According to the myths of Ancient Persia (modern-day Iran), there were two beings that influenced human life: the wise Ahura Mazda and the wicked Ahriman. The struggle for power between these two beings helped people explain the presence of evil in the world, and also showed them that it is up to humans to choose a way through life: a virtuous path or a wicked one.

ASIA

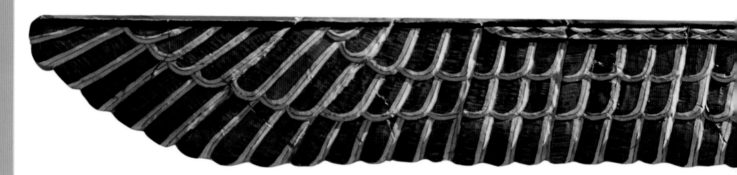

The first god Zurvan ("Time") longed for a son, but doubted his ability to create. Eventually he made two sons, Ahura Mazda ("Wise Lord") and Ahriman ("Destructive Spirit"). Before these sons emerged, Zurvan predicted that his first-born would build the world and rule over it. His sons heard this prophecy while still in Zurvan's body, and Ahriman forced himself out into the world before Ahura Mazda to claim the role of the creator. Ahura Mazda was pale and sweet-smelling at birth as he was born out of Zurvan's optimism, while Ahriman, born out of Zurvan's doubts, was dark and foul-smelling.

CREATION OF THE WORLD

Zurvan had no choice but to bestow the title of creator to Ahriman as he was the first-born. However, Ahriman was unable to create anything, and lost his place as the ruler and creator to Ahura Mazda.

Now was the time for Ahura Mazda to begin his task of giving the universe its form. He created the sun, moon, and stars, and then made six immortals, including Vohu Manah ("Good Mind"), to make other beings and help him rule. Finally, he created Gayomart, the first human, and gave Vohu Manah the job of making Gayomart good.

AHRIMAN'S REVENGE

Things went well for Ahura Mazda and the universe for some time. However, the wicked Ahriman was jealous of Ahura Mazda, and produced demons and dangerous creatures to disrupt the work of his brother. Ahura Mazda was able to repel the attacks of these demons, and cast Ahriman out into the darkness, away from the world he had created. This made Ahriman more resentful, so he created the evils of starvation, disease, pain, and death, and brought them into the world Ahura Mazda had created. Ahriman also took away

Ahura Mazda   Ahriman

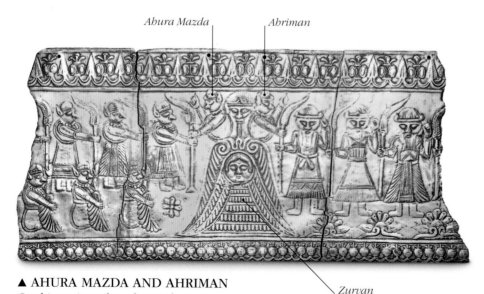

▲ **AHURA MAZDA AND AHRIMAN**
On this ancient silver plaque, the twin deities Ahura Mazda and Ahriman emerge from the body of the first god Zurvan, who stands in the center.

Zurvan

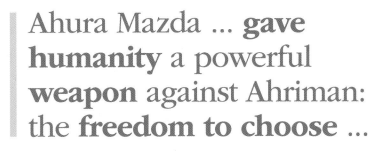

Ahura Mazda ... **gave humanity** a powerful **weapon** against Ahriman: the **freedom to choose** ...

The figure holds a ring of leadership.

The circle represents the sun.

▲ THE FARAVAHAR
This emblem is an important symbol of the Zoroastrian religion as a reminder of one's purpose in life and to accept Ahura Mazda as the only god.

Loops on either side of the Faravahar represent good and evil.

the fertility of the land, destroying crops and poisoning the soil. He then gave diseases to Gayomart, ensuring that the first human was made mortal and would eventually die.

THE HUMAN RACE

The first human, Gayomart, was unable to have children on his own. Ahura Mazda did not want this to be the end of humankind, so he took some of Gayomart's seed and created a human couple, Mashya and Mashyoi. This pair would be able to have children, ensuring the survival of humankind. Ahura Mazda also realized that Ahriman was indestructible and would continue to harm the humans.

Seeing no way to keep him away from his creations, Ahura Mazda trapped the wicked spirit on Earth, but gave humanity a powerful weapon against Ahriman: the freedom to choose between a good or evil path through their lives.

People believe that ever since then, these two opposing forces have been locked in conflict. This power struggle will continue until the end of time, when Ahura Mazda will return with a new god, Saoshyant ("the Saviour"), who will be able to defeat Ahriman and make all of humankind wise and good.

◄ GAYOMART
The first human was seen as the first king of the Persian people. Here he is shown with the people in his court, planning an attack on Ahriman.

Rustum and Sohrab

Tales about the heroic warrior Rustum unfold in the Persian epic poem *Shahnama* (*The Book of Kings*). Based partly on the history of the early Persian Empire, the legend describes how the great hero Rustum defends his people from powerful enemies and monsters alike. One tragic episode tells the story of Rustum's unfortunate battle with his son, Sohrab, showing the waste of life involved in warfare.

Rustum was the son of the legendary Persian warrior Zal and the princess Rudaba. As a child, Rustum possessed amazing strength and was trained in warfare by his father when he grew older. As a fighter, Rustum was so brave and skillful that his heroics could inspire his comrades and help them win any battle. When Kay Kavus, the emperor of Persia, was captured by the demons of Mazandaran, Rustum was sent to rescue him. Riding his famous horse Rakhsh, Rustum set out on his mission. During his journey, he had to undertake seven quests.

These included encounters with powerful beasts as well as battles with skilled enemies, such as the champion fighter of Mazandaran. When he finally reached his destination, Rustum had to slay both Div-e Sepid (see p.190), the leader of the demons, and his entire army, before rescuing Kay Kavus.

RUSTUM AND TAHMINA

Once when Rustum was out hunting, his horse Rakhsh was stolen. Sad at losing his faithful companion, Rustum followed Rakhsh's tracks until he arrived at the kingdom of Samangan. The king of Samangan welcomed Rustum as his guest and assured him that a horse as famous as Rakhsh would be found in no time. The king also introduced the young warrior to his daughter Tahmina. Rustum and Tahmina fell in love, and before long, it became apparent that Tahmina was going to have Rustum's child.

After a while, Rakhsh was found, and Rustum prepared to be on his way. Before leaving, however, Rustum gave Tahmina a jeweled amulet and asked her to give the ornament to their child. Tahmina gave birth to a boy, whom she named Sohrab. When the child was older, his mother handed him the amulet and told him about the father he had never met. Sohrab grew up to be a great warrior

▼ KILLING THE DRAGON
Among the quests on Rustum's mission to free Kay Kavus was an encounter with a dragon. Rustum fought hard and cut off the beast's head.

himself, and he soon gained fame as the best fighter in the army of King Afrasiab, the ruler of Turan.

THE WAR AGAINST PERSIA

After Turan declared war on Persia, Sohrab led a force that attacked a castle belonging to the Persians. Messengers from the castle rode quickly to the Persian emperor, telling him that they were besieged by a warrior as mighty and skillful as their own Rustum. The emperor realized that his only hope of defending his kingdom was to send Rustum into battle.

When King Afrasiab found out that Persia's greatest warrior was entering the fight, he was worried. Afrasiab encouraged Sohrab to challenge Rustum, hoping the young man would kill the hero, a move that would significantly weaken his enemy and make it easier for Afrasiab to take over Persia.

THE *SHAHNAMA*

The *Shahnama*, written in c.1010 CE by the Persian poet Firdausi, describes the history of Persia (modern-day Iran) from mythical times up until its conquest by Islamic forces in c.650 CE. The book is full of stories of mythical beasts and noble warriors, and contains tragic tales like that of the ill-fated Sohrab.

◄ THE DEMON OF MAZANDARAN
King Kavus's captor was a huge demon called Div-e Sepid ("White Demon"), who was skilled in magic. Rustum rescued Kavus by killing the demon.

THE FATAL CHALLENGE
After Rustum arrived on the battlefield, the two sides fought bravely, but eventually it became clear that the best way to settle the conflict would be for the two heroes to fight in single combat. When Sohrab challenged him to a duel, Rustum accepted, knowing that it would be certain death for one of them, but unaware that he was about to fight his own son.

Rustum and Sohrab began their duel and fought for a whole day with no clear victor. When they resumed their struggle the next day, Rustum struck a blow so hard that it threw Sohrab down and broke his back. As he lay dying, Sohrab showed Rustum the jeweled amulet his mother Tahmina had given him and told Rustum that his father would avenge his death. Devastated, Rustum realized that the young warrior he had killed was, in fact, his own son.

> ## Rustum and Sohrab began their duel and **fought for a whole day with no clear victor**.

▼ THE TRAGIC END
Unknown to one another, Rustum and his son Sohrab met for the first time on the battlefield and fought each other to the bitter end.

The sky god and his creations

The early Mongolian people of northeast Asia lived in harmony with nature, believing they shared their world with many sacred spirits, known as *tengri*. Chief among these spirits was Mongke Tengri (or simply Tengri), who created the first humans. Tengri's story tells how an evil force prevents his creations from becoming immortal.

In the beginning, Earth was inhabited only by animals. The chief spirit and sky god Mongke Tengri decided to create the first man and first woman to populate the world. He made their bodies and covered them with soft hair. Mongke Tengri was happy with these creations and wanted them to live forever. For this, he would need to fetch water from the Spring of Immortality. Tengri wanted to ensure that the humans would be safe while he was away, so he ordered a cat and a dog to watch over them.

MONGKE TENGRI ▶
The fierce sky god was the creator and protector of humanity. He is usually shown brandishing a weapon, ready to fight any demons that could harm his creations.

SPOILED PLANS

Meanwhile, the god of the Underworld, Erlik Khan, had been watching the sky god and his creations. A sworn enemy of Mongke Tengri, he decided to ruin the sky god's plans. As soon as Tengri was out of sight, Erlik Khan lured away the cat with a bowl of milk and the dog with a piece of meat. Erlik Khan then polluted the first man and woman with impurities.

When Tengri returned, he was furious to discover what had happened. He punished the animals by making the cat lick all the body hair off the humans, except for the hair on their heads, which had not been polluted. Tengri then made the cat stick this hair onto the dog. He then washed the humans with the water he had brought from the Spring of Immortality, hoping this would purify them and make them live forever. However, Erlik Khan's impurities could not be washed off, and the humans could not gain everlasting life. Mongke Tengri sent the first man and woman out into the world to populate it, knowing that every generation of humans that was born would eventually die.

MONGOLIAN SHAMANS

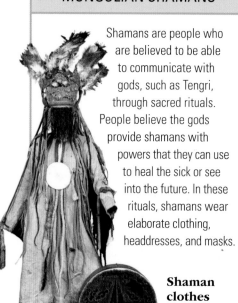

Shamans are people who are believed to be able to communicate with gods, such as Tengri, through sacred rituals. People believe the gods provide shamans with powers that they can use to heal the sick or see into the future. In these rituals, shamans wear elaborate clothing, headdresses, and masks.

Shaman clothes and ritual drum

Erlik Khan was **a sworn enemy** of Mongke Tengri, and **decided to ruin his plans.**

The eagle's food

Mongolian myths frequently attempt to explain the natural world that people saw around them. Many of them feature animals, and tell of how they received their different qualities. One Mongol story explains why eagles eat snakes and why wasps buzz.

Of all the flying creatures on Earth, the eagle Khan-Garid was the mightiest. It thought that it should have the best-tasting food to reflect its status as king of the birds, but wondered what that might be. Khan-Garid decided to give the daunting task of finding the perfect food to two smaller flying creatures: the wasp and the swallow. It told them to fly around and taste every creature on Earth, before returning to report their findings. This would help the eagle decide which would make the tastiest meal.

In present-day Mongolia, eagles are specially trained to hunt animals for people.

THE SWALLOW'S TRICK

While the wasp flew around enthusiastically, biting every living thing it could find, the swallow forgot about the task, and spent all its time flying, singing, and enjoying the beautiful day.

When the two met later, the swallow asked the wasp what it thought tasted best. The wasp said that of all the creatures it

▲ THE FEARSOME SNAKE
The swallow chose the snake as the perfect food for the eagle hoping this would protect the king of the birds from humans.

had bitten, humans tasted the best. The swallow was worried by this, because it thought that attacking people could put the king's life in danger. To keep the wasp from passing on this information to the eagle, the swallow bit off the wasp's tongue. As a result, the only noise the insect could make was a meaningless buzz.

The clever swallow then went to Khan-Garid and told it that the snake tasted best. The king of the birds then decided to make this its food of choice. Since that time, all descendants of the eagle have hunted snakes and eaten them.

▼ THE GOLDEN EAGLE
In Mongolia, eagles are believed to be descendants of the mighty Khan-Garid. The golden eagle is a large, powerful bird, and hunts small mammals and reptiles.

HORSES IN MONGOLIAN MYTHS

Mongols were nomads, traveling long distances on horseback, so a horse was an important possession. Many Mongol deities are shown riding horses, including Kubera, the god of wealth and good fortune, and the sky spirit White Lightning Tengri, whose swift passage across the sky on his white steed was said to be the bright bolts of lightning.

Kubera shown as a horseman

Great queens

There are many remarkable queens in myth and legend, from rulers of the Underworld to legendary leaders on Earth. Gentle and loving or warlike and adventurous, they play major roles in many of the world's most popular stories.

▶ FRIGG
The queen of the Aesir (sky gods), Frigg is one of the most powerful Norse deities. She is the goddess of love, fertility, and the household.

◀ GUINEVERE
One tale about Queen Guinevere, the wife of King Arthur of Britain, describes her as being descended from a noble Roman family. Her relationship with Sir Lancelot brings about the downfall of Arthur's court.

◀ ISIS
As the first queen of Egypt and wife of the god Osiris, Isis is at the heart of Egyptian mythology. She is seen as the ancestral mother of all the pharaohs.

HIPPOLYTA ▶
In Greek mythology, Hippolyta is the queen of the Amazons, a tribe of fearless warrior women. She leads them in many epic conflicts.

Hippolyta's belt is a gift from her father, the god Ares.

◀ MEDB
The ambitious Medb of Connaught is a warlike queen in Irish mythology. She leads her people against their rival, the kingdom of Ulster.

◀ **CLYTEMNESTRA**
The powerful queen of Mycenae, Clytemnestra (on the left), is ruthless and determined, and is best-known for killing her husband Agamemnon.

NÜ WA ▲
After the universe comes into existence, the Chinese creator goddess Nü Wa populates Earth by creating the first humans out of yellow clay and mud.

Nü Wa is sometimes shown with a snake's body.

SEE ALSO

- The labors of Hercules pp.30–33
- The trial of Orestes, pp.58–59
- Aeneas's destiny, pp.60–61
- Loki and Balder, p.70
- Cúchulain's fate, pp.82–85
- Sir Lancelot's betrayal, p.95
- The great flood, p.129
- Rama's journey, pp.158–161
- The death of Osiris, pp.172–177

▲ **DIDO**
Queen Dido establishes the North African city of Carthage and rules it well. She falls in love with the Roman hero Aeneas, and tragically ends her life when he leaves for Latium.

◀ **RAMBHA**
In Hindu mythology, Rambha is the queen of the Apsaras, a group of female spirits in heaven. She is famed for her dancing and musical skills.

KAIKEYI ▶
One of the three queens of Ayodhya in the Hindu epic Ramayana, Kaikeyi is Rama's stepmother. She plays a part in bringing about his exile.

Pan Gu creates the universe

In Chinese mythology, the creation of the universe combines the violence and strength of the primal god Pan Gu with the gentler, nurturing way of the mother goddess Nü Wa. Pan Gu makes the universe out of chaos, while Nü Wa creates the first humans.

◀ **THE CREATOR GOD**
Pan Gu separated the dark elements of the Yin from the light elements of the Yang to create the cosmos, bringing order to the universe.

THE FIRST PEOPLE

A gentle goddess named Nü Wa now appeared. Impressed by the beauty of the cosmos around her, she wanted people to live in the world. She took some clay and molded it into the first humans. Nü Wa made many of them, and gave them the power to have their own children, ensuring that Earth would always be populated.

Before the beginning of time, only formless chaos existed. Gradually, this chaos gathered inside a cosmic egg, where the lone creator god Pan Gu was sleeping. He slept long and deeply, before finally awaking from his slumber.

ORDER FROM CHAOS

Displeased by his dark and dreary surroundings, Pan Gu broke free from the cosmic egg, sending the swirling elements of chaos flying in different directions. He then conjured up a massive ax (see p.117), and used it to separate the opposing forces of Yin and Yang. This caused the darker, heavier Yin elements to sink and form the land, while the lighter Yang elements floated upward and mixed together to produce the sky. Anxious to keep Earth and sky separate, Pan Gu stood between them, and raised his arms to push the sky higher still. With every passing day, the sky rose higher and the land grew thicker. Pan Gu himself grew taller to keep up with the expanding universe.

When the universe was fully made, Pan Gu's eyes became the sun and moon; his hair fell into pieces that made the stars; his flesh and bones formed the soil and mountains; and his blood formed the lakes and rivers.

NÜ WA ▶
The goddess Nü Wa observes the world from the clouds in this carving.

When **the universe** was fully made, **Pan Gu's eyes** became the **sun and moon ...**

The great flood

Several accounts of the Chinese creation story continue with what happens when a great flood is unleashed on the world, drowning all of humanity. Most of these stories tell us how the goddess Nü Wa comes to Earth's rescue, and ensures that life is restored to the world.

The first humans, made by the goddess Nü Wa (see opposite), thrived on Earth until they were swept away in a great flood. This flood had occurred because a gap in the heavens was letting in too much rain.

Nü Wa decided to do something to end this destruction. She melted some colored stones and plugged the gap with the mixture. This ended the flood, but the goddess was saddened by the fact that there were no longer any people living on Earth. Nü Wa and her husband, the god Fu Xi, decided to have many children together so that Earth could be repopulated once more.

CREATORS OF HUMANKIND ▶
Nü Wa (left) and Fu Xi brought human life back to the world. They are often shown in serpentlike forms.

The Three Officials

Among the heavenly gods of Daoism, a Chinese belief system, are a trio known as the Three Officials ("Sanguan" in Chinese). These important deities are second in rank to the Jade Emperor, the ruler of Heaven, and each is responsible for governing one of three separate realms.

After the creation of humanity, the Jade Emperor (see pp.130–131), who ruled heaven, looked down on Earth and saw that its people were growing in number. He decided that the people needed guidance to make sure they lived together peacefully, so he sent three godly rulers down from heaven. The first of these officials was named Tian Guan ("the Ruler of Heaven"), a figure so important that he was second-in-command to the Jade Emperor himself. Tian Guan brought happiness, freedom, and prosperity to the people of Earth.

Tian Guan

Di Guan   **Shui Guan**

◀ HEAVENLY OFFICIALS
As bringers of happiness, fortune, and health, the Three Officials are widely worshipped in China.

Next came Di Guan ("the Ruler of Earth"), who judged the actions of the people and who could forgive sins. The third of these principal officials was Shui Guan ("the Ruler of the Waters"). He taught the people how to drain the land for farming and avoid floods, as well as how to cure diseases. These three heavenly officials have been worshipped by the Chinese people ever since.

The Jade Emperor's court

The ruler of Heaven, the Jade Emperor is the supreme deity in Chinese mythology. There are different stories about him, some of which say that he created the universe and the human race. The most common version, however, describes him as a virtuous human who becomes immortal and rules with a vast group of other deities in Heaven.

▲ **XI WANGMU**
Also known as the Queen Mother of the West, the Emperor's wife Xi Wangmu is one of the most powerful deities, with the ability to grant immortality to people (see p.135).

ASIA

The Jade Emperor began life on Earth as a mortal man. He had been born to a king called Ching Teh and a queen named Pao Yüeh. The royal couple had longed for a child for years but had not been blessed with one. One day, Pao Yüeh went to a temple and asked the priests to pray for her so that she might have a child. That night she dreamed that Laozi, the father of Daoism, visited her carrying a baby.

In due course, the queen gave birth to a son, Yühuang, who became the emperor of China when his father died. Yühuang ruled well, combining good judgement and kindness. Once he had ensured that his people were prospering, Yühuang gave up the throne to lead a life of meditation and prayer. He had been such a good ruler on Earth that, upon his death, he became the immortal Jade Emperor, the supreme ruler of Heaven. His wife, Xi Wangmu, shared the job with him.

HEAVENLY HELPERS

The Jade Emperor gathered around him a large number of other immortals (see pp.132–133) to act as his helpers. This heavenly administration ensured that the world of the immortals ran smoothly. In addition, each deity had a specific role in helping the people on Earth. Among

◄ **KITCHEN GOD**
Families burn an image of Zao Jun at the end of every year. They believe that the smoke rising from the burning image carries a report of their behavior to heaven.

the prominent ones were Yue Lao, who took care of couples, especially those who were newly married, and Longwang, the god of rain, who looked after the seas and rivers that were vital for both food and transportation. The most important assistant to the Jade Emperor was a deity named Zao Jun. He was also known as the Kitchen God because mortals kept a picture of him in their kitchens. His place in the heart of the home meant that he provided the closest link between Heaven and Earth.

CHINESE BUDDHISM

The Jade Emperor appears as a deity in Chinese religions such as Buddhism, Daoism, and folk religion. Chinese Buddhists consider him the ruler of one of the Buddhist heavens, and see the Buddha himself as an immortal, rather than a real person, the monk Siddhartha Gautama.

RULING IN HEAVEN ▶
Just like a mortal Chinese emperor who rules with the help of administrators, the Jade Emperor, too, has a whole court of deities who act as his officials.

The Eight Immortals

In Chinese mythology, the Eight Immortals (*Ba Xian*) were a group of legendary beings with exceptional abilities. They began life as humans and became immortal by devoting themselves to the Daoist faith, an ancient way of living in harmony with nature.

Li Tieguai

- **Also known as:** Li T'ieh-kuai
- **Shown with:** Gourd, iron crutch

An old man who walked with an iron crutch, Li Tieguai was kind and gentle. He carried a hollow gourd (dried shell) containing medicines, and used these to heal sick people he met on his travels. Li Tieguai studied with Laozi (the founder of Daoism), and was a follower of Daoism for 40 years, pursuing his faith single-mindedly and often going without food.

Zhongli Quan

- **Also known as:** Chung-li Ch'uan
- **Shown with:** Fan

Zhongli Quan was a soldier who fled to the hills after facing defeat in a battle. There he met a wise man who taught him the ways of Daoist magic. Zhongli Quan had a magical fan, which he would use along with his extensive knowledge of alchemy, to raise the dead or produce gold coins for the poor and needy.

Zhang Guolao

- **Also known as:** Chang Kuo-lao
- **Shown with:** White mule, drum

Zhang Guolao was an adviser to several emperors and lived to a very old age. He made a special wine out of herbs and plants that had healing properties, and shared this wine with the other immortals. Zhang Guolao was a master of the martial art Qigong, which involved both physical exercise and spiritual meditation. He rode a magical white mule that could be folded into paper when not in use.

Lü Dongbin

- **Also known as:** Lü Tung-pin
- **Shown with:** Sword, horsehair fly whisk

Lü Dongbin was a Daoist poet and scholar. The most famous of the Eight Immortals, he was a master of "internal alchemy," the use of Daoist magic to prolong life and create a spirit body that could become immortal. Lü Dongbin was also a gifted warrior who could subdue evil spirits with his magic sword.

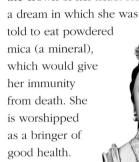

The Eight Immortals are still worshipped by Daoists today, and often appear in popular culture in China.

He Xiangu

- **Also known as:** Ho Hsien-ku
- **Shown with:** Lotus flower, ladle

He Xiangu is said to have been the daughter of an herbalist (someone who makes medicine from plants). She was born with six long hairs on the crown of her head. He Xiangu had a dream in which she was told to eat powdered mica (a mineral), which would give her immunity from death. She is worshipped as a bringer of good health.

Cao Guojiu

- **Also known as:** Ts'ao Kuo-chiu
- **Shown with:** Pair of castanets, official's writing equipment

Cao Guojiu was a relative of an empress. His brother Cao Jingzh made use of his powerful royal connections to gain influence over people, but Cao Guojiu used his position to help others. Upset by his brother's abuse of power, Cao Guojiu left the imperial court and set out to live alone. On his way, he met the two immortals Zhongli Quan and Lü Dongbin, who taught him Daoist magic.

Lan Caihe

- **Also known as:** Lan Ts'ai-ho
- **Shown with:** Flute, flower basket

Usually portrayed as a woman, Lan Caihe loved flowers and was considered a deity by florists. She is said to have gained much Daoist wisdom from Monkey (see pp.136–139), and ascended to Heaven on the back of a swan.

Han Xiangzi

- **Also known as:** Han Hsiang-tzu
- **Shown with:** Chinese flute (dizi)

A musician and composer, Han Xiangzi is believed to be the great-nephew of Han Yü, a famous scholar and writer from the Tang dynasty. Han Xiangzi studied Daoist magic under Lü Dongbin and became his assistant. He was a patron of musicians, especially players of the Chinese flute, or dizi, which he also played himself.

Han Xiangzi carries his flute.

YI SHOOTS THE SUNS
With his distinctive red bow and white arrows, Yi rescued humankind from a disastrous drought by shooting the suns out of the sky.

Yi, the heavenly archer

Ancient China was prone to both floods and droughts. Chinese mythology has many stories about how the gods helped people overcome these disasters. One involves the heavenly archer Yi, who becomes a hero for preventing a devastating drought, but pays a heavy price for refusing his reward of immortality.

A long time ago, there were ten suns in the sky, all of which were the children of Di Jun, the emperor of the Eastern Heaven, and Xi He, the goddess of the sun. Each day, one of the ten suns would take its turn to shine in the sky, spreading warmth across the land, and helping the crops ripen and people thrive.

Over time, the suns grew weary of this routine, and one day they decided to all rise together. This spelled disaster for the land: the crops shriveled and died, rivers dried up, and people began to suffer in the extreme heat.

HEAVENLY HELP

The emperor of China, Yao, was in despair and prayed to Di Jun and Xi He for help. Hearing Yao's prayers, the heavenly couple told the ten suns to stop rising together, but the suns were enjoying each other's company in the sky, and would not listen to their parents. To teach them a lesson, Di Jun decided to call upon his most talented archer, Yi. The heavenly emperor asked Yi to travel to Earth and shoot the suns out of the sky. The archer brought with him his wife Chang'e, but by the time they had arrived on Earth, all the suns had set. Yi met Emperor Yao and together they waited for sunrise.

SHOOTING THE SUNS

The next day, the ten suns rose to shine together and the heat became unbearable again. Yi aimed his bow and arrow at the first sun and shot at it. As its light went out, the emperor and Yi saw an enormous bird fall from the sky. They were amazed to see that this bird was shaped like a crow (see p.148), but was golden in color and had three feet instead of two. They realized that the crow was the spirit of the first sun and that it had used its wings to propel the sun across the sky.

The archer continued shooting down the remaining suns until just one sun shone in the sky. At last, the land cooled to a bearable temperature, the crops recovered, and the people could live comfortably once again. The heavenly deities were delighted at Yi's feat. Xi Wangmu, the Queen Mother of the West (see p.130), gave him the elixir of immortality as a reward for restoring life on Earth. However,

> **China's first robotic spacecraft sent to the moon was named *Chang'e 1*, after the goddess.**

▶ **CHANG'E**
The moon goddess Chang'e would gaze down lovingly at Earth, where her husband Yi still lived.

Yi did not want to be separated from his wife Chang'e, so he did not take the elixir and decided to live with her on Earth.

TO THE MOON

The couple lived happily until one day, when Chang'e was alone, a disciple of Yi broke into their house to steal the elixir. Chang'e swallowed the elixir to keep it away from the intruder. As soon as she had done so, Chang'e became immortal and flew to the nearest heavenly body, the moon. When Yi discovered what had happened, he was saddened by the loss of his wife. However, in order to honor her, he set up a tradition of offering Chang'e's favorite foods to the moon each year on the day of her departure from Earth. From this point on Chang'e came to be worshipped as the goddess of the moon.

The adventures of Monkey

A mischievous trickster called Monkey is one of China's most colorful mythical characters. Always landing himself in trouble, Monkey's eventful travels take him from the Underworld to Heaven, and finally on a quest to bring the Buddhist scriptures from India to China.

Of all the monkeys, the one known simply as Monkey was the cleverest and most cunning. He could change his shape and size, and was highly skilled in martial arts. Monkey attained these skills by training under a Daoist master, but his teacher soon banished him to his home in the forest as punishment for his mischievous behavior.

In the forest, however, the other monkeys treated him like royalty, as they were completely in awe of Monkey's clever tricks. They organized a feast to celebrate Monkey's return, during which he got drunk and fell asleep. While he was sleeping, the king of the Underworld kidnapped Monkey and took him to that dark realm. Even in the Underworld, Monkey could not stop making mischief. He found a book in which the fate of every mortal creature was written down. It said that Monkey would live for 342 years. Hoping it would make him immortal, he crossed out his name in the book.

IN HEAVEN

Word of Monkey's misconduct reached the ears of the ruler of Heaven, the Jade Emperor (see pp.130–131). He grew worried when he heard that Monkey was seeking immortality and decided to bring him to Heaven to keep an eye on him. He made Monkey guard the heavenly garden in which the Peaches of Immortality grew, hoping this would keep Monkey busy. One day, the other deities organized a feast for the empress of Heaven, Xi Wangmu (see p.130), but the troublesome trickster was not invited. Monkey was furious, so he ate all the Peaches of Immortality to teach the others a lesson.

Monkey was now sure that he had gained immortality and announced that he was going to take over Heaven. The Jade Emperor was alarmed, and asked the Buddha, the wisest of all

◀ **HEAVENLY PEACHES**
The Peaches of Immortality took 3,000 years to ripen and were very precious to the gods. The Jade Emperor trusted Monkey with the important task of guarding them.

The foursome **traveled** through a magical landscape of **dragons and demons**.

ASIA

◀ WARRIOR'S ARMOR
Monkey is called Sun Wukong in Chinese, and is sometimes shown wearing the armor of a powerful warrior.

People born under the Chinese Zodiac sign of the monkey are considered good leaders.

immortals, for advice. When the Buddha questioned Monkey's intentions, the cunning trickster said that he deserved to be the ruler of Heaven because he was more powerful than anyone else and could even travel thousands of miles in a single leap. The Buddha held Monkey in the palm of his hand and asked him to demonstrate this incredible ability.

To Monkey's shock, when he jumped, he could not even escape the Buddha's hand and merely landed on the wise immortal's fingers. As punishment for his pride, Monkey was imprisoned inside a magic mountain and only set free 500 years later when he had repented.

HEADING WEST

A new adventure awaited Monkey upon his release. The monk Xuanzang was going on a long and challenging journey westward to India, to collect the Buddha's writings. As the monk was a gentle man, the gods decided that the skilled fighter Monkey should accompany him on this difficult task. The pair were given two more companions: Zhu Wuneng, a heavenly army marshal who had

been banished to Earth in the form of a pig, and an exiled heavenly general called Sha Wujing.

Together, the foursome traveled through a magical landscape inhabited by dragons and demons. Their trip was perilous, but they were successful in bringing the scriptures to China. These were used to teach the people about the Buddhist faith. As a reward for his bravery, Monkey was finally granted immortality.

XUANZANG'S QUEST ▶
The monk Xuanzang was keen to travel to the west because he was unhappy with the incomplete texts on Buddhism that were in use in China at the time.

TEMPLE ART
A painting from the Great Buddha Temple in Gansu Province, China, shows the monk Xuanzang on his journey to India to bring back the Buddha's teachings. With him are Monkey (center left) and Zhu Wuneng (center), the piglike heavenly army marshal.

Izanagi and Izanami

The story of Japan's creation is found in *Kojiki* (*Record of Ancient Matters*), the oldest surviving book of Japanese myths and traditions, first published in 712 CE. It describes how Japan is created not by one god, but by the couple Izanagi and Izanami. The pair also bring into being the *kami* ("spirits of nature") that play a major role in Japanese mythology.

In the beginning there were only three deities. Not much is known about this mysterious trio, except that they contained all the energy needed for creation. These deities gave birth to several generations of gods before the god Izanagi and goddess Izanami were born. This pair represented the masculine and feminine forces that were needed to bring the world into being. Izanagi and Izanami stood on a bridge, which spanned dark Chaos below. Izanagi took a spear (see p.117) and churned the Chaos until some of the elements came together and formed an island surrounded by water. The creator deities then decided to marry and make this island their home.

THE WRONG CEREMONY

The pair began the marriage ceremony, which required both to say their marriage vows, with

◄ **THE CHURNING OF THE WATERS**
Izanagi used a giant spear called Amenonuhoko *("heavenly jeweled spear") to churn the watery Chaos below him and form the first island of Japan.*

Two sacred rocks in southern Japan called Meoto Iwa symbolize the marriage of Izanami and Izanagi.

the man speaking first. However, Izanami was the first to speak, and though the couple completed the ceremony, the other gods refused to accept their marriage, as the correct custom had not been followed. The first child born to the couple, Hiruko, was born without limbs and bones—a sign that all was not well. Izanagi and Izanami then repeated the ceremony, speaking in the accepted order, and this time their marriage was approved by all.

Izanami now gave birth to all the features of Earth: trees, mountains, lowlands, seas, rivers, and even winds. Each of these had its own spirit, called a *kami*, and thousands of these spirits spread out all over the world. The creator goddess also gave birth to all the remaining islands of Japan.

Finally, Izanami gave birth to the fire god Kagutsuchi. Unfortunately, the goddess perished in the child's

flames and descended to Yomi, the Underworld. Angry at the fire god, Izanagi killed Kagutsuchi with his powerful sword.

JOURNEY TO YOMI

Izanagi was distraught at the loss of his wife, and decided to travel to Yomi to bring her back. When he reached the Underworld, however, he was disturbed by the sight of Izanami's body, which had already started to decay and was covered in maggots. Izanagi realized that Izanami could not be brought back to Earth and so prepared to leave Yomi. The creator god's trespass into the Underworld had been noticed by Emma-O, the ruler of the dead, and his demons. As Izanagi was still alive, he was not allowed in the land of the dead, so Emma-O's demons chased Izanagi to attack him. To save himself, the god threw rocks at the demons, which magically changed into food as they

▲ **EMMA-O**
The fearsome ruler of the Underworld judged the fate of the dead, sending the good souls back to Earth to be reborn and keeping the sinful ones.

▲ **WEATHER SPIRITS**
Born from Izanami, Raijin (left) and Fujin (right) are two of the oldest kami. *Raijin is the* kami *of thunder and lightning, while Fujin is the* kami *of the wind.*

fell. These morsels distracted Izanagi's pursuers, allowing him to hurry to the doorway of the Underworld. What Izanagi did not know was that Izanami had followed him the whole way, hoping to return to Earth. Izanagi failed to see her, and blocked the doorway with a large stone as soon as he had passed through, trapping Izanami in Yomi forever.

FORMS OF *KAMI*

The Japanese believe that *kami* can take different forms and live within the creatures or geographical features they are said to control. Some occupy mountains or rivers, while others take the form of animals or birds, like the *karasu-tengu*, or crow spirit (left).

141

▲ SUSANO-O
Banished from heaven for his ill-treatment of Amaterasu, the storm god Susano-O spent the rest of his life on Earth.

Amaterasu and the mirror

The Shinto religion of Japan has many thousands of deities, and one of the best known is Amaterasu, the goddess of the sun. Her name comes from the Japanese words that mean "shining in heaven." A popular story describes what happens when she clashes with her violent brother, Susano-O, the god of storms, and how this conflict puts Japan at risk.

Amaterasu was the child of the creator deities Izanagi and Izanami (see pp.140–141). She was born after Izanagi returned from his visit to the Underworld, leaving his wife Izanami there. Izanagi's visit to this dangerous region had made him unclean, so he bathed to purify himself. When Izanagi washed out his left eye, his daughter Amaterasu appeared; his son Tsukuyomi was born when Izanagi rinsed his right eye; and Susano-O came into existence when Izanagi cleansed his nose.

Amaterasu, the sun goddess, was so dazzling that she would scorch Earth if she stayed, so Izanagi asked her to ascend into the sky. From this distance, her light could warm the world more gently, and make life thrive. The goddess had a special interest in farming, and once Earth was warm enough, she taught the people of Japan how to grow rice.

THE GODDESS IN HIDING

Amaterasu's brother Susano-O, longing to find his mother Izanami, became resentful when he was not allowed to visit the Underworld. He showed his frustration by unleashing violent storms, which damaged Amaterasu's rice crops. This angered the sun goddess and she sulkily hid inside a cave, blocking the entrance with a giant rock. Without her powerful light, the world fell into a deep darkness in which no crops grew and only evil spirits thrived. This worried the gods, and they decided to lure the goddess out of the cave.

PLAYING A TRICK

The gods gathered together outside Amaterasu's hiding place, and Omohi-kane, the god of wisdom, devised a cunning plan to trick the goddess into coming out. He had the other gods hang a mirror and jewels on

◀ SHINTO MIRROR
Many Shinto temples have a sacred mirror to honor the moment when Amaterasu saw her reflection for the first time and was awestruck.

a tree outside the cave. Omohi-kane then asked the dawn goddess Ama-no-uzume to put on a dance show to amuse everyone. Omohi-kane hoped to arouse Amaterasu's interest by the bursts of laughter from the gods. When the sun goddess asked about the uproar, she was told that there was a goddess more beautiful than her outside. Unable to resist, Amaterasu peered out of the cave, caught her reflection in the mirror, and was dazzled by it. The gods took advantage of this and pulled her out of the cave, and light was restored to the world once again.

> Amaterasu is considered to be the original ancestor of the imperial family of Japan.

LEAVING THE CAVE ▶
After pulling Amaterasu out, the other gods sealed the entrance to the cave behind her to ensure that the goddess could never hide there again.

The fox-wife

In Japanese myths, animals often have supernatural powers. The fox is thought to possess great intelligence and the ability to shape-shift. A popular story tells how a rice farmer accidentally marries a fox, and how the creature cleverly shows him the best way to grow rice.

ASIA

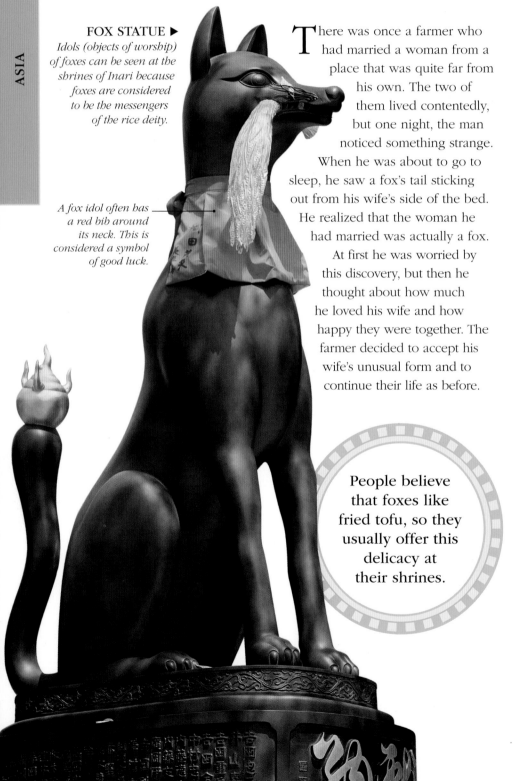

FOX STATUE ▶
Idols (objects of worship) of foxes can be seen at the shrines of Inari because foxes are considered to be the messengers of the rice deity.

A fox idol often has a red bib around its neck. This is considered a symbol of good luck.

There was once a farmer who had married a woman from a place that was quite far from his own. The two of them lived contentedly, but one night, the man noticed something strange. When he was about to go to sleep, he saw a fox's tail sticking out from his wife's side of the bed. He realized that the woman he had married was actually a fox. At first he was worried by this discovery, but then he thought about how much he loved his wife and how happy they were together. The farmer decided to accept his wife's unusual form and to continue their life as before.

People believe that foxes like fried tofu, so they usually offer this delicacy at their shrines.

GROWING RICE

The woman repaid her husband's devotion by showing him how to cultivate rice so that it grew upside-down, into the soil rather than above ground. This way, the rice was largely invisible to the tax collector who visited their farm— and because he did not know how much rice the farmer was growing, he could not collect any tax. The fox-wife's cleverness had helped her husband prosper.

THE RICE DEITY INARI

The female form of Inari

The Shinto deity Inari (who is depicted both as male and as female) is the god of rice, Japan's most important food crop. Some people believe that every year Inari comes down to the rice fields, bringing water from the fresh mountain streams, to help the crop grow. Foxes are said to be Inari's helpers.

The good deeds of Okuninushi

Many Japanese myths illustrate the way humans and *kami* (spirits) interact with each other. The tale of gentle Okuninushi is a famous example, showing how kindness can bring unforeseen rewards.

OKUNINUSHI SHRINE

Many people worship Okuninushi as a Shinto god. They believe that he has the ability to bring happiness to a marriage. A shrine in the Izumo province of Japan is dedicated to him. It is said that each October, all the gods leave their homes and gather at his shrine.

Okuninushi was a kind man who lived in the Izumo province of Japan with his 80 brothers. The brothers were all rivals for the hand of a princess, Yaga-mi-hime, who lived in the far-off coastal province of Inaba. They decided to travel to Inaba, so that the princess could choose one of them as a husband. On the journey, the brothers treated Okuninushi poorly by making him carry all the luggage. Although this was unfair, Okuninushi accepted the task because he did not want to make trouble.

UNEXPECTED ENCOUNTER

When the brothers arrived at the seashore, they met a rabbit that had lost its fur and was shivering and shaking with cold and pain. Okuninushi's brothers laughed at the poor rabbit's misfortune, and told it to bathe in salt water to heal its furless skin and then stand in the wind to dry itself.

Okuninushi knew that this was a cruel trick, because the salt water would sting the rabbit's soft skin, and the wind would make its skin crack, causing it unbearable pain. Okuninushi told the creature to bathe instead in the fresh water of the river, and then to dry itself by rolling in the soft, furry spikes of the cattail plant.

Pleased with this act of kindness, the creature revealed that it was actually a *kami* (see p.141), and declared that Yaga-mi-hime would be Okuninushi's bride. The other brothers were so bitterly jealous of Okuninushi that they killed him, but the gods revived the gentle hero, allowing him to marry the princess and triumph over his wicked brothers.

◄ MEETING THE RABBIT
The rabbit had been attacked by beasts in the water while crossing the sea. When Okuninushi heard of the rabbit's plight, he decided to help out.

Kintaro

The legendary hero Kintaro (meaning "golden boy") is a wonder-child, whose strength and heroic deeds are described as greater than those of most Japanese warriors. Although he is the subject of ancient legends and modern comic books, Kintaro may have been based on a real samurai warrior named Sakata Kintoki, who lived in medieval Japan.

ASIA

There was once a heroic warrior called Kintoki, who held an important position at the Japanese emperor's court. Kintoki fell in love with a young woman and the two of them got married, but Kintoki's happiness was short-lived because some people spread rumors about him. These angered the emperor, who exiled Kintoki and his wife to a forest. The couple built a home there, and Kintoki's wife was soon expecting their first child. However, tragedy struck when Kintoki died before the baby was born.

LIFE IN THE FOREST
Kintoki's wife gave birth to a boy and named him Kintaro. Even as a baby, Kintaro possessed amazing strength, and by the time he was eight years old, he could cut down trees as quickly and easily as experienced wood-cutters. Because Kintaro spent a lot of time in the forest, he got to know many wild creatures, and became friends with the bear, monkey, and

◄ **FIERCE FIGHTER**
To protect Japan, Kintaro wrestled and overcame a vicious dragon by tearing its monstrous jaws apart.

hare. He refereed wrestling contests between his animal friends, and gave rice cakes to both the winners and losers, keeping them contented.

◄ **FRIENDLY MATCH**
Kintaro's animal friends, the hare and the monkey, competed in a wrestling match, and the wonder-child acted as a judge.

MIGHTY KINTARO
Kintaro used his great strength to protect his friends from woodland monsters, such as the giant earth-spider, a creature that trapped victims in its web and slowly poisoned them. All the forest animals believed that the bear was the strongest among them, but on one occasion Kintaro built a bridge over a river by pulling down a tall tree with his bare hands. Even the bear could not match this feat, and it became clear that Kintaro was the strongest of the forest dwellers.

When a passing stranger saw Kintaro tear down the tree, he was impressed, but thought he might be able to beat the young boy in an arm-wrestling contest. The stranger proposed a challenge, which Kintaro accepted and then won easily. The mystery opponent identified himself

as Sadamitsu, a great samurai warrior, who was also a follower of a lord called Raiko. When Sadamitsu introduced Kintaro to Raiko, the lord invited the boy to become one of his samurai followers. Kintaro accepted the offer, and soon joined the Four Braves, a small group of the best and bravest samurai that protected Japan from its enemies. Kintaro was now a hero not just of the forest, but of all Japan.

▼ **KINTARO AND URABE SUETAKE**
Urabe Suetake was a member of the Four Braves, a group of samurai who were known for their strength and skill in combat.

Creatures in myth

Myths and legends are full of fascinating beasts that often combine the features of more than one real animal. These sometimes terrifying creatures may prey on unwary people or carry off sinners to the Underworld. However, a few beasts are kind, protecting those they favor or aiding the gods in their work.

Garuda is often portrayed with eagle-like wings.

▶ HARPY
Monsters called harpies have women's heads and birds' wings in Greek and Roman myths. They steal food, abduct people, and lead wrongdoers such as murderers to their punishment in Tartarus, deep in the Underworld.

MANTICORE ▶
This beast from Persian mythology has a human head attached to the body of a lion. A manticore has a triple row of sharp teeth with which to devour its victims.

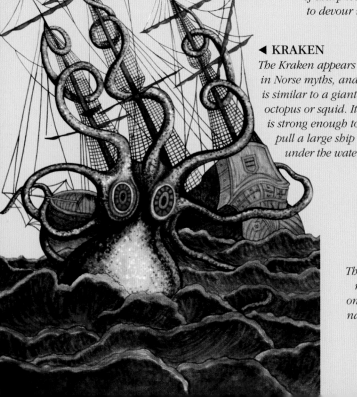

◀ KRAKEN
The Kraken appears in Norse myths, and is similar to a giant octopus or squid. It is strong enough to pull a large ship under the water.

◀ THREE-LEGGED CROW
In Chinese mythology, a three-legged golden crow represents the sun. People say it sometimes flies down to Earth to find food. There are similar crows in Korean and Japanese myths.

Scylla has a tail like that of a snake.

SCYLLA ▶
The terrifying Scylla of Greek myth is a monster who was once a nymph. She lives by a narrow stretch of water, and snatches sailors from ships to eat them.

◄ GARUDA
Birdlike Garuda is a protective creature sometimes described as king of the birds in Hindu mythology. It symbolizes power, military strength, and speed.

▲ SIRRUSH
This creature from Mesopotamia represents Marduk, the god of Babylon. It has a serpent's head and a dragon's body, which is covered in scales.

The Japanese thunder god Kashima usually stops Namazu from moving.

NAMAZU ►
This beast is a giant catfish that lives deep under the land of Japan. When it moves, the country suffers earthquakes.

◄ AIRAVATA
Hindu mythology describes how Airavata, a white elephant with many heads, carries Indra, the leader of the Devas (gods). Airavata can create rain clouds by sucking up water from the Underworld.

◄ CHIMAERA
This fire-breathing Greek monster has three heads: a lion's head in the front, a goat's head in the middle, and a snake's head at the end of its tail.

SEE ALSO
- Bellerophon and Pegasus, p.40
- Jason and the Argonauts, pp.42–43
- Odysseus journeys home, pp.54–57
- Marduk creates Babylon, p.108
- Yi, the heavenly archer, pp.134–135
- The churning of the ocean, pp.152–153

Saraswati is the Hindu goddess of knowledge and the arts. She is the source of all learning and grants wisdom to humans.

Brahma, the creator

Brahma, the creator deity, is part of a triad of supreme gods in the Hindu mythology of South Asia that also includes Shiva and Vishnu. Brahma came into being on a lotus flower that emerged from Vishnu, before starting on the enormous task of creating the universe and all forms of life in it.

Before the world came into being, the supreme deity Vishnu slept on a serpent named Shesha Naga that floated on the primal ocean. Alongside Vishnu was his wife, the goddess Lakshmi (see p.207). After he awoke, Vishnu focused his energy into making a lotus flower that sprouted from his navel. When the lotus bloomed, it revealed the creator god Brahma inside it. Brahma opened his eyes and saw the emptiness around him. He then set about the task of creating the world.

MAKING THE WORLD

Brahma imagined the universe, and it began to take shape. Using his mind, he created four sons called the Kumaras, and then thought up more sons called Prajapatis. These divine beings were ten in number, including two named Marichi and Daksha. Marichi had a son named Kashyapa, who married several of Daksha's daughters, including Aditi, Diti, and Kadru. Aditi gave birth to the Devas (gods), including Surya (the sun god) and Indra (the rain god); Diti to the Asuras (demons); and Kadru, to the Nagas (serpents), including Vasuki (see pp.152–153). The sun, the stars, and the planets also came into being.

THE FIRST WOMAN

Meanwhile, Brahma had made Shatarupa, the first woman, from his own body. He was so captivated by her beauty that he grew another three heads so that he could admire her in whichever direction she went. Shatarupa kept changing her form in order to get away from Brahma, but he continued to pursue her. When she flew upward to escape him, Brahma grew a fifth head so he could look toward the sky. Furious at Brahma's behavior, the god Shiva appeared in his Bhairava form to cut off his fifth head (see p.154). Brahma eventually realized his mistake, and with Shatarupa's help, he created all the other creatures in the world. Brahma then created the first man, Manu, from his body. He was the ancestor of all humans that would live on Earth. Shatarupa later took the form of the goddess Saraswati, who became Brahma's wife.

It took Brahma millions of years to complete his work. Hindus believe that Shiva will one day end the world, and that it will be made again by Brahma. This cycle of destruction and creation will continue endlessly.

▲ THE CREATOR'S WORK
Vishnu and Lakshmi observed Brahma as he sat on the lotus flower and started his task of creation.

YAGYA

The sacred Hindu texts called the *Vedas* describe the important ceremony of *yagya*, in which worshippers offer tributes to the gods in a holy fire. This is believed to be one way to please them and get blessings. Another way is prayer. The god Brahma was known to grant gifts and abilities to anyone—mortal humans, the Devas, and even the Asuras.

Yagya involves agni, or fire

BRAHMA ▶
The creator is usually shown with four heads. He also has eight hands, four of which hold the Vedas, *which are ancient Hindu texts.*

The churning of the ocean

In Hindu mythology, the Devas (gods) and Asuras (demons) are half-brothers who are constantly at war. Sacred texts called the *Puranas* reveal the events that unfold when the two enemies forge a temporary alliance in their quest for the *amrita* ("nectar of immortality").

> Both Asuras and Devas are called Asuras in early versions of the ancient texts called the *Vedas*.

The sage Kashyapa was the father of two important groups of deities with the sisters Aditi and Diti, daughters of Daksha (see p.150). Aditi gave birth to the Devas (gods), while Diti was the mother of the Asuras (demons). The Devas lived in Swargaloka (Heaven), and were led by the mighty rain god Indra. Many of them controlled natural elements: Agni controlled fire; Surya, the sun; and Varuna, water. Their enemies were the Asuras, evil creatures that inhabited Patalaloka, the Underworld, and were led by the demon king Bali. The two sides were forever in conflict.

AN UNLIKELY ALLIANCE

When a sage named Durvasa offered a garland of flowers to Indra, Airavata (see p.149), the rain god's elephant, threw it to the ground. Furious Durvasa cursed Indra for showing him disrespect, and the Devas grew weaker. Seizing this opportunity, Bali led the Asuras into battle. They defeated the Devas and took control of Swargaloka. The Devas went to Vishnu (see pp.162–163) for help in defeating the Asuras, and following his advice, they approached the Asuras and offered to share the *amrita* ("nectar of immortality") equally

◀ BALI
A worshipper of Vishnu, the mighty Bali led the Asura army in their conquest of Heaven and Earth.

The Devas hold the serpent called Vasuki by its tail.

... the **nectar of immortality** was hidden **under a cosmic ocean** ...

with them. This liquid was hidden under the waters of a cosmic ocean and it needed the combined efforts of the two sides to raise it from the depths. The Asuras were tempted by the possibility of becoming immortal and so agreed to join forces with the Devas. What they did not know was that Vishnu had secretly promised the Devas that the *amrita* would be theirs alone.

THE OCEAN IS CHURNED

The Devas and Asuras placed a mountain called Mandara in the middle of the cosmic ocean. It started to sink, so to hold it in place, Vishnu appeared as a turtle named Kurma (see p.162),

◀ **THE MOUNTAIN**
Mount Mandara was heavy and would have sunk in the ocean when the churning started had it not been for Kurma the turtle holding it up.

and sat below it. Then the two sides wound a serpent called Vasuki around the mountain to act as a rope. Each held one end and took turns to pull. The mountain began to rotate, churning the ocean's waters. This went on for thousands of years.

The work of the Devas and Asuras was threatened when the serpent Vasuki spat out *halahala,* a deadly poison that could destroy all of creation. The Devas and Asuras called on the god Shiva (see pp.154–155) for help. He saved the day by drinking the *halahala,* but before he could swallow it, his wife Parvati (see p.156) stopped the poison in his throat. The poison turned Shiva's throat blue, and so he came to be called Neelkantha ("the blue-throated one").

Over time, many treasures emerged from the ocean and were quickly claimed. Some of these included a holy cow called Kamadhenu and the divine flowering tree Parijat, which

◀ **KAMADHENU**
The cow called Kamadhenu had the power to grant wishes. She is called the mother of all cows.

were taken by the Devas, while others, such as a seven-headed horse called Uchchaihshravas and a powerful bow called Sharanga, were grabbed by the Asuras.

When a pot of the *amrita* finally emerged, the two sides fought each other bitterly for it. The Asuras caught hold of the pot first, so the desperate gods sought Vishnu's help once more. He appeared as a female named Mohini (see p.28), who used her charms to distract the Asuras long enough to take back the pot of *amrita* and distribute the nectar among the Devas. Their strength restored, the Devas defeated the Asuras and took back control of Swargaloka and the world.

The Asuras hold the serpent by its upper body.

Vasuki releases a deadly poison called halahala.

Shiva, the destroyer

To maintain order in the universe, the supreme god Shiva plays the part of the "destroyer"—he crushes evil when it threatens the world. One of the triad of supreme deities, Shiva is known for his great wisdom and incredible strength. He has taken on many avatars (forms), while his divine energy has given rise to many beings.

The strands of Shiva's hair fly loose in this energetic dance.

Rudra

- **Also known as:** No known alternative
- **Shown with:** Trident

Many Hindus consider the ancient weather god Rudra to be an early version of Shiva. The word *rudra* means "roarer"—Rudra was a destructive deity, linked with howling winds and raging storms. Worshippers of Shiva use prayer beads made from the berries of a tree called Rudraksha ("eye of Rudra").

The hourglass-shaped drum produces the sounds made at the beginning of the universe.

Bhairava

- **Also known as:** Mahakaala Bhairava
- **Shown with:** Garland of skulls around his waist, human skulls in his hand

When Brahma chased after the first woman, Shiva became angry and took the form of fierce Bhairava, the god of terror and fear. Bhairava cut off Brahma's fifth head as punishment (see p.150). He then wandered the world using Brahma's skull as a begging bowl.

Nataraja

- **Also known as:** Narteshvara
- **Shown with:** Serpent, crescent moon, drum, fire

As Nataraja ("Lord of dance"), Shiva defeated Apasmara, the Asura (demon) of ignorance. He crushed the demon under his right foot as he performed the Ananda Tandava ("the cosmic dance of joy") within a circle of fire. This represented the victory of knowledge over ignorance, and its depiction is one of the most famous in Hindu mythology.

The demon lies subdued.

Tripurantaka

- **Also known as:** Tripurari
- **Shown with:** Bow and arrow

Three Asuras each received from Brahma the gift of a city that moved around in the sky and that could only be destroyed by a single arrow hitting all three cities. Now fearless, the demons attacked the Devas (gods) and humans. In his Tripurantaka form, Shiva destroyed the cities with a single shot from his bow.

The flame in Shiva's hand represents agni *(fire), which is considered holy.*

Ardhanarishwara

- **Also known as:** Ardhanarisha
- **Shown with:** Trident, mirror

One story tells that Brahma was inspired to create the first female after a vision of Shiva as Ardhanarishwara. This avatar is half man, half woman, and it resulted from the union of Shiva and the goddess Parvati, an avatar of the goddess Mahadevi (see p.156). It represents the coming together of the male and female energies.

Gajasurasamhara

- **Also known as:** Gajantaka
- **Shown with:** Trident, deer, weapons

The Asura Gajasura took the form of an elephant. He tormented the worshippers of Shiva, and scared even the gods. Shiva defeated the demon as the avatar Gajasurasamhara, and put an end to his reign of terror. Shiva then killed the powerful demon before wearing his thick skin.

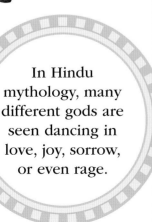

In Hindu mythology, many different gods are seen dancing in love, joy, sorrow, or even rage.

Andhakasura

- **Also known as:** Andhaka
- **Shown with:** Fangs, sickle

One day Shiva's wife Parvati playfully covered his eyes. As the world turned dark, a drop of sweat from Shiva's forehead fell to Earth, creating a blind Asura called Andhakasura. He was blessed with Shiva's divine energy and went on to conquer the world, but was killed by Shiva for his misdeeds.

The great goddess

Hindus believe in a supreme female deity called Mahadevi ("great goddess"). She has many avatars (forms): as Parvati, she is a gentle goddess, but when angered, she can turn into destructive Kali. She can also become mighty Durga, a warrior who destroys evil.

▲ CALMING KALI
To stop Kali's rampage, Shiva lay down in her path. When Kali stepped on him, she came back to her senses and then stuck out her tongue in shame.

Also known as Shakti, the vital cosmic force, Mahadevi is the central goddess in Hindu mythology. The protector of the world and the destroyer of evil, she watches over the universe with Shiva (see pp.154–155).

GENTLE PARVATI

Mahadevi was born as Parvati, the gentle daughter of Himavana, the god of mountains. Parvati worshipped the god Shiva for a long time before they met. Eventually the pair were married, and Parvati had a calming influence on Shiva, who was known for his temper.

Once, she playfully covered Shiva's eyes, which turned the world dark (see p.155). Shiva then grew a third eye in the middle of his forehead, which restored light to the world.

The couple had two sons, Kartikeya and Ganesha (see p.206). Ganesha was close to his mother. One day, he stood guard outside her room as she bathed. When Shiva wanted to meet her, Ganesha blocked his path. Furious Shiva cut off Ganesha's head, but regretted his actions when he saw Parvati's distress. The goddess asked Shiva to go and bring her the head of the first animal he met. Shiva brought her the head of an elephant and put it on Ganesha's body, bringing him back to life as the elephant-headed god.

KALI THE DESTROYER

The angry form of Mahadevi was Kali. A destructive force, Kali once killed an entire army of Asuras (demons). Yet she continued to be so filled with rage that she began killing every being in her path. Shiva helped the Devas (gods) calm Kali.

DURGA THE WARRIOR

The Devas were once defeated in battle by a shape-shifting Asura called Mahishasura. He had been blessed by Brahma (see pp.150–151) so that he could not be hurt by Devas, Asuras, or mortal men. He did not ask for protection from women because he did not think a female could hurt him.

The demon terrorized Heaven and Earth, so Vishnu, Brahma, and Shiva combined their energies and prayed to Mahadevi, who appeared as the warrior goddess Durga. The gods gave her all their weapons. As Durga battled Mahishasura, he changed into a lion, then an elephant, and finally a buffalo. After a long fight, she finally pinned him down and killed him using Shiva's trident. The demon had, indeed, been killed by a woman.

▲ PARVATI AND GANESHA
Ganesha was devoted to Parvati. When she was bathing, he stopped anyone from approaching her, even her husband Shiva.

FIGHTING MAHISHASURA ▶
The demon became a buffalo to evade Durga, but she cut off the buffalo's head, forcing the Asura back into his original form.

Rama's journey

The *Ramayana* is a Hindu epic poem that tells the story of the good Prince Rama, who has to journey to the kingdom of Lanka to rescue his wife Sita from King Ravana, an Asura (demon). This popular tale highlights the importance of values such as loyalty and duty, and continues to be retold in the Indian subcontinent and beyond in the form of books, plays, and dance performances.

The ten-headed Asura king Ravana was the fearsome ruler of the island kingdom of Lanka. He prayed to Brahma (see pp.150–151) for 10,000 years, and when the creator deity appeared, Ravana asked to be blessed so that neither Devas (gods) nor Asuras (see pp.152–153) could hurt him. In his arrogance, he did not ask protection from attacks by people, because he did not think a human could hurt him. With Brahma's blessing, Ravana was now more powerful than ever before, and

wreaked havoc in the world and in Heaven, defeating even the Devas. To kill him, Vishnu (see pp.162–163) decided to appear on Earth as the human prince, Rama—his seventh avatar (form).

RAMA AND HIS BROTHERS

King Dasharatha of the kingdom of Ayodhya had three wives—Kaushalya, Sumitra, and Kaikeyi (see p.127)—but no son. In order to have a son, he performed a holy ceremony called a *yagya* (see p.150). Soon his queens were blessed with sons: Kaushalya gave birth to Rama, Sumitra to

Lakshmana and Shatrughana, and Kaikeyi to Bharata. The four princes grew up studying ancient texts and learning to use weapons, and Rama became a skillful archer.

When he was older, Rama went to the kingdom of Mithila. King Janaka of Mithila had organized a contest for the hand of his daughter, Sita, who was a human avatar of the goddess Lakshmi

▼ WINNING SITA'S HAND
Using his immense strength, Rama not only lifted and strung Shiva's bow with ease, but also broke it in the process. Janaka was impressed and decided that Rama had won Sita's hand.

Rama considered it his duty to follow his father's wishes, and went into exile.

(see p.207), Vishnu's wife. Janaka had a holy bow that had belonged to the god Shiva (see pp.154–155), and he declared that the person who could lift and string the bow would marry his daughter. Many princes tried and failed, but Rama was able to string the bow easily. Rama and Sita were married, and they returned to Ayodhya.

When Dasharatha decided to announce Rama as the heir to his throne, his wife Kaikeyi reminded him of a vow he had once taken to grant her two wishes. Kaikeyi asked for her son, Bharata, to become the next king, and for Rama to be exiled. Dasharatha was unhappy about this but unwilling to break his vow, so he did as asked and banished Rama for 14 years. Rama considered it his duty to follow his father's wishes and went into exile, to a forest called Panchavati. He was accompanied by his wife Sita and his half-brother Lakshmana, who were both loyal to him. When Bharata learned of the injustice done to Rama, he refused to be crowned king and instead looked after Rama's kingdom until his return.

> Hindus believe that the modern city of Ayodhya in north India is the site of Rama's kingdom.

SITA IS ABDUCTED

Over the years, Rama, Lakshmana, and Sita grew used to living a simple life in the forest. They lived in a small cottage near a settlement of hermits, and the brothers would often protect the hermits from attacks by demons. One day, an Asura called Shurpanakha,

who was Ravana's sister, saw the two brothers and was attracted to them. However, they rejected her advances, and so she attacked Sita in anger. While protecting Sita, Lakshmana cut off Shurpanakha's nose, and the demoness fled to her brother in pain and rage. She encouraged him to take revenge on the princes for her humiliation and told him of Sita's beauty. Ravana decided to kidnap Sita.

One of Ravana's demons changed into a golden deer and walked past Rama's cottage. When Sita saw the deer, she asked Rama to bring it to her. Rama told Lakshmana to stand guard and went off in search of the deer, which lured him deep into the forest. After Rama had been absent for a long time, Sita grew worried and asked Lakshmana to find him. Before leaving her alone, Lakshmana drew a protective charmed circle around the cottage and forbade Sita from crossing it. After he had gone, Ravana transformed himself into a beggar and approached Sita. He pretended to be weak and hungry, and persuaded Sita to step over the line to give him food. As soon as she did this, Ravana turned back into his ten-headed form and

▲ TRICKING SITA
Ravana could not cross the charmed protective circle set by Lakshmana, so he had to trick Sita into stepping over it.

carried her off to Lanka on his flying chariot. In Lanka, Ravana imprisoned Sita in a garden and began trying to win her affections.

THE SEARCH FOR SITA

Rama and Lakshmana began a frantic search for Sita. Their quest led them to Kishkindha, the kingdom of the Vanaras, a tribe of powerful monkeys. This kingdom was in turmoil as two brothers, Sugreeva and

◀ TEN HEADS
While praying to Brahma, Ravana cut off his head as a sacrifice to the creator. Pleased at this, Brahma blessed him, and a new head appeared along with the old one. Ravana repeated this until he had ten magical heads.

Vali (see p.223), fought over its throne. Rama came to Sugreeva's aid by killing Vali, and in return, Sugreeva promised to help in the search for Sita. At Kishkindha, Rama also met Hanumana, the great warrior of the Vanaras, who had the abilities of flight and shape-shifting. Hanumana became devoted to Rama, and set out to find Sita. In his search, he flew over the southern sea and reached the island of Lanka. He then transformed into a small monkey and continued looking for Sita. When he found her in the garden,

miserable and lonely, he told her that Rama was coming to rescue her. Hanumana then allowed himself to be captured by Ravana's soldiers, who set his tail on fire. The monkey was able to escape and return to Rama, but not before setting the city on fire.

THE FINAL BATTLE

Now that he finally knew where Sita was, Rama assembled an army of Vanaras and began marching toward Lanka to meet Ravana in battle. To reach the island, the Vanaras built a

▲ LANKA ON FIRE
When Hanumana's tail was lit, he swept through the city, spreading a fiery trail of destruction through Lanka.

bridge of stone over the sea. On Rama's side were warriors such as Lakshmana, Hanumana, and Sugreeva. Vibheeshana, one of Ravana's brothers, joined forces with Rama because he believed that Ravana was in the wrong.

In the forefront of Ravana's Asura army were fierce commanders such as his son, Meghnath, and his brother, Kumbhakarna, a giant who slept for half the year and stayed awake for the other half. The two sides fought a series of battles over a number of days. During one battle, Meghnath killed Lakshmana, significantly weakening Rama's army. Hanumana flew to Mount Dronagiri in the Himalayas to find a magical herb called *sanjeevani booti* that could

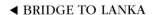
◄ BRIDGE TO LANKA
The Vanaras wrote Rama's holy name on each stone in the bridge. This kept the stones from sinking into the sea.

revive Lakshmana. Once he had taken this herb, Lakshmana came back to life and was able to kill Meghnath in their next encounter. Kumbhakarna woke up and began crushing Rama's forces in his path, but the prince eventually killed him. Rama now faced the ten-headed Ravana on the battlefield, and each of them called on all of their strength for this final battle. Unfortunately for Rama, each time he cut off one of Ravana's heads, another grew magically in its place. The two warriors fought for a long time, but finally Rama fired a divine weapon called the *Brahmastra* at the Asura king, killing him.

The Hindu festival of Dussehra celebrates Rama's victory over Ravana's forces.

THE RETURN OF RAMA

Following his triumph over the evil forces of Ravana, Rama was reunited with Sita and together they returned to Ayodhya along with Lakshmana and Hanumana. The city was lit up with lamps to mark Rama's return to Ayodhya as its king. Under his wise and fair rule, the kingdom prospered. Sita had been separated from Rama for such a long time that some people in Ayodhya began to question her loyalty to the king. Bowing to popular opinion, Rama reluctantly sent Sita away to live in the forest. There she gave birth to twin boys, Lav and Kush (see p.223). Many years later, the boys met their father there and he asked them to come back to his kingdom with their mother. Sita refused to return, and asked the Earth goddess to take her. At this, the ground opened up and swallowed Sita. Saddened at his loss, Rama returned to Ayodhya with his children. After his death, Rama and Sita were reunited as the deities Vishnu and Lakshmi.

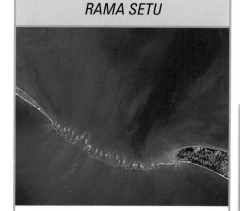

RAMA SETU

Known to Hindus as *Rama setu* ("Rama's bridge"), this natural ridge of limestone sits between India (left) and Sri Lanka (right), extending for 30 miles (48 km) under the sea. Many believe this to be the ruins of the mythical bridge built to transport Rama's army to Lanka.

ASIA

▼ THE GREAT WAR
The Asura army had the benefit of chariots and elephants, while Rama's forces fought mainly on foot during their long war with Ravana.

Avatars of Vishnu

Tales from the sacred Hindu texts called the *Puranas* describe how Vishnu, one of the three supreme deities, preserves the world by defeating the forces of evil and restoring order. In times of trouble, he appears on Earth in different avatars (forms). Of these avatars, Hindus consider ten to be the most important; they believe the tenth avatar will come in the future.

Matsya is sometimes shown as half man, half fish.

Kurma

- **Also known as:** Vishnu's second avatar
- **Shown with:** Discus and conch shell

When the Devas (gods) and Asuras (demons) set aside their differences to churn the cosmic ocean together in their quest for *amrita* ("nectar of immortality"), Vishnu appeared as the turtle Kurma to help them (see p.153). He sat at the bottom of this ocean, balancing a mountain on his back, while the two sides rotated the mountain. This churning motion revealed many treasures.

Matsya

- **Also known as:** Vishnu's first avatar
- **Shown with:** Discus, conch shell, mace, lotus flower

In his first avatar, Vishnu appeared on Earth in the form of a fish, and was known as Matsya. He warned Manu (see p.150), the first human, of a coming flood. Under his guidance, Manu saved one of each kind of plant and animal. Matsya took them to safety when the world was flooded.

Kurma is sometimes shown as half man, half turtle.

Varaha

- **Also known as:** Vishnu's third avatar
- **Shown with:** Discus, conch shell, mace, lotus flower

When the Asura Hiranyaksha stole Earth and hid it under a cosmic ocean, Vishnu appeared as the fearsome Varaha, who had the head of a boar and the body of a man. Varaha swam to the bottom of the ocean and raised Earth out of the water on his tusks while he fought and killed the Asura.

Narasimha

- **Also known as:** Vishnu's fourth avatar
- **Shown with:** Long claws, various weapons

The Asura Hiranyakashipu became almost invincible after praying to Brahma (see pp.150–151) and began tormenting Vishnu's followers. To kill him, Vishnu turned into Narasimha, who was half man, half lion.

Vamana

- **Also known as:** Vishnu's fifth avatar
- **Shown with:** Wooden umbrella

When the Asura Bali defeated the Devas, Vishnu became the holy dwarf Vamana. Bali agreed to grant him the ground he could cover in three paces. Vamana grew into a giant and covered Earth and heaven in two strides. With the third he covered Bali's head, defeating him.

ASIA

Parashurama

- **Also known as:** Vishnu's sixth avatar
- **Shown with:** Ax

Vishnu took the form of the warrior sage Parashurama when a group of warriors began terrorizing people. As this avatar, Vishnu was able to kill the evil warriors.

Rama

- **Also known as:** Vishnu's seventh avatar
- **Shown with:** Bow and arrows

As the virtuous prince Rama, Vishnu defeated and killed the Asura king Ravana, as described in the epic the *Ramayana* (see pp.158–161). He broke Shiva's sacred bow in a competition to win the hand of his future wife, Sita.

Krishna

- **Also known as:** Vishnu's eighth avatar, Gopala
- **Shown with:** Flute, peacock feather

To kill an Asura called Kansa, Vishnu was born as Krishna. He grew up to be a cowherd and loved a woman called Radha, who was an avatar of the goddess Lakshmi (see p.207). Krishna also helped the Pandavas in their war against the Kauravas (see pp.164–167).

Buddha

- **Also known as:** Vishnu's ninth avatar
- **Shown with:** Top knot of hair

Many Hindus consider the Buddha to be an avatar of Vishnu. He is a wise man who protects the knowledge of the sacred Hindu texts called the *Vedas* and encourages all to be nonviolent.

Kalki

- **Also known as:** Vishnu's tenth avatar
- **Shown with:** Sword

Hindus believe that the Kalki avatar of Vishnu will appear at the end of the current age. Riding on a white horse, Kalki will wield a flaming sword as he destroys the forces of evil. He will then restart the cycle of life.

The Great War

The epic poem called the *Mahabharata* narrates the tale of cousins, the Kauravas and Pandavas, who struggle for power and eventually fight a great and terrible war for the kingdom of Hastinapura. The longest poem ever written, this story about *dharma* ("the correct way of living life") includes the teachings of the god Krishna, which are at the heart of Hinduism.

King Shantanu of the Bharata dynasty ruled over the kingdom of Hastinapura. He had a warrior son named Devavrata from his marriage to the goddess Ganga. When the king fell in love with Satyavati, a fisherwoman, she agreed to marry him if he promised to make her children the heirs to the throne of Hastinapura instead of Devavrata. Shantanu hesitated, but Devavrata vowed to never marry, have children, or want the throne. This sacrifice, or *bhishma pratigya* ("terrible oath") earned Devavrata the name Bhishma ("terrible").

THE THREE PRINCESSES

Satyavati and Shantanu had a son called Vichitravirya. When the boy grew up, Bhishma was asked to find wives for him. Bhishma kidnapped the three princesses of the kingdom of Kashi—Amba, Ambika, and Ambalika—for his half-brother. Amba wanted to marry another king so Bhishma let her go, but she was rejected by her suitor. Instead, she asked Bhishma to marry her, but he refused because of his oath. Amba was furious at all these rejections, so she killed herself, vowing to be born again to take her revenge on Bhishma. Ambika and Ambalika were married to Vichitravirya, but he died childless.

Amba was enraged on being taken by force.

▲ **THE ABDUCTION**
When Bhishma kidnapped the three princesses of Kashi, he dishonored them and their suitors. As a result, the king Amba wanted to marry rejected her.

Satyavati had a son named Vyasa from a previous marriage, who lived as a hermit. She called Vyasa to have children with the princesses. When Ambika saw this wild hermit, she shut her eyes out of fear. This meant that her son, whom she called Dhritarashtra, was born blind. Ambalika turned pale in fright on seeing Vyasa, and had a weak boy named Pandu. Dhritarashtra was heir to the throne of Hastinapura, but because he was blind, Pandu became king.

THE PANDAVAS

Pandu had two wives, Kunti and Madri, but was cursed to never have children. After his wives prayed to the Devas (gods) for offspring, Kunti had three sons—Yudhishthira, Bheema, and Arjuna—while Madri had two, Nakula and Sahadeva. The five sons of Pandu came to be called the Pandavas. Dhritarashtra had married Gandhari, who gave birth to 100 sons, known as the Kauravas, and one daughter, named Duhsala. The eldest Kaurava was Duryodhana. When King Pandu died, the Pandavas were left in the care of Dhritarashtra, who took the throne.

The two sets of cousins quarreled frequently. They all trained in warfare under the sage Drona. Bheema and Duryodhana became known for their strength, Arjuna for his skill in archery, and Yudhishthira for his honesty.

◄ **GANDHARI**
Gandhari was devoted to Dhritarashtra. She blindfolded herself for life so that she could experience the world as her husband did.

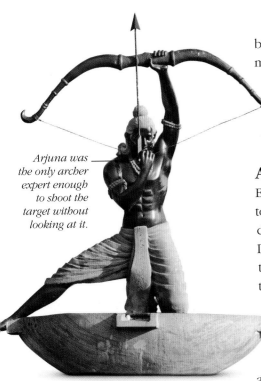

Arjuna was the only archer expert enough to shoot the target without looking at it.

▲ **WINNING DRAUPADI**
In the contest, Arjuna successfully shot at the eye of a mechanical fish moving on the ceiling by looking at its reflection in a pool of oil on the ground.

When the cousins grew up, Dhritarashtra made Yudhishthira the heir to the kingdom. However, Duryodhana believed the kingship to be his birthright, so he plotted with his brothers to kill the Pandavas. Dhritarashtra had given the Pandavas a separate palace to live in, but it was made of flammable materials. The Kauravas planned to burn the palace at night, but the Pandavas learned of the conspiracy against them and escaped with Kunti, just as their palace was set ablaze.

The Pandavas and Kunti wandered from place to place disguised as a poor family. One day, while in the neighboring kingdom of Panchala, the brothers heard of a contest that the king was holding for the hand of his daughter, Draupadi. Arjuna won the competition and

▶ **A DANGEROUS GAMBLE**
During the game of dice, the Kauravas taunted Yudhishthira, which made him reckless and gamble more with every turn.

brought Draupadi back to meet his mother. Without seeing the prize that he had won, Kunti told Arjuna to share it with his brothers. The princess of Panchala was therefore married to all five brothers.

A GAME OF DICE

Eventually the Pandavas returned to Hastinapura. King Dhritarashtra divided the kingdom between Duryodhana and Yudhishthira to keep the peace. The Pandavas established the city of Indraprastha, which prospered under Yudhishthira.

However, jealous Duryodhana challenged Yudhishthira to a game of dice in which he cheated and won, tricking Yudhishthira into losing everything—his jewels, his palace, his brothers, and even his wife. Duryodhana then tried to have Draupadi humiliated in public, but she was protected by the divine

SHADOW PUPPETRY

Episodes from the *Mahabharata* are retold across South Asia in many ways, including films and theater. In Indonesia, the story is told by traditional shadow puppetry, called *Wayang Kulit*. Two-dimensional carved figures are projected onto a backlit screen while the puppeteer narrates the story.

powers of Krishna, the eighth avatar (form) of the supreme deity Vishnu (see pp.162–163). As punishment for Duryodhana's actions, Bheema vowed to kill every Kaurava single-handedly.

ASIA

THE *BHAGAVAD GITA*

The *Bhagavad Gita* is a sacred Hindu text in the *Mahabharata* that contains Krishna's speech to Arjuna on *dharma* ("the correct way of living life") and sacred duty. His words filled Arjuna with renewed determination.

Krishna as Arjuna's charioteer

The Pandavas were then banished for 13 years, during which time they found shelter in forests. When they returned, Duryodhana refused to give up his kingdom. The stage was now set for a violent conflict between the Pandavas and Kauravas.

A TERRIBLE WAR

As the cousins prepared for war, the armies of various kingdoms lined up on either side. The Kauravas were led by Bhishma, and had the help of Drona the sage and a fearsome warrior named Karna. Arjuna and Duryodhana both sought the support of Krishna, who offered them each a choice: Krishna's army or Krishna himself. Duryodhana chose the army, while Arjuna asked for Krishna's personal support, and so Krishna became Arjuna's charioteer and guide in the Great War. When the armies finally faced each other, Arjuna felt uncertain about fighting his own family. However, Krishna encouraged him and reminded him of his sacred duty as a warrior (see box).

The war raged for 18 days on the battleground of Kurukshetra. Thousands died, but the Pandavas knew they could not win as long as Bhishma led their enemies. Following Krishna's advice, on the tenth day, Arjuna let a warrior called Shikhandi drive his chariot. Shikhandi was the princess Amba reborn as a woman but raised by her father as a man. Noble Bhishma would never attack a woman, and so on seeing Shikhandi, he put down his weapons. This allowed Arjuna to defeat him easily.

Drona then took charge of the Kaurava forces. Krishna told the Pandavas how to defeat him, by spreading a rumor that Drona's son

Ashwatthama had been killed. In reality, Bheema had killed an elephant with the same name as the boy. When Drona heard this rumor, he asked the honest Yudhishthira if it was true. The eldest Pandava struggled for a moment because he could not lie, and then told Drona

◀ BED OF ARROWS
Arrows fired by Arjuna rained down on a defenseless Bhishma, who had put down his weapons. The arrows held the warrior above the ground of the battlefield.

▼ THE LAST KAURAVA
*The rules of war did not allow
warriors to hit below the waist. To
defeat Duryodhana, Krishna told
Bheema to cheat by attacking his thigh.*

The
Mahabharata is
ten times as long
as the Greek epics
Iliad and *Odyssey*
combined.

*Duryodhana did not think
Bheema would hit his thigh
and so was taken by surprise.*

easy target for Arjuna. With Krishna
by their side, the Pandavas ultimately
emerged victorious. Bheema had kept
his word and killed all the Kauravas
by himself until there was only
Duryodhana left. On the final day of
the war, Bheema killed Duryodhana.
With his death, the Great War was
finally over and the Pandavas
became rulers of Hastinapura.

JOURNEY TO HEAVEN

After ruling for 36 years,
Yudhishthira set out across
the Himalayas for Swargaloka
(Heaven), along with his
brothers and Draupadi. On this
difficult journey, his companions
fell from the mountains one by one,
until he was the only member of his
family left by the time he reached the
gates of Heaven. Eventually he was
reunited with his family in Swargaloka.

▲ THE WAY TO HEAVEN
*On their journey to Heaven, the Pandavas
traveled for days on dangerous rocky paths
through the mountains of the Himalayas.*

loudly that Ashwatthama had indeed
been killed. What Drona did not
hear was Yudhishthira muttering
under his breath that it might have
been an elephant or a man. Drona
stopped fighting in grief and
was killed in one swift strike by
Dhristadyumna, Draupadi's brother.

Next to lead the Kauravas was
Karna, the secret son of Kunti, born
to her with the blessing of Surya
the sun god before her marriage to
King Pandu. Kunti had abandoned
Karna as an infant, but before the

war, she pleaded with him not to
fight the Pandavas, who were his
half-brothers. He promised not to
harm any of the Pandavas except
for Arjuna. During his fight with
Arjuna, Karna fired a divine weapon
at him. Seeing it approach, Krishna
pushed hard on the floor of
Arjuna's chariot, making it sink into
the ground slightly. As a result, the
weapon missed Arjuna's head and
instead hit his crown. Later, when
the wheels of Karna's chariot became
stuck in the ground, he became an

On the final day ...
**Bheema killed
Duryodhana.
With his death,
the Great War
was finally over.**

AFRICA

The mythology of Ancient Egypt is known to us through written records and artifacts that are thousands of years old. These give us a fascinating insight into this civilization of long ago. By contrast, the stories from living cultures such as the Maasai and the San help explain ways of life, customs, and practices that continue today.

Nephthys, a protector goddess of the dead, features on the base of this painted sarcophagus from c. 1100 BCE, found at an archaeological site in eastern Egypt.

◀ GEB, NUT, AND SHU
While Geb, the earth god, lay beneath, the sky goddess Nut curved her body high above him to form the sky. The god Shu held the two apart, to provide space for life between them.

Nut's arched body is covered with stars.

Shu represents air or wind as he stands between the sky and earth.

Geb has a greenish body, which symbolizes plant life.

Ra's creation

There are several versions of the Ancient Egyptian creation story, each of which describes how all beings emerged from an endless sea. The principal creator deity is Ra, the sun god, who creates the world with the help of his children and grandchildren.

In the beginning, there was an infinite sea. Out of the water rose Ra, the sun god, by uttering his own name. Ra sneezed and Shu, the god of dry air, emerged from his nose. He then spat and Tefnut, the goddess of damp air, appeared. Ra sent the two deities on a journey across the sea.

THE WORLD IS BORN

While Shu and Tefnut were away, Ra made some of the sea retreat to reveal a dry island, known as the Benben stone (see p.99). Ra stood on the stone and brought into being the plants and animals. He first imagined them, and as he called their names, they emerged from the water. Ra also created Ma'at (see pp.180–181), the goddess of harmony and fairness, who brought order to his creations. Ra then took out his eye and shaped it to form the goddess Hathor

(see p.180). He sent Hathor to look for Shu and Tefnut, and bring them back. When she returned with them, Hathor saw that another eye had replaced her on Ra's face. Realizing she was no longer needed, she wept, and out of her tears, the first people were born.

Shu and Tefnut, meanwhile, had two children: Nut, the sky, and Geb, who was the earth. This pair of gods together created the stars, but this

angered their father Shu because they had not asked for his permission. Shu separated the two, but the young gods wanted to be reunited so that they could continue the work of creation. They asked the god Thoth (see p.178) for help, and he brought Geb and Nut back together. They then created many of Egypt's greatest gods and goddesses.

PHARAOHS

The Ancient Egyptians saw their rulers, or pharaohs, as gods in human form. These rulers were a link between the worlds of humans and the gods. The people believed that when the pharaohs died, they joined the sun god and lived in the sky forever.

Ptah's creation

The creation story from the Egyptian city of Memphis centers on Ptah, the god of craftsmanship, architecture, sculpture, and metalworking. The Ancient Egyptians believed that Ptah was the ancestor of the great architect Imhotep, who lived between 2700 and 2601 BCE.

A skilled craftsperson first imagines a creation and then gives it form using different materials such as stone or metal. In the same way, the Egyptian god Ptah made all things in the world with his mind and his hands.

THE FIRST CREATIONS

The first beings created by Ptah were the gods and goddesses of Egypt. He first imagined the shapes of these deities, then gave them form with his skillful hands. Ptah also named these gods and goddesses. Unlike a human craftsperson, Ptah had the power to give life with his speech, and as he named the deities, they came to life.

Next, Ptah created all the other beings that inhabit Earth, including all plants and animals. He made some of these by carving them

CREATOR KING ▶
Although his myth portrays him as a craftsman, Ptah is often shown as a kingly figure holding a scepter, which indicates his great importance in the Egyptian creation story.

from stone, and others by casting them in metal. All creations were then given life when Ptah pronounced their names.

THE FIRST CITIES

Finally, Ptah made the places where people live, and was worshipped as the founder of many Ancient Egyptian cities. The greatest among these was the country's capital, Memphis. At the heart of this city, Ptah created a shrine for himself, which became the most popular center for his worship.

HEART AMULET ▶
The Egyptians thought that a person's mind was located in the heart, and that the god Ptah's heart was where he imagined all his creations.

Unlike a human craftsperson, Ptah had the power to give life with his speech.

The death of Osiris

The story of the god Osiris and his brother and rival Set was popular among the Ancient Egyptians. It follows King Osiris's miraculous triumph over death and his son Horus's struggle to regain his rightful place as Egypt's ruler. This myth confirmed the Egyptians' belief that their royal leaders were descendants of gods, and gave them hope of a life after death.

Osiris and Isis, the first king and queen of Egypt, ruled well and were loved and respected by their people. Their peaceful reign, however, was short-lived. Envious of his brother's power, Set planned for Osiris's downfall. His jealousy became so great that he decided to kill his brother and take the throne for himself. He tricked Osiris into climbing into a large wooden chest, then slammed the lid tightly shut, locked it, and threw it into the Nile River.

"Osiris" is the European version of the Egyptian name "Usir," which means "powerful" or "mighty."

BACK FROM THE DEAD

Isis discovered that her husband had disappeared, and began searching for him. However, by the time she had found the chest and hauled it from the river, Osiris appeared to be completely lifeless. Isis took his body, intending to bring him back to life. When Set found out about her plan, he stole Osiris's body and chopped it into pieces. He then scattered all the parts across Egypt to ensure that his brother could never be revived.

◀ ISIS
The goddess of motherhood and healing, Isis was widely worshipped. Like many Egyptian deities, she carried an ankh (an Egyptian symbol of life) in her hand.

Isis and her sister Nephthys were horrified at what Set had done, but were determined to revive Osiris. They gathered almost all the pieces of Osiris's body and held them together with bandages. His body became whole again with the help of Thoth and Anubis (see p.52), the gods of Duat,

▶ REVIVING OSIRIS
Isis and Nephthys watched as Anubis, the god of the dead, embalmed the body of Osiris to preserve it as the first mummy.

Isis kneels beside her husband's body.

Nephthys waits by Anubis as he performs his ritual.

EGYPTIAN ROYALTY
As the first king of Egypt, Osiris was always shown holding a crook (left) and a flail (right), which were symbols of his royal authority.

MUMMIFICATION

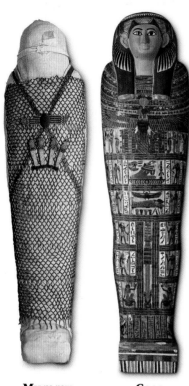

Mummy   **Case**

The ritual of mummification involved the preservation of a dead person's body to allow it to carry on in the afterlife (see pp.178–179). The body was cleaned, treated with preservative salts, bound in linen cloth, and enclosed in a decorated case. This case could then be placed in a chest called a sarcophagus, like the one that Set gave Osiris.

the Underworld (see pp.178–179). Osiris had become the first mummy. Isis then transformed herself into a falcon and, hovering above the wrapped body, beat her wings rapidly to breathe life into her husband. Osiris survived long enough for the couple to have a child, Horus. Unfortunately, all these efforts could not keep Osiris alive for long, and he soon left Earth for Duat.

THE WICKED SET

With Osiris in Duat, Set was able to take over the throne of Egypt. Although Horus was the rightful king, Isis was fearful of what Set would do to him, and so fled to safety with her child. Set was convinced that he had no further threats to worry about and continued to rule Egypt. When Horus grew up, he found out what his wicked uncle had done. He decided to reclaim the throne and avenge his father's death. Set and Horus fought, but Set soon realized that Horus was stronger and more intelligent than him. Refusing to accept defeat, on one occasion Set blinded Horus while he was asleep.

Fortunately, Isis was able to use her healing powers to restore her son's eyesight. Having failed to hurt Horus physically, Set tried to turn the other gods and goddesses against his nephew by spreading lies about him. The deities knew of Set's evil and devious character, and most refused to accept his words. Some of them, however,

> Set soon realized that **Horus was stronger and more intelligent** than him.

supported Set—they believed he had a legal claim to the throne because he had been born before Osiris.

THE COMPETITION

Set suggested that they resolve the matter of who should be king by competing in a boat race along the Nile River. However, he insisted that the vessels used in the race be made of stone to make the challenge difficult. Horus decided to play a trick on Set. He made his boat from wood, but covered it so that it looked like stone. Set, on the other

THE FALCON ▶
Although he could take human form, Horus was often portrayed as a falcon, to emphasize his role as the sky god.

▶ **SET**
The villainous Set was depicted as a beast with a pointed beak or muzzle, two fur tufts coming out of his head, and a straight tail.

The **gods and goddesses** finally realized that **Horus was truly worthy** and made him king.

hand, cut off stone from a mountaintop and used it to make his boat. While Set's stone boat sank, Horus raced toward the finish line in his lighter vessel. Set then transformed into a hippopotamus, swam underneath Horus's boat, and overturned it to make sure that his nephew, too, failed to complete the race. The gods and goddesses, however, realized that Horus was truly worthy and made him king, while the wicked Set was sent away in disgrace.

HORUS AND OSIRIS
After he became king, Horus found many ways to honor his father Osiris. On one occasion, he tried to give Osiris his restored eye, in the hope of bringing him back from Duat. The other gods admired Horus's dedication to his father. Horus eventually became the sky god and took the

form of a falcon. His eyes were said to be the sun and moon. His father Osiris came to be known as the most honest and just of the gods, and became the supreme judge in Duat (pp.178–179), deciding what should happen to the souls of dead people when they entered his realm.

Ancient Egyptian pharaohs, or kings, were worshipped as the god Horus in human form.

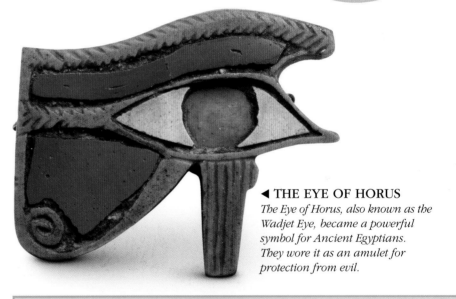

◀ **THE EYE OF HORUS**
The Eye of Horus, also known as the Wadjet Eye, became a powerful symbol for Ancient Egyptians. They wore it as an amulet for protection from evil.

THE TEMPLE OF OSIRIS

The story of Osiris gave hope of life after death, so the god came to be widely worshipped in Ancient Egypt. The center for his worship was in the city of Abydos in Upper Egypt, where his temple was beautifully decorated (left) with scenes from his life. Not much is known about the workings of this temple, but it is believed that its priests performed rituals to ensure that the god looked favorably upon the souls being judged in Duat (see pp.178–179).

TEMPLE TO HORUS

Part of the Kom Ombo temple in Egypt is dedicated to the sky god Horus. In this wall carving, the figure with the head of a hawk and a sun disk headdress represents Ra-Horakhty, a combination of Horus and the sun god Ra.

The Egyptian afterlife

Ancient Egyptians believed in life after death. Their myths explained the importance of preparing the body for the afterlife in Duat, the Underworld, and reminded them that judgement of their past actions awaited them there.

AFRICA

In Ancient Egyptian mythology, when a person died, their life force (*ka*) and their soul (*ba*) left their body. These would have to return to the body in the afterlife for the person to be able to live on. For this continued existence,

the physical body was preserved with the heart still inside it, in a ritual process called mummification (see p.174).

After mummification, the dead person's soul began a journey through Duat, which was ruled

by the god Osiris (see pp.172–177). The journey through Duat was not an easy one, as this place was full of poisonous snakes and lakes of scorching flames. The soul eventually made its way to the Hall of Two Truths. The god Anubis (see p.52)

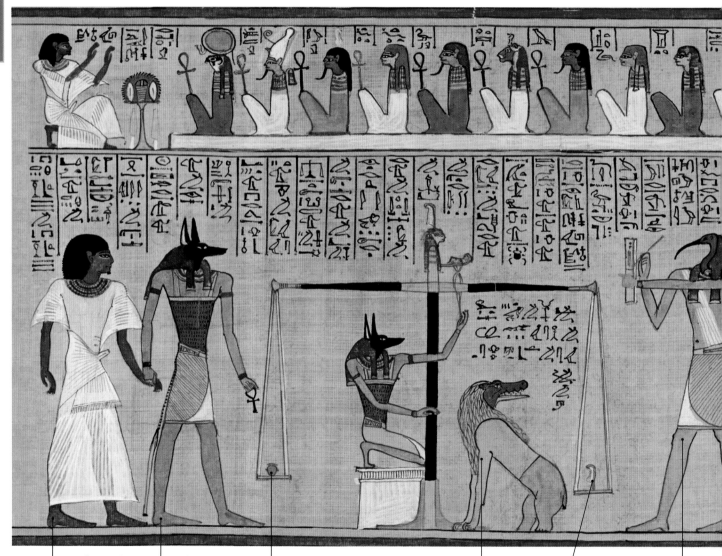

Hunefer's soul begins its journey through Duat.

Anubis leads the soul into the Hall of Two Truths.

Hunefer's heart is placed on one side of the balance.

Ammut is part lion, part hippopotamus, and part crocodile.

Ma'at's feather is placed on the other side of the scale.

Thoth, scribe of the gods, records the judgement on clay tablets.

led the soul into this hall, where it was judged by Osiris and 42 Assessor gods.

FEATHER OF TRUTH

The main ritual in this hall was the weighing of the dead person's preserved heart. In the middle of the hall stood a huge weighing scale, on which the heart was weighed against a feather from the goddess Ma'at (see pp.180–181), who represented truth and justice. A good person's heart would be lighter than this feather, but a heart heavy with sins committed in the living world would outweigh the feather.

Ammut (see p.53), the devourer of the dead, gobbled up the heart of a sinner—this meant the death of the soul and no chance of an afterlife. On the other hand, if a soul passed this test, a person would live forever in Duat.

CANOPIC JARS

During mummification, a person's vital organs were removed, preserved in salts, and stored in containers called canopic jars. Burying these jars with the mummy was believed to help the soul live on in Duat.

▼ JUDGEMENT OF HUNEFER
Hunefer was a scribe in c. 1300 BCE. This painting from his copy of the Book of the Dead *(a collection of spells) shows his soul's journey to the afterlife.*

Each Assessor god is responsible for judging if a particular sin, such as murder, had been committed.

The Eye of Horus (see p.175) has the form of a falcon, and represents health and restoration.

Seated in his shrine, Osiris oversees the judgement.

Hunefer's soul passes the feather test, and is presented to Osiris.

The god Horus, the son of Osiris and Isis, leads the soul to Osiris's shrine.

Four canopic jars (see above) contain the preserved organs of Hunefer.

Isis, the goddess of motherhood and healing, is dressed in white. She stands with Nephthys, the protector of the dead.

Egyptian goddesses

Many of Egypt's goddesses were worshipped as protectors of women and children. Some were revered as goddesses of war and hunting. These deities often took on animal form—some were gentle, like Hathor the cow, while others were fearsome, like Renenet the cobra.

Ma'at wears an ostrich feather, which is symbolic of truth, according to Ancient Egyptian beliefs.

Hathor

- **Also known as:** Eye of Ra, Sekhmet
- **Shown with:** Scepter, sun disk, sistrum (rattle-like musical instrument)

The gentle mother goddess Hathor often took the form of a cow or of a woman wearing a cow-horn headdress. She also acted as the eye of the sun god Ra (see p.170), watching over the world. On one occasion, Hathor transformed into the warlike, lion-headed goddess Sekhmet, whom Ra sent to Earth to punish humanity for rebelling against him.

Bastet

- **Also known as:** Bast, Ubaste
- **Shown with:** Sistrum (rattle-like musical instrument)

This goddess originally took the form of a lioness but later turned into a cat. Although she was less fierce as a cat, Bastet was still able to protect her husband, the sun god Ra, against sinister deities or spirits, such as the vicious snake-god Apophis.

The Ancient Egyptians mummified dead cats in honor of the goddess Bastet.

Taweret

- **Also known as:** Tuat
- **Shown with:** The "sa" symbol, which stands for "protection"

The goddess Taweret had the head of a hippopotamus, a creature known for its aggressive nature. She was the protector of women in childbirth, guarding them from evil spirits. Taweret also guided the souls of the dead on their journey to the Underworld (see pp.178–179).

Ma'at is often shown with wings that stretch along each arm.

Ma'at

- **Also known as:** Mayet
- **Shown with:** Ostrich feather

All Egyptians were expected to follow the paths of truth and justice, and Ma'at was the deity who represented these virtues. She valued order and fairness over anarchy and chaos. In Ancient Egypt, the people called their pharaoh "Lord of Ma'at": he was expected to be just and balanced in all his judgements, just like the goddess herself.

Meskhenet

- **Also known as:** Mesenet
- **Shown with:** Two-horned symbol

Meskhenet was the goddess of motherhood and mainly looked after women and infants during childbirth. She sometimes took the form of a brick with a woman's head. Egyptian women would stand on bricks or squat on them when giving birth.

Neith

- **Also known as:** Net
- **Shown with:** Scepter, shield, crossed arrows

Known as "the terrifying one," Neith was both a creator deity and the goddess of war and hunting. She was said to make weapons for warriors and to look after them in battle. The symbol for her name resembled a loom, so she also became the goddess of weaving.

The symbol for Neith's name includes a pair of bows bound together.

Renenet

- **Also known as:** Renenutet
- **Shown with:** Sun disk, baby

The cobra-headed goddess Renenet was the deity of nourishment and the harvest. Her name means "to nurse" or "to rear": she was a nurse who raised and protected pharaohs from birth to death. This powerful goddess was capable of destroying enemies with just her gaze.

The tricks of Anansi

Anansi the spider is a trickster-hero from West Africa, and stories about his pranks are widely told. Though he is small and not physically strong, Anansi uses his intelligence and cunning to outwit many humans and animals. Many of the stories about him also feature the creator deity Nyame.

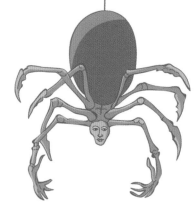

▲ ANANSI THE SPIDER
Spider silk is extremely strong, so Anansi was able to trap hornets and a leopard by weaving a web.

The sky god Nyame sat high in the sky, far away from the animals and people that he had made. On Earth, the people worked all the time, in a never-ending day, without the chance to rest. They grew exhausted and complained bitterly. When Anansi the spider heard their complaints, he decided to take action. He quickly spun a thread high into the sky and climbed up it to talk to Nyame. After hearing about the people's woes from Anansi, the creator made night, so that the people had the opportunity to take a break from work and to sleep. However, many people were frightened of the dark, so Anansi returned to talk to the sky god. This time Nyame created the moon to provide some light at night. Now the people were happy, but they shivered in the cold of the night. Anansi contacted Nyame once again, and the creator made the sun to warm the land. When the sun shone all day, the ground became parched and the scorching heat was too much for the humans. This time Anansi asked Nyame to make something to moisten the earth and cool the people, and so the sky god brought the refreshing rain. At first the ground flooded and some people drowned. Anansi went to Nyame one more time. The god drained away the flood waters, and at last the people were happy.

NYAME'S STORIES

Anansi had helped solve all the people's problems, but he was still not satisfied. He was jealous

◄ SPIDER ART
The traditional craft items of West Africa, such as this bronze beaker from Nigeria, often feature images of a spider, showing Anansi's popularity.

The **sky god thought** it would be **impossible** for a **spider** to **catch all these creatures**.

SUN AND MOON MASKS

Masks showing the sun (far left) and the moon are common in West Africa, as they recall Anansi's role in the creation of night and day.

Sun

Moon

than the snake. To prove the spider wrong, the python came out of hiding and lay down next to the stick. Anansi quickly tied the serpent to his staff, preventing it from escaping. To catch the leopard, Anansi dug a deep hole and covered it with branches. The unsuspecting leopard fell into the pit, and Anansi wove an intricate web around the animal to trap it.

When Anansi took the creatures to Nyame, the sky god was highly impressed. He kept his promise and declared that all the stories of the world now belonged to Anansi.

of Nyame, who owned all the stories in the world. The spider longed to be able to tell stories on Earth and asked the creator god if he could buy them from him. Nyame decided to set a difficult challenge for Anansi and said he could have the stories in exchange for three things: some hornets, a python, and a leopard. The sky god thought that it would be impossible for a mere spider to catch all these creatures, and that he would be able to keep the stories to himself.

> Anansi is a god in the Vodou religion, which is widely practiced in Haiti.

TRAPPING THE ANIMALS

Anansi set out to look for the animals and soon came across the hornets' nest. Holding a hollow calabash (bottle gourd) in his hand, the spider took a large banana leaf and held it over the nest. As he poured water over the leaf, the hornets were fooled into believing this was the rain. He then offered them his calabash as a shelter. As soon as the hornets flew into the gourd, Anansi wove a thick web to seal the top so that the insects could not escape.

Anansi now went to the python carrying a long stick and loudly proclaimed that this staff was longer

BR'ER RABBIT

When people from Africa were taken to the Caribbean as slaves, their stories found new settings. Tales featuring the Jamaican character Br'er Rabbit are identical to those about Anansi. The rabbit, too, is a trickster who uses his cunning to outwit larger and stronger rivals.

◀ DANGEROUS TARGET

Nyame sent Anansi to capture the rock python, the largest snake in Africa, confident that the spider would fail in his task.

The creation of Ife

The sacred stories of the Yoruba people from West Africa feature many gods and spirits, including a supreme god called Olorun (also known as Olodumare), meaning "almighty." In the Yoruba creation story another god named Obatala descends from the sky and creates the land and living beings with Olorun's help.

THE PALM TREE

The palm tree is known among the Yoruba people as the "tree of life"; they believe all the plants and trees sprang from the very first palm nut. The palm provides people with oil that is widely used in cooking. People also make palm wine and use the tree's wood and leaves to craft items such as furniture and mats.

AFRICA

In the beginning there was only the sky and an endless expanse of water. The supreme god Olorun ruled the sky and the goddess Olokun ruled the waters below. Many other gods lived in the sky, but they were not as skilled or as wise as Olorun. One of these deities, called Obatala, wanted to improve Olokun's realm by adding dry land, with hills, valleys, forests, and living creatures. When Obatala sought Olorun's permission, the supreme god sent him to his son, Orunmila, the god of knowledge and wisdom, who could help Obatala reach the water and carry out this task. Orunmila suggested that Obatala make a gold chain to lower himself down to the water below. He gave Obatala sand in a snail's shell, a palm nut, a white hen, and a black cat, and told him how he should use these things.

THE DESCENT

Obatala lowered himself down on the chain, and sprinkled the sand on the water, creating the first land. He then placed the hen on the land, which scratched at the sand,

scattering it everywhere. More land formed wherever the sand fell, and soon there was a large stretch of it. Obatala called the land Ife, and built a house for himself on it. The god then planted the palm nut to grow the first tree and settled down in the house with the black cat as his companion.

After a while, Obatala decided he wanted human companions, too. He formed clay figures, and Olorun breathed life into them to create the first humans. When the other gods saw this new world, many of them climbed down to live there. Olorun told the gods to protect the humans.

WEAVING CONTEST

The people and gods built villages on the land and lived happily. Only Olokun, the sea goddess, was unhappy. The creation of land had reduced the amount of water in the world, thereby diminishing her power. She unleashed a devastating flood to destroy the land, but Orunmila pushed the waters back and stopped the flood. Furious, Olokun challenged

Olorun to a weaving contest. The sea goddess thought that she would win easily, as she was the most skillful weaver of all the deities. She hoped her victory would show the other gods that she was greater than Olorun.

Although Olorun took no notice of the challenge, Olokun was determined to prove her skill. However, each time Olokun started weaving, the chameleon Agemo, who was the messenger of the gods, changed its skin color to match the goddess's work. Olokun realized that even the humble Agemo could produce colors that equalled her best efforts. She accepted defeat and recognized Olorun as the supreme god.

◀ OBATALA
The god Obatala is shown as an old man dressed in white, which symbolizes purity. He usually carries a staff representing truth.

◀ OÒNI OF IFE
Yoruba kings (Oòni) protect the sacred land of Ife, and are believed to be the descendants of the gods. The Yoruba often carve bronze heads to honor their kings.

185

The first cattle

For the Maasai people of Kenya, cattle provide their main source of food and clothing. While there are many stories about how the Maasai came to own cattle, one tale describes how the gods gave the Maasai cattle as a gift, guiding them to a more settled way of life.

There was once a man from the Dorobo people who shared his land with an elephant. The two lived in peace with each other, until the day the elephant gave birth to a calf. When the Dorobo man approached them, the elephant feared for her baby and attacked him. The Dorobo man killed the mother elephant in self-defense, and the calf fled in fear, leaving the man alone on his land.

The calf ran until it met Le-eyo, a man from the Maasai tribe, and told him what had happened to its mother. On hearing the tale, Le-eyo went to the Dorobo man's land and was surprised to find him talking to Naiteru-kop, the messenger of the gods. Le-eyo hid behind some bushes and heard Naiteru-kop telling the man to come to a clearing in the forest the next morning, where the gods would give

the Dorobo man a great gift. Le-eyo decided to get to the meeting place before the Dorobo man in order to seize this gift for himself.

A GIFT FROM THE SKY

Early the next morning, Le-eyo arrived at the meeting place. When Naiteru-kop saw Le-eyo, he mistook him for the Dorobo man. He told Le-eyo to go home and build a fence around his hut, and then wait inside the hut. The messenger god insisted that Le-eyo remain indoors, no matter what he

heard. Le-eyo went home and did as asked, and soon he heard a terrifying, thundering noise outside his hut. Curious, Le-eyo could no longer stay indoors, and went out to investigate. He was amazed to find that the sky god Enkai had lowered an enormous strip of animal hide down to Earth, on which a herd of cattle had come down to Le-eyo's land. Le-eyo took the cattle and reared them as instructed by Enkai. Ever since, the Maasai have lived as cattle herders, while the Dorobo live in the old way, as hunters.

◀ **MAASAI SETTLEMENTS**
Traditional Maasai houses are arranged inside a circular fence made from thorns, to protect the cattle and people inside from wild beasts.

▼ **MAASAI CATTLE**
In Maasai culture, the number of cows a person owns indicates how rich they are, and the cows are often used as currency.

The eland and the coming of night

▲ SAN ROCK ART
For the San people, the eland is a sacred animal and often a symbol of strength. The people made rock paintings depicting the eland as a part of their sacred ceremonies.

The traditional way of life for the San people of southern Africa is one of hunting and gathering. Their story of the first eland hunt (an eland is a type of antelope) explains the coming of night into the world.

Long ago, in the Kalahari Desert of southern Africa, a creator named Mantis made the first eland, a young calf that scurried off in fear. Mantis was fascinated by his creation, so he tracked down the terrified animal and fed it some honey. He raised the eland with great care, rubbing its coat of fur with a honeycomb until it shone, and continued to feed it honey until the eland was a full-grown animal. Mantis then left to gather food for himself.

Curious about why Mantis was taking all the honey, another being called Kwammang-a followed the creator to the place where he had left the eland. When Kwammang-a saw the animal, he killed it with a bow and arrow and divided the meat among his followers. Taking a liking to the taste of meat, Kwammang-a's followers decided that, from then on, they would be hunters.

When Mantis returned and saw the people cutting up his beloved creation, he was overcome with grief. He pierced the eland's gall bladder and out poured darkness, covering the world. He then threw the empty gall bladder into the sky and it became the moon. Since then, the days have been divided into day and night. Kwammang-a and his followers were pleased about Mantis's actions, because they could use the light of the moon to hunt at night.

> The oldest ancestors of the San people lived in Africa about 100,000 years ago.

▲ EXTRACTING HONEY
The San people extract honey from the honeycombs of wild bees nesting in trees. The creator deity, Mantis, nourished the eland with honey, and so it plays an important role in the religious rituals of the San.

187

/Kaggen and the world tree

The creator god of the San people of southern Africa is /Kaggen. The story of creation describes how he brings people and animals to the surface of the world, and how fire destroys the relationship between them.

Long ago, all the people and animals lived beneath the land with their creator /Kaggen, who had the power of shape-shifting and often took the form of a praying mantis. In this underground world, the humans and beasts understood each other very well, and the people themselves lived in peace, with no arguments. There was enough food, and even though there was no sun, it was always warm and bright. While life went on pleasantly here, /Kaggen wondered if his creations could live above ground and set about making this happen.

▲ PRAYING MANTIS
The San consider the mantis to be sacred because the insect has an upright, praying posture. They believe it to be a form of /Kaggen.

A NEW WORLD

/Kaggen's first act was to create an enormous tree on the ground. Its branches stretched across the world and right up into the sky, and its roots penetrated deep into the earth. This magnificent tree came to be known as the "world tree." Under the shelter of the tree's branches, /Kaggen dug a long

THE SAN

The culture of the San of the Kalahari Desert is more than 30,000 years old. Although they were hunter-gatherers at first, the San eventually learned to grow crops and rear cattle. The rock paintings and cave art of these people are thousands of years old and are considered to be the best records of their history and culture.

San cave art

KALAHARI TREE
Large trees that grow in the Kalahari Desert provide people with food and materials for houses, just like the "world tree" that formed a home for many creatures in the San creation story.

The San language has "click" sounds, usually written with symbols such as "/" or "!".

▲ FIRE RITUALS
While the first people needed fire for warmth and light, present-day San also gather around a fire to sing, dance, and perform healing rituals.

tunnel, which ran down past the roots to the underground realm of the people and animals. He led the first man and then the first woman through the tunnel, bringing them to the upper world. Before long, the other people followed. When they emerged from the mouth of the hole, they looked in amazement at the beautiful world around them. Then /Kaggen encouraged all the animals to come to the upper world. Some creatures rushed up the tree's roots and climbed straight onto its branches, where they made homes. Others came more reluctantly, with /Kaggen's help.

THE FIRST FIRE

When all the people and animals had gathered around /Kaggen, he told them that from then on this new world would be their home. He said everyone could have a happy life here, but warned them to never make fire, because it would destroy this new existence. They agreed, and the mantis went away, but kept an eye on his world from afar.

At first, the people were happy, but when the sun went down, darkness crept over the land and the new world grew colder. The people did not have eyes like those of animals that could see in the dark. They became frightened and, forgetting /Kaggen's warning, made a fire to warm themselves and bring light. As soon as they had broken their promise to /Kaggen, the people found that they could no longer understand or talk to the animals. The beasts themselves were terrified by the fire and ran away. Animals have been scared of people ever since—the friendship that once existed between humans and beasts has never returned.

Magical beings

Some mythological characters, such as witches, wizards, sorcerers, and demons, have magical powers that they can use to help or hinder the plans of gods and humans alike. Their actions often change the course of events, bringing about intriguing twists and turns in the lives of those around them.

◀ YAMA-UBA
In Japanese mythology, Yama-Uba is a cunning spirit who lives on remote mountain-tops or in dense forests. She is known to attack strangers, but also cares for lost children.

▲ BÁBA YAGÁ
Many myths from Slavic countries describe Bába Yagá as a witch who can change her shape at will, but she usually appears as an old woman flying through the air.

The brave warrior Rustum fights Div-e Sepid.

MEDEA ▶
The sorceress Medea is the granddaughter of the Titan Helios in the mythology of Ancient Greece. She is skilled at making magical potions and ointments. She helps the hero Jason in his search for the Golden Fleece.

DIV-E SEPID ▶
In Persian mythology, the demon king Div-e Sepid is a giant of enormous strength. He can create storms that hurl rocks, tree trunks, or chunks of ice at his enemies.

The demon's leg is severed in the struggle.

SEE ALSO

- Jason and the Argonauts, pp.42–43
- Odysseus journeys home, pp.54–57
- The impossible quest, pp.74–77
- The sword in the stone, pp.92–93
- Bába Yagá, the witch, p.100
- Rustum and Sohrab, pp.122–123
- Rama's journey, pp.158–161

◄ VÄINÄMÖINEN

The mythical Finnish hero
Väinämöinen can enchant with
his music. He uses this power to
steal the magical object called the
sampo to help his people.

Uther Pendragon,
King Arthur's father

Väinämöinen's
magical kantele
lulls people to sleep.

MERLIN ▲

The most famous wizard in the
legends from Britain and France,
wise Merlin has the ability to foresee
the future. He is an adviser to
King Arthur and his family.

Ravana has 20
hands, each carrying
a unique weapon.

▲ CIRCE

The enchantress Circe from
Greek mythology combines
herbs and spells to turn her
enemies into animals. She
can also use her powers to
darken the sky by hiding
the moon or the sun.

RAVANA ►

In Hindu mythology, the
ten-headed Asura (demon)
Ravana can shape-shift into
any form. In the epic Ramayana,
he uses this ability to lure and
abduct Sita, the wife of Rama.

191

The adventures of Mwindo

The story of Mwindo, a child with the powers of a superhero, is a traditional tale of the Nyanga people of the Democratic Republic of the Congo. The epic tells of the boy's fights with mighty enemies, and how he travels to the Underworld and to the sky. The story teaches respect for the gods and that all animals are sacred.

The first written version of the Mwindo epic was published in 1969 by Belgian scholar Daniel Biebuyck.

Mwindo's flyswatter is made of a buffalo tail and has a wooden handle.

Shemwindo was the chief of a tribe of the Nyanga people. He and his wife Nyamwindo had a son called Mwindo, who was a wonder-child. He could walk, talk, and foretell the future as soon as he was born, and could also fly through the air. Many people were terrified of Mwindo's supernatural powers—even his own father feared him. Shemwindo was also worried that Mwindo would one day take over his kingdom, and so he tried to kill his son. He failed in his attempt because of the boy's amazing strength, and so Shemwindo's tribespeople worked together to seal Mwindo inside a drum and throw it in a river. Fortunately for the child, Shemwindo's sister Iyangura found the floating drum further downstream and rescued Mwindo.

◀ MWINDO
This strong wonder-child is sometimes portrayed as a more adult heroic figure in modern representations. He is shown with his magical flyswatter, which had the power to deflect other weapons.

Mwindo could walk, talk, and foretell the future as soon as he was born ...

AFRICA

TO THE UNDERWORLD

Mwindo vowed that he would return home to challenge his father to a fight. Iyangura persuaded Mwindo to take some warriors with him, so he went to the house where his mother's brothers lived. They sided with Mwindo against his wicked father. The warriors forged armor for Mwindo and accompanied him to the chief's house, where they killed many of his followers. However, Shemwindo himself escaped to the Underworld.

Mwindo followed his father to the land of the dead, where he was challenged by its fearsome ruler, Muisa. At first, Muisa did not let him approach Shemwindo, until mighty Mwindo defeated Muisa in a fight using his flyswatter. When the boy was finally allowed to meet his father, Shemwindo apologized to Mwindo for trying to kill him. Accepting his apology, Mwindo used his miraculous powers to bring the chief's dead followers back to life. The pair then returned to Earth, and decided to split their kingdom in two, so that they could each rule one half.

▲ TEACHING MWINDO
Taking the form of a hedgehog, Nkuba taught Mwindo a valuable lesson about the importance of animals.

ORDEALS IN THE SKY

Mwindo gained a reputation for protecting his followers from danger. Once when Mwindo's men went hunting, a dragon attacked and ate them. Mwindo cut the beast open and released the hunters from the dragon's belly. Although the people praised Mwindo for his bravery, the dragon's death angered Nkuba, also known as Lightning Master, who was a friend to the beast.

Nkuba transformed himself into a hedgehog and told Mwindo that all animals were sacred to the gods and should be respected. As Mwindo had offended the gods, the Lightning Master made him travel to the sky, where he had to endure many terrible ordeals as punishment.

ORAL RETELLINGS

The Nyanga people have never written down the story of Mwindo. Instead, the epic is mainly passed on from one generation to the next by reciting it as a performance. The tale is accompanied by singing, dancing, and drumming. Many traditional stories across the world have survived in this way.

When he was finally allowed to return to Earth, Mwindo explained to his people that animals should not be harmed unnecessarily. From then on, Mwindo ruled over his people well, and always remembered to treat both animals and gods with respect.

Cowrie shells are a symbol of power and wealth in Africa.

▶ POWERFUL BELT
Muisa, the ruler of the Underworld, had a magic belt that could crush anyone it hit. Only Mwindo's flyswatter was more powerful.

THE AMERICAS

Myths from the Americas evoke the ancient civilizations of the Aztecs and Incas, as well as those of the Maya and Taíno, whose descendants still live in the region today. These stories are filled with lively characters and bizarre creatures, as well as gods and goddesses that govern the weather, farming, and much more.

The Aztec god of rain and fertility, Tlaloc, was believed to bring both rain and droughts. This terra-cotta container features the head of the deity.

The Feathered Serpent

Quetzalcoatl was one of the most important gods for the Aztecs, who lived in present-day central Mexico from c. 1300 to 1521 CE. One of the stories about him tells of the destruction of the world, and Quetzalcoatl's journey to the Underworld to bring back human bones with which to create more people. He also gives humankind the gift of maize (corn), which was the main crop cultivated by the Aztecs.

Quetzalcoatl took on the guise of Ehecatl to enter the Underworld.

In the beginning there were two deities: the god Ometecuhtli and the goddess Omecihuatl. The pair went on to have four sons: Huitzilopochtli, the god of war; Xipe Totec, the god of farming and springtime (see p.200); Tezcatlipoca, the god of judgement and sorcery; and Quetzalcoatl, a shape-shifter who, as Ehecatl, was the god of light and wind. Quetzalcoatl usually took the form of a serpent, but with feathers instead of scales covering his body, so he was also known as the Feathered Serpent.

The four sons created all the other gods and goddesses and then made the world, including all the animals, plants, and people in it. However, the brothers constantly fought with each other, which meant that the world was destroyed and recreated repeatedly. Each terrible destruction was different from the last. First, jaguars wiped out the world, then the wind, a fire, and lastly flood. After the world had been destroyed for the fourth time, Quetzalcoatl killed a vicious sea monster called Tlaltecuhtli with the help of his brother Tezcatlipoca, and used its body to make the world once more.

Quetzalcoatlus, a giant flying reptile that lived millions of years ago, is named after Quetzalcoatl.

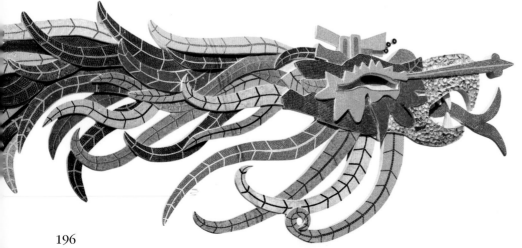

◀ PLUMED SERPENT

The word quetzal *meant both "feathered" and "precious" in the Aztec language. This famous Mexican wall mural depicts the god Quetzalcoatl in his feathered serpent form.*

Mictlantecuhtli is shown covered in red spots, which represent blood.

◀ EHECATL IN THE UNDERWORLD

Although Mictlantecuhtli had agreed to give Ehecatl the bones, he still asked him to perform a near-impossible task, hoping the god would fail.

of the Underworld agreed to this request, but on the condition that Ehecatl travel around Mictlan four times using his powerful winds to blow a horn made from a conch shell. Ehecatl found a shell, but it had no holes for him to blow into. Undeterred, the god asked worms to bore holes in it, and placed a swarm of bees inside to make it sound louder. He then traveled around the Underworld four times, blowing the conch shell as Mictlantecuhtli had instructed. His task now complete, Ehecatl claimed a pile of bones. As he was leaving Mictlan, he accidentally dropped the bones, and before he could pick them up again, a quail pecked at them. When he returned to Earth, he changed back into Quetzalcoatl, and gave the bones to the goddess Cihuacoatl, who ground them into a powder. All the gods then poured their blood onto the powdered bones, and from this mixture Quetzalcoatl created the new humans. What he did not realize was that the quail's pecking had damaged the bones. This meant that the people he made grew to be different sizes and were doomed to die.

REMAKING HUMANS

After he remade the world, Quetzalcoatl thought about how to remake the humans again. He realized that he would need the right materials: human bones. When he could not find any on Earth, Quetzalcoatl transformed himself into Ehecatl and set off to search for them in Mictlan, the Underworld.

After he had entered Mictlan, Ehecatl asked its ruler, Mictlantecuhtli, for some human bones. The god

THE GIFT OF GRAIN

Quetzalcoatl was concerned about his people and wanted to help them. One day, he saw some ants carrying a maize kernel and followed them until they disappeared into a crack in a mountain called Popocatepetl. The serpent god was curious about what lay inside the mountain, so he turned himself into an ant to crawl through the crack. Inside was a vast cave full of various seeds and grains. Quetzalcoatl realized that this food could feed all humans. He tried to break open the mountain and failed, so he asked the other gods for help. The gods used rain and lightning to break open Mount Popocatepetl, and maize and other grains were scattered across the land to provide food for the people.

MAIZE

Quetzalcoatl giving people the gift of maize

Before growing maize, the Aztecs ate only roots or the animals they could kill. The swampy land where they settled was not suited to farming, so the Aztecs constructed islands where they could plant their crops. They believed maize had been given to the first Aztecs by Quetzalcoatl himself.

AZTEC CODEX
The god Quetzalcoatl sits surrounded by ritual symbols in this page from the Codex Borbonicus, *an Aztec book from c. 1500 CE. The codex is written on a piece of bark paper more than 46 ft (14 m) long and contains hundreds of colorful figures.*

Aztec nature deities

Farming, particularly of the crop maize, was important to the Aztecs. They had many nature deities who had the power to control the sun, rain, and the fertility of the soil, and worshipped these gods to ensure perfect weather and plentiful harvests.

Chicomecóatl

- **Also known as:** Xilonen
- **Shown with:** Ears of maize in hands

Chicomecóatl was the goddess of food, drink, and fruitfulness. She looked after the growth of plants and blessed the crops during the harvest season. However, her name, which means "seven serpent," was a warning about her destructive side: if angered, she could destroy the world.

Xipe Totec

- **Also known as:** Tlatlauhca
- **Shown with:** Blood-stained knife, stripped skin

Xipe Totec was the god of agriculture, plant life, and the seasons, especially springtime. He was said to have removed his own skin—revealing an inner golden body—to provide food for humankind. This was believed to represent the way the seeds of the maize crop shed their outer layer.

Tlaloc

- **Also known as:** Chaac (Maya)
- **Shown with:** Lightning bolt wand, ritual water jug

This important Aztec god shares many of the characteristics of Chaac, a deity of the earlier Maya people. While the Aztecs worshipped Tlaloc as the god of the life-giving rains, they also feared his ability to bring storms. Usually portrayed as a man with long fangs, he could also take the form of an amphibian such as a frog, or a water bird such as a heron.

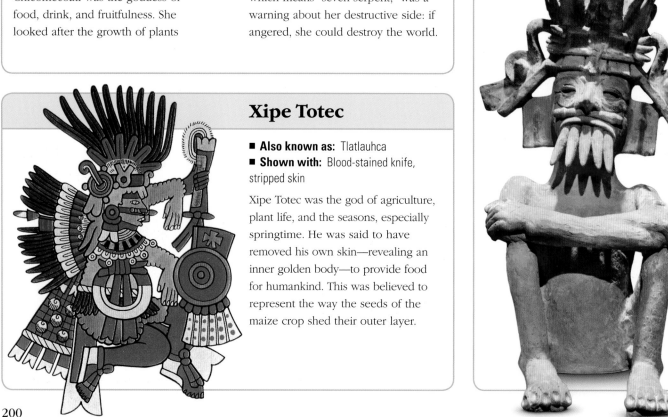

Tonatiuh

- **Also known as:** The Fifth Sun
- **Shown with:** Eagle and jaguar

The sun god Tonatiuh was worshipped as the ruler of Tollan, the Aztec Heaven. The people believed that he was the fifth incarnation of the sun, and his worship often involved human sacrifice. This god was usually represented by a colored disk, sometimes with hands or claws that held human hearts— those of the victims who were sacrificed in his name.

Centéotl

- **Also known as:** Centeocihuatl
- **Shown with:** Maize headdress

The maize god Centéotl had yellow skin, like the ears of maize themselves. His name means "dried maize still on the cob." When Aztec farmers sowed maize seeds, they did a ritual dance in the god's honor to make them sprout. They repeated this dance throughout the growing season. The farmers believed that this ritual would encourage Centéotl to bless the crops and produce a good harvest.

Coatlicue

- **Also known as:** Teteoinnan ("Mother of the Gods")
- **Shown with:** Skirt made of snakes

The primal Earth goddess Coatlicue was a fearsome character. She had two fanged serpents for a face, and wore a necklace consisting of hands, hearts, and a skull. In an alternative creation story, Coatlicue gave birth to the moon goddess and the gods of the stars. These children murdered her, but as she was dying she gave birth to Huitzilopochtli, the god of war and the sun, who was born fully grown and armed. Huitzilopochtli avenged his mother by killing his sister and brothers.

The Hero Twins

The creation of humankind and the adventures of the Hero Twins, Hunahpu and Xbalanque, form the main part of a Maya story called *Popol Vuh* (*Book of the People*). An oral telling was probably written down by the Quiché Maya (a people living in midwestern Guatemala), before being translated into Spanish by a Spanish priest in c.1700 CE. This remains one of the best early accounts of Maya mythology.

In the beginning the world was empty. Then the first gods came into being, including Gucumatz, the god of the sea, and Huracan, the sky and wind god. Gucumatz and Huracan decided to create humankind to populate Earth. However, the very first creatures they made were unable to speak the names of the gods, managing only to utter a few meaningless sounds. These creatures therefore became the first animals. The gods decided to try again, and this time chose to make humans out of clay. However, these beings turned out to be limp and voiceless, and dissolved away in water.

After two failed attempts, the creators were unsure of what to do next, and so they decided to seek help from the gods Xpiyacoc and Xmucane, who were known for their wisdom. Xpiyacoc and Xmucane told Gucumatz and Huracan to try making men from wood and women from reeds. The gods did so, but these humans refused to worship their creators. Infuriated, Huracan unleashed a flood on Earth, washing away these creatures. The deities realized that the time was not right for humans to come into the world.

Gucumatz and Huracan create humans out of clay.

Some of the clay beings dissolved soon after being made.

THE CREATION OF HUMANS ▶
This modern interpretation of the Maya creation story is by famous Mexican artist Diego Rivera. The creators mold the first human while Tohil, patron god of the Quiché, looks on.

PLAYING BALL

The wise gods Xpiyacoc and Xmucane had twin sons named Hun Hunahpu and Vucub Hunahpu. The twins spent all their time gambling and playing ball, and they made so much noise that it annoyed the gods who ruled over Xibalba, the Underworld. These gods challenged the twins to a ball game, hoping to entice them to enter Xibalba. The gods were confident that the twins would lose the game, after which the deities could kill them. The twins accepted the challenge and went down to Xibalba, but discovered the perils of the Underworld as soon as they entered. When they tried to sit on a bench, they found it to be scorching hot, which made them jump up immediately. On their first night in Xibalba, the twins were made to stay in a place called the Dark House, where they had only a flaming torch and two cigars to provide light. When the gods

> The **gods were confident** that the **twins would lose** the game, after which the **deities could kill them**.

of the Underworld came to check on the twins in the morning, they saw that the cigars had been smoked and the torch had burned out. They declared that the brothers would have to be punished for the loss of their property, and took the twins to the ball court, where they put them to death. The gods buried the brothers, but kept Hun Hunahpu's head and hung it up in a calabash tree as a warning.

THE HERO TWINS

Xquic, the daughter of one of the gods of Xibalba, was picking fruit from this tree when Hun Hunahpu's head spat at her and made her pregnant. Months later, Xquic gave birth to twins named Hunahpu and Xbalanque, who came to be known as the Hero Twins. Like their father Hun Hunahpu and uncle Vucub Hunahpu, the Hero Twins liked to spend their days playing ball.

Early versions of the *Popol Vuh* would have been written in Maya picture-writing.

When the twins heard how the gods of Xibalba had killed their father and uncle, they decided to avenge the deaths. They made a lot of noise while playing ball to annoy the gods. As expected, the angry gods summoned the Hero Twins to the Underworld, hoping to kill them.

BALL GAME

The Maya ball game was played in large stone courts. Two opposing teams tried to get a small rubber ball through stone rings placed on the side walls that acted as goals. Players were not allowed to touch the balls with their hands or feet, and could only use their knees, elbows, or hips.

DEFEATING THE GODS

As soon as Hunahpu and Xbalanque arrived in Xibalba, the gods set them a series of challenges. They had to spend each night in a different house, which was home to one deadly force or another. As well as the Dark House, there was also the Razor House, which contained moving blades and razors, and the Cold House, which was freezing and covered in ice. Others included the Jaguar House, packed with hungry jaguars; the Fire House, which was ablaze with scorching flames; and the House of Bats, which was filled with deadly, shrieking bats. The Hero Twins survived each of these terrifying houses, using their wits to stay alive: they used fireflies for light in the Dark House, and hid in their blowpipes (a hollow tube used for firing darts) to stay away from the bats in the House of Bats.

When the gods of Xibalba saw that the Hero Twins had survived the terrors of all these houses, they decided to challenge the twins to a ball game. This pleased the brothers, because they loved the game and believed they had a good chance of winning. However, they were caught off guard when they saw that the vicious creatures from the House of Bats had been let loose around the ball court. As the twins played, one of the bats swooped down and took off Hunahpu's head. Rather than accept defeat, Xbalanque carved a new head from a gourd and put it on Hunahpu's body. The twins then continued playing, using Hunahpu's real head as a ball. These antics distracted the gods, which gave Xbalanque the chance he needed to reattach his brother's proper head to his body. The twins continued playing, and won the match.

The Ancient Maya believed that everyone, even good people, had to visit the Underworld after death.

THE MAGICIANS OF XIBALBA

No sooner had the twins triumphed than the angry gods of the Underworld decided to kill them. Although they were aware of the gods' plan, the brothers did not resist as they were put to death. Their remains were thrown into a river. The gods had not, however, killed the spirit of the Hero Twins, and so the two were reborn as catfish, before changing back to their old selves.

The Hero Twins now lived in the Underworld and developed supernatural powers, which brought them great recognition as magicians. One of their tricks involved Xbalanque

The Hero Twins developed **supernatural powers**, which brought them **great recognition as magicians**.

apparently killing Hunahpu by taking off his head and rolling it along the floor, before reattaching the head and bringing his brother back to life. The gods of the Underworld did not know these brothers were the Hero Twins, and so they begged the twins to perform this trick on them as well. Xbalanque then cut off the heads of the gods, but refused to bring them back to life, proclaiming that, at last, there would be no more sacrifices to the deities of Xibalba.

▲ MAIZE GOD
The Maya believe that maize was used to make the first humans. Some think the maize god was Hun Hunahpu, the father of the Hero Twins.

THE FINAL CREATION

The Hero Twins now rose into the sky, and became the sun and the moon. The universe was finally in order. The creators gods, Huracan and Gucumatz, decided to try making humans again, this time using maize (corn). This attempt was successful, and the world was soon populated with humankind. The gods then taught the humans how to behave well toward each other, and these people went on to have children and live together in harmony.

◀ HERO TWINS
Painted pottery found in Maya settlements often shows the Hero Twins. This example has inscriptions in Maya picture-writing running around the top.

205

Fate and fortune

Many cultures have deities who are believed to control people's luck, fate, and fortune. These gods and goddesses often feature in groups of three. Their ability to bring about sudden, and sometimes terrible, changes in fortune made people fear and worship them.

▲ THE MOIRAI
In Greek mythology, the three Moirai are goddesses of fate who spin the thread of a person's life and cut it when the time comes for them to die. They are called Clotho (right), Lachesis (center), and Atropos (left). In Roman myth they were known as the Parcae.

▼ THE NORNS
Three wise women called the Norns decide the fate of everyone in the Norse cosmos. They also draw from the Well of Fate to water the roots of the world tree, Yggdrasil.

Ganesha always holds an ax with which to destroy any obstacles in his path.

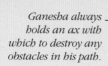

◄ SHAI
The Egyptian god of fate is Shai. He decides how long a person should live, and is present when the soul is judged in Duat, the Underworld.

◄ GANESHA
The elephant-headed Hindu god Ganesha (see p.156) is known to remove obstacles. This god of good fortune is also associated with knowledge and learning.

LAKSHMI ▶
The Hindu goddess Lakshmi is said to grant wealth and good fortune to her worshippers. She is the wife of the supreme Hindu deity Vishnu.

CAMAXTLI ▶
Camaxtli is the Maya god of fate, hunting, and war. Some Maya stories claim he is the god who first gave fire to humans.

FORTUNA ▶
In Ancient Roman mythology, Fortuna is the goddess of fate and luck. She is often portrayed with a cornucopia (a horn full of flowers and fruit), which represents riches and fruitfulness.

The lotus symbolizes fortune and plenty.

◀ **GEFION**
In Norse mythology, Gefion is the goddess of farming and the wealth of the land, and is especially associated with plowing. Her followers believed she brought good luck.

◀ **SANXING**
Shou (far left), Lu (center), and Fu (right) are the Sanxing ("Three Stars"). Worship of these Chinese gods is thought to bring long life, status, and financial success.

207

The five eras of creation

According to the Taíno people of the Caribbean island of Hispaniola, the creation of the universe spanned five eras. Each era reflects a stage in the Taíno people's history. Unusually, the story finishes in the real historical past in 1492CE, with the arrival of European settlers, who bring an end to the Taíno way of life.

In the beginning there was a supreme god called Yaya. When Yaya's son rebelled against his authority, the god killed him. Yaya placed his son's bones inside an enormous gourd and hung it from a hook on the ceiling of his house.

A few days later, Yaya noticed that the bones had turned into fish, which were swimming in some water inside the gourd. Yaya's wife cooked some of the fish from the gourd, and together they enjoyed the meal.

One day, Yaya's enemies visited his home while the god and his wife were away. Seeing the gourd unattended, they looked into it and saw the fish. Yaya's enemies ate them hurriedly, fearing the supreme god's return. When they saw Yaya

Taíno sun

▲ SUN AND MOON
The sun and moon were sacred to the Ancient Taíno, worshipped for their power to transform other beings. The pair would not appear together because if they did so, one might transform the other.

Taíno moon

► GOURD CONTAINER
Many gourds grow in the Caribbean islands. Some have hard skins, which is why they were hollowed out and used as containers for water or food by the Ancient Taíno.

coming back, they tried to hang the gourd back in its place, but it fell on the ground and smashed open, spilling the water all around. The water spread across Earth and formed the Caribbean Sea. This was the end of the First Era of creation.

THE FIRST HUMANS

There were two caves on Hispaniola, an island in the Caribbean Sea. At the beginning of the Second Era, the sun and the moon rose from one of these caves. The first humans emerged from the other cave; they were all men. When they saw fish swimming in the sea, they decided to catch some to feed themselves. Some of the men set out to fish, while the others stayed behind to guard the caves.

The sun watched over these first humans as they carried out their tasks, and punished those who neglected their duties or angered him. When some of the men returned home early from fishing, the sun transformed them into trees. The sun also saw a man taking a break from guarding the caves, and turned him into stone. The next day, one

man tried to go fishing before the sun came out, but the sun spotted him and changed him into a bird that sings at dawn. This was the end of the Second Era of creation.

In the Third Era, women appeared to keep the men company and start families. Soon the island of Hispaniola had a large population, and the people lived well by fishing and growing crops.

AGE OF EXPLORATION

In the Fourth Era, the humans began to explore the land, and even traveled to other islands in the Caribbean Sea. Some people stayed on the newly discovered islands and started new settlements. People learned how to grow the cassava plant for food and to build villages; they also invented their own language.

The Taíno lived happily and in peace until the beginning of the Fifth Era, when European settlers arrived on the Caribbean islands. This was a terrible time for the Taíno, because the Europeans treated them badly

The name "Taíno" means "good" or "noble" in the Taíno language.

► HUMMINGBIRD
Taíno myths describe how the sun has the power to transform any creature. In one story, the sun changes small, buzzing flies into tiny, brightly colored birds, creating the first hummingbirds.

and brought diseases that killed many of the Taíno people. The end of the Fifth Era marked the destruction of Taíno society and their traditional way of life.

> # The sun **watched over the first humans** ... and **punished** those who **neglected their duties**.

TAÍNO FISHERMEN

Fish were the main source of food for the Ancient Taíno people. They built dugout canoes and made nets to fish. They also developed ways of storing their catch, using cages made of cane that they built in rivers.

European color engraving of Taíno cooking fish

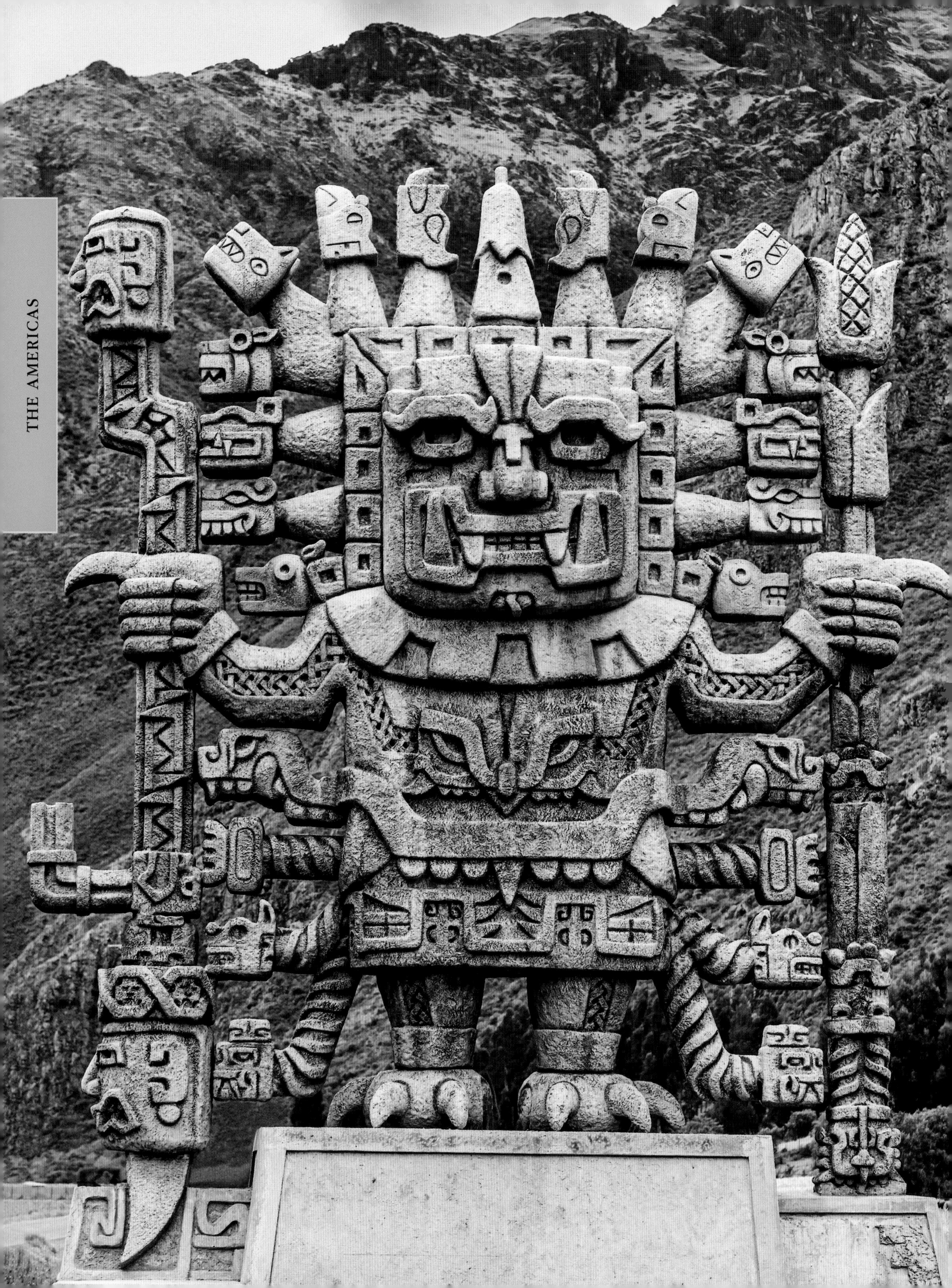

Inca beginnings

Several myths describe the origin of the Incas (a culture from a region of South America now in Peru), but the most famous is a story that involves the creator god Con Tiki Viracocha. In this version, the god hands over his creations to Manco Capac, the first ruler and ancestor of all Inca kings.

The ancient city of Cuzco, where Manco Capac set up his empire, later became the Inca capital.

In the beginning, the supreme god Viracocha emerged from the waters of Lake Titicaca (in modern-day southern Peru) and created the sun, moon, and stars. The god had several children, such as Inti (see p.213), who ruled over the sun; Mama Kilya (see p.212), the goddess of the moon; and Pachamama (see p.212), who became the goddess of Earth, and helped plants to flower and bear fruit. Next, Viracocha created the first creatures, a tribe of giants, who would live on the land surrounding the lake. However, the giants did not have the power of thought. These senseless creatures treated the land poorly and disappointed Viracocha, so he washed them away in a devastating flood.

THE FIRST PEOPLE

After the flood waters had drained away, Viracocha began the process of creation once again. He took some stones, and shaped and breathed life into them to make the first humans. Viracocha placed these beings in a cave with three entrances, and told them to wait inside until the time was right for them to emerge into the world. When that time came, from the first entrance came the first man,

Manco Capac, and his wife Mama Ocllo, together with a number of their relatives. They became the first Inca rulers. Then from the other two entrances of the cave emerged more people: those that would farm the

▲ MANCO CAPAC
The first Inca ruler is often shown with a golden staff bearing the symbol of the sun because, in some versions of the myth, he was sent by the sun god Inti to rule the Incas.

land and those that would serve the royal family. When these first humans established settlements, Viracocha taught them how to live. He gave them a variety of languages and showed them how to grow crops for food. Viracocha then sent them out to establish more towns and villages across the land. When he had taught them all he could, Viracocha vanished into the waters of the ocean.

VIRACOCHA RETURNS

After some time had passed, Viracocha returned to Peru disguised as a beggar to check on his creations. Earth's inhabitants failed to recognize him and ignored his advice. This saddened the god and in the end he left the world.

It is said that one day Viracocha will return and punish humanity for not obeying him. He will engulf them in another great flood, just as he had done with the giants.

◀ CON TIKI VIRACOCHA
Wearing a ceremonial mask, the creator god holds thunderbolts in his hands in this stone sculpture in Cuzco, Peru.

MACHU PICCHU

The mountaintop complex of Machu Picchu is the most famous ruin from the Inca civilization. The complex is believed to have been used as a ceremonial site or royal palace by the Inca rulers. It was built around 1450 CE, and abandoned in c. 1500 after the Spanish invasion.

Inca deities

Some of the most widely worshipped gods and goddesses of the Inca civilization were closely connected to the everyday life of the people. They governed the weather, ensuring there was enough water for crops to grow, and also looked after the farmers and their cattle.

Mama Kilya

- **Also known as:** Mama Quilla
- **Shown with:** Semicircular headdress

The goddess of the moon was called Mama Kilya. She ruled the sky with her brother, the sun god Inti (see opposite). The Incas used the phases of the moon to calculate the days of the month. To the Incas, a lunar eclipse meant that Mama Kilya had been attacked by an enemy, so they would throw weapons at the sky to protect her.

Modern representation of Pachamama

The Incas were the first people to grow the potato, over 7,000 years ago.

Pachamama

- **Also known as:** Paca Mama
- **Shown with:** Potatoes and coca leaves

The earth deity Pachamama was the goddess of mountains and earthquakes. She also looked after the fertility of the soil, and farmers worshipped her while planting their crops in the hope of a good harvest. In recent times, Pachamama has come to be associated with the figure of Mother Nature.

Urcuchillay

- **Also known as:** No known alternative
- **Shown with:** Multicolored fur

The god Urcuchillay protected animals, and his worshippers were mostly cattle herders who hoped that he would look after their livestock. Urcuchillay often took the shape of a llama, so the herders made gold figurines of llamas as offerings to the god. The Incas also worshipped the constellation Lyra, because its arrangement of stars appeared to take the form of a llama.

Inti

- **Also known as:** Apu-punchau
- **Shown with:** Rays of the sun around his head

Inti, the sun god and ruler of the sky, was the most powerful of all Inca gods. He was also called the "leader of the daytime," who not only warmed the land with his rays but was actively involved with the people. In one story, he helped the first Inca ruler, Manco Capac (see p.211), decide where to build Cuzco, the capital city of the Incas. He gave Manco Capac a golden stick and told him to build the city wherever the stick would sink into the ground.

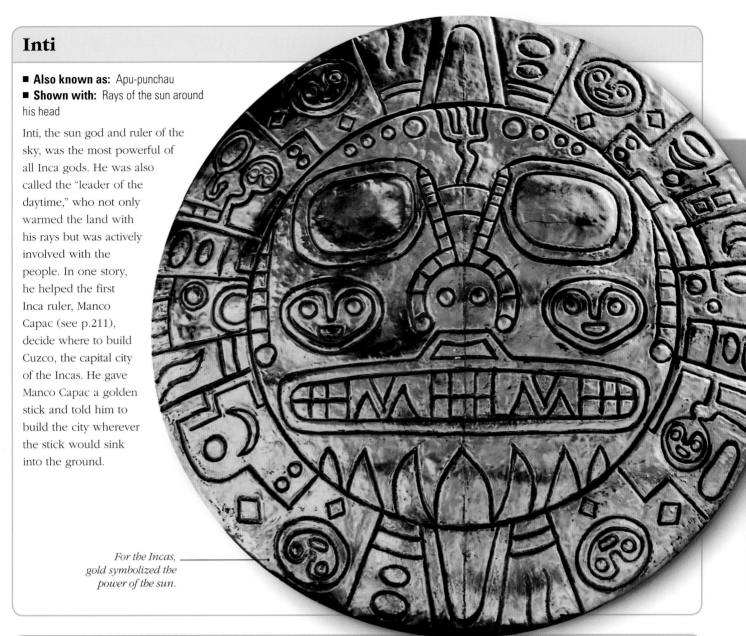

For the Incas, gold symbolized the power of the sun.

Catequil

- **Also known as:** Apocatequil
- **Shown with:** Lightning bolt

The god of stormy weather, Catequil created thunder by striking the clouds with his spear and club. He had great destructive power and could predict future events. These qualities meant that the Incas carried his image into battle for good luck. It was said that Catequil's priest—his representative on Earth—foretold the final defeat of the Incas by the Spanish conquerors in 1572 CE.

Illapu

- **Also known as:** Illapa, Apu Illapu
- **Shown with:** Headdress covering face

The weather god Illapu was worshipped as the bringer of rain. One myth describes how Illapu's sister stored the Milky Way, which the Incas called the "river of the sky," in a jug until its water was needed on Earth. Illapu fired a bolt of lightning from his slingshot and struck the jug, making a loud roar of thunder. As the jug shattered into pieces, water fell to the earth as rain.

The beggar god

Among the Yauyos people of the Andes, Coniraya Viracocha is said to be the creator of the world, but he is best known as a trickster god. He has great powers, although sometimes when he intervenes in human life, things do not turn out as planned.

Coniraya Viracocha often visited Earth disguised in the ragged clothes of a beggar in order to observe his creations. The god wandered from place to place and, one day, saw a woman named Cavillaca. Coniraya wanted to marry her, but when he approached her, Cavillaca did not want anything to do with him because he looked like a beggar. Annoyed at this rejection, Coniraya gave Cavillaca a magical fruit that would make her pregnant, and in time, she gave birth to a baby boy. A year later, Cavillaca invited all the male gods to her home, so that she could find out who the father was. When the child saw Coniraya, he identified the beggar god as his father by climbing onto his lap. Shocked at this revelation, Cavillaca ran away with her son, finding refuge with Pachacamac, the god of fire and rain.

Coniraya was upset at being separated from his son, so he set off in pursuit. Along the way he met various animals and asked them for help. He gave the creatures different qualities according to what they told him: he gave the condor a long life because the bird encouraged the god's search, but made the skunk smell revolting because it said Coniraya would not find his son. Unfortunately, the skunk's words turned out to be true. When Coniraya caught up with Cavillaca, he discovered that both mother and child had been turned to stone.

HUACAS

For the early people of South America, huacas were sacred places where their ancestors were honored in religious ceremonies, often using vessels like the one below. Huacas could be temples, settlements, mountains, or even the mummified remains of important dead people.

Astronomers have named a large crater on the dwarf planet Ceres after the god Coniraya.

▼ RUINS OF PACHACAMAC
The ancient settlement of Pachacamac in Peru was home to people who worshipped the god of the same name.

The Forest Mother

The Warao people of the Orinoco Delta in Venezuela spend much of their lives on the river in dugout canoes. One of their stories describes the invention of the first canoe and its transformation into a figure called the Forest Mother.

Two sisters lived on the banks of the Orinoco River. One of them had a baby whom she named Haburi. When an evil spirit killed the baby's father, the sisters fled their home with Haburi to avoid the same fate. Eventually they entered a forest, where they came across a house. Here lived an old frog-woman named Wauta, who possessed magical powers. Wauta transformed Haburi into an adult. Haburi then cut down a large tree and hollowed out and shaped its trunk to create the first dugout canoe. Haburi, his mother, and his aunt pushed the canoe into the Orinoco River, and paddled until they arrived at the Northern World Mountain, where they decided to settle.

The canoe lay unused until one day it magically changed into a snake-woman. The Warao people who lived here called her Daurani, or the Forest Mother. She made her home on Earth, and became the first shaman of the Warao people. These shamans came to be known as *wishiratu* ("masters of pain") because they used their knowledge of traditional medicine to heal.

▲ **DUGOUT CANOE**
The Warao use the wood of the Cachicamo tree to build dugout canoes. They believe the canoes are copies of Haburi's original one.

The creation of night

Wanadi is the creator deity of the Yekuana people of the upper Orinoco River. They believe that he is in conflict with a demon called Odosha.

Wanadi was the supreme being who wanted only good creations on Earth, but he had a great rival, the foul demon Odosha, who was a force for evil. On one occasion, Wanadi tried to impress Odosha by displaying superior power: his control over life and death. To do this, he created a woman, Kumariawa, then killed her. After she had been buried, Wanadi asked a parrot named Kudewa to guard the grave, because the woman would come back to life and he did not want Odosha to influence his creation. Wanadi also gave his nephew Iarakaru a medicine pouch carrying the darkness of the night, and instructed him to never open it. The god then went off hunting. When Kumariawa began to rise from her grave, jealous Odosha set her on fire, burning her to her bones. The parrot screeched a warning, but Wanadi was too far away to hear it. Odosha also forced Iarakaru to open the medicine pouch, causing darkness to descend on the world. Wanadi was disappointed at his failure to prevent Odosha's actions and returned to the heavens. However, the Yekuana people believe that he will return one day to defeat Odosha.

THE PARROT'S CALL ▶
Orange-winged parrots live in the tropical regions of South America. They have a screamlike call, similar to Kudewa's cry.

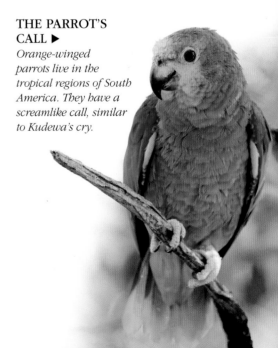

OCEANIA

Spreading across thousands of miles, Australia and the surrounding Pacific islands are rich with sacred stories from a number of different living cultures. Though diverse, these tales have many deities in common, such as nature gods and tricksters. They also share features such as respect for ancestors and heroes, as well as a close connection with the landscape.

This wood carving by Maori artist Cliff Whiting depicts the Maori weather god Tawhiri struggling to control the wind, shown here as blue spirals, during a storm.

Greedy Lumaluma

Lumaluma is the sacred creator and ancestor of the Gunqinggu people of Arnhem Land in northern Australia. He arrives from the sea in the form of a whale, transforms into a human, and becomes a culture hero by teaching the people the sacred rituals that will be central to their lives. However, Lumaluma can also be dangerous: he is greedy and often devours all the people's food.

Lumaluma was originally a whale, but took the form of a man when he came ashore at Arnhem Land. There he met two women whom he befriended. They agreed to marry Lumaluma, and the three of them began a journey inland to the west. As they traveled, Lumaluma taught sacred rituals to the people they met along the way. As some of these rituals had to be performed indoors, he also taught them how to build huts using the leaves and branches of trees. The people of Arnhem Land respected this sacred being for his teachings.

THE HUNGRY HERO

Lumaluma had a whale-sized appetite. Whenever he saw people gathering food such as yams or honey, or hunting for kangaroos, his mouth would begin to water. To satisfy his hunger, he created laws by which any food that he

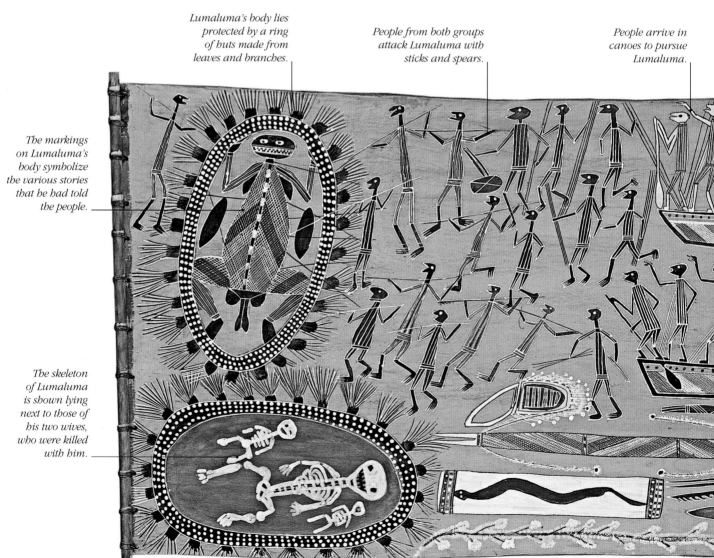

Lumaluma's body lies protected by a ring of huts made from leaves and branches.

People from both groups attack Lumaluma with sticks and spears.

People arrive in canoes to pursue Lumaluma.

The markings on Lumaluma's body symbolize the various stories that he had told the people.

The skeleton of Lumaluma is shown lying next to those of his two wives, who were killed with him.

claimed was "sacred" could not be eaten by anyone but him. The people became hungry and resentful at this abuse of his sacred powers, and so they decided to take action.

Large groups of people chased after Lumaluma, and when they caught him, they wounded him with their spears and sticks. They then propped his body up against a tree and bound it tightly to the trunk. The people gathered leaves and branches to build a ring of huts around Lumaluma's body, because although they were angry with him, they also recognized that he was sacred and that his body had to be treated with respect.

LAST WORDS OF WISDOM

The attacks on Lumaluma continued. When he was close to death, he asked his attackers to stop, so that he could finish teaching them the remaining rituals. Once he had taught them all he knew, Lumaluma asked the people if they had understood everything. The people assured him that they had, and on hearing this, the sacred being died.

The people of Arnhem Land gathered all the objects that Lumaluma had used in the sacred ceremonies: his stone ax, his spear-thrower, and a clapper with which he made sounds to accompany the rituals. They untied Lumaluma's body and carried it to the ocean's edge, where the tide carried it off into the ocean. Once he was out in deep water, the sacred being came back to life and became a whale once more.

ABORIGINAL DREAMTIME

In the sacred stories of the Aboriginal and Torres Strait Islander people, the "Dreamtime", or "Dreaming", was a period when ancestors created many of the land's features and life forms. These are existing beliefs that give meaning for everything in the world. People often carve sacred designs on small stones or pieces of wood to show their connection to the Dreamtime.

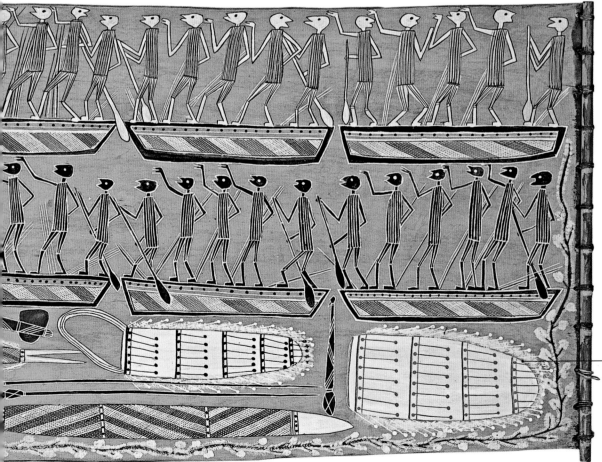

◄ **THE ATTACK**
In this Aboriginal painting by Danny Nalorlman Djorlom, an artist from the Gunqinggu people of Arnhem Land, Lumaluma is attacked by two groups of people. Each group is shown wearing different body paint.

Dilly bags (traditional baskets made of woven pandanus) hold the ritual objects used by Lumaluma and the people.

The Rainbow Serpent

Many Aboriginal peoples from Australia tell stories of the Rainbow Serpent (also known as the Rainbow Snake), a powerful and dangerous creature that can create life as well as cause great destruction. It has a long body and can stretch and curve itself to produce a shape that resembles a rainbow. This creature plays a key role in creating the geography of Australia and helps the first people come into the world.

As the Rainbow Serpent slithered across the land, its weight and the movement of its body carved out valleys in Australia's landscape. The soil that piled up at the sides formed the country's hills and mountains.

The Rainbow Serpent had a great appetite. One day it attacked three birds, swallowing them whole. Once they were inside the snake, the birds decided to try and escape by pecking at the side of the creature's belly. One of the birds managed to make a large enough hole for them to escape and as the three birds pushed

their way out through the snake's skin, they changed shape and became the first humans.

Although it was known mainly for its life-giving ability, the Rainbow Serpent could also be a destructive force. On one occasion, a fisherman noticed some unusual black fish bones that had been left behind after some men had finished eating. He recognized the bones as those of a rare fish that he had been searching for. Angry that such a fish had been eaten, the fisherman cried out to the Rainbow Serpent, who appeared as a great colored arch extending from the sky to Earth. When it saw what had happened to the rare fish, it, too, was furious and caused a great flood to sweep over the land. Eventually the water receded and drained into the holes that the Rainbow Serpent

▲ TAIPAN
The Rainbow Serpent is also called Taipan, a name used for a type of poisonous Australian snake.

had made on the landscape, forming the first rivers and billabongs (lakes) of Australia.

BRIDGE TO THE SKY

The Rainbow Serpent also helped bring knowledge of sacred rituals to the people. It formed a bridge to the sky using its body, allowing some people to travel skyward so that they could learn these rituals from the spirits and ancestors who lived there. The people who made this journey came to be known as shamans. They were regarded with respect by the Aboriginal people, because they had gained not only the knowledge of rituals but also miraculous healing skills and the ability to see into the future.

A DANGEROUS CREATOR ▶
With power over life and death, the Rainbow Serpent is both worshipped and feared for its ability to create and destroy humans.

The **Rainbow Serpent appeared** as a great **colored arch** extending from the **sky to Earth**.

ABORIGINAL ART ▶
Many paintings, such as this work by Keith Kaapa Tjangala, show the Rainbow Serpent slithering over the landscape of Australia as it creates various natural features.

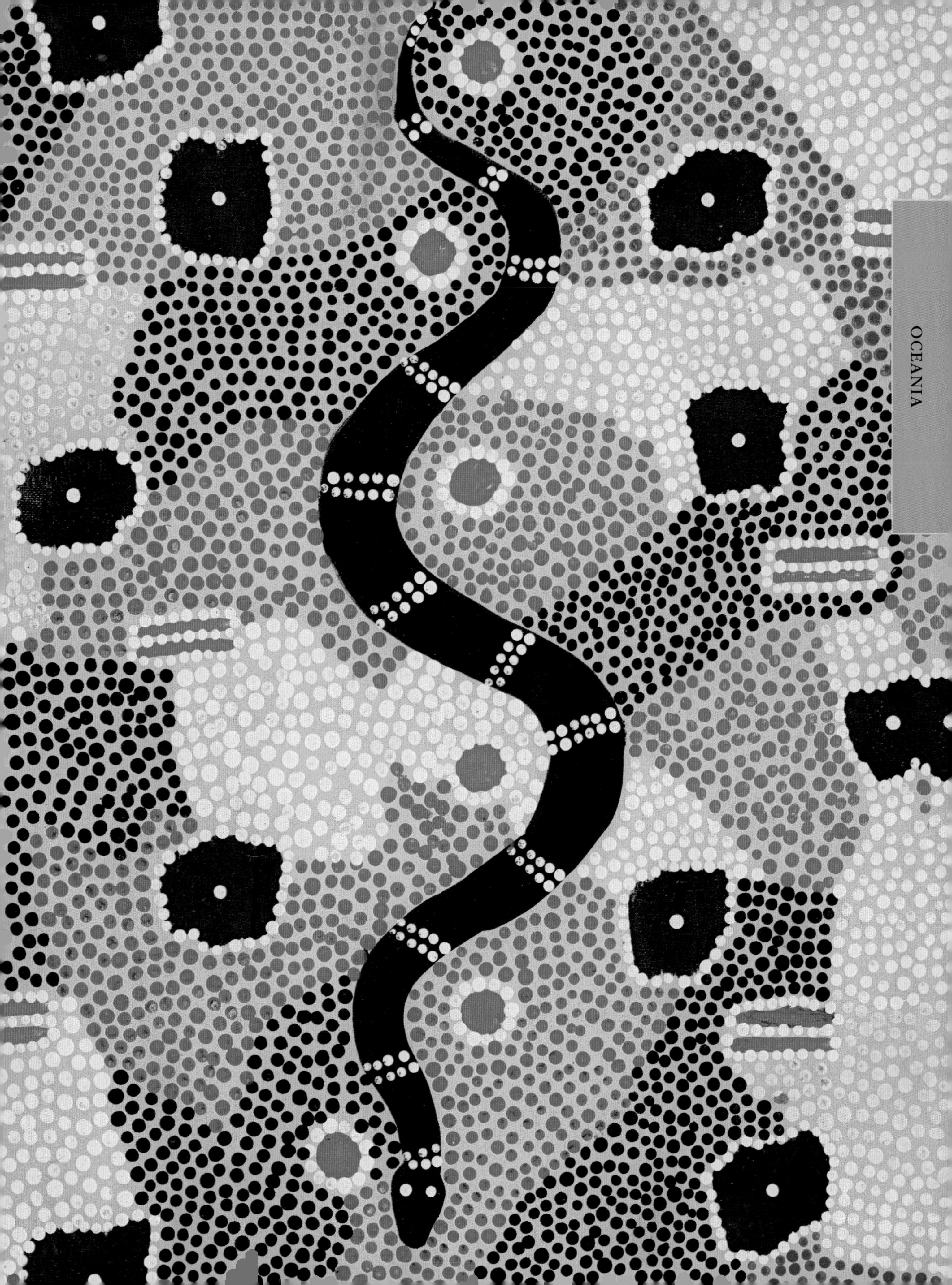

Mythological siblings

Cultures across the world have many myths featuring brothers and sisters. These siblings may be similar in character or represent opposites, such as good and evil. While some siblings bring prosperity by working together, others cause only devastation because they fight each other.

▲ THE HERO TWINS
In Maya mythology, Hunahpu and Xbalanque are twins with special powers who defeat death. They use their love of the Maya ball game to trick the gods of the Underworld.

▲ THE PLEIADES
In Greek mythology, the Titan Atlas and the sea nymph Pleione had seven daughters, collectively known as the Pleiades. They are turned into a group of stars by Zeus. A seven-star cluster in the night sky is known by their name.

Ahura Mazda

A winged beast possibly symbolizing Ahriman

▲ AHURA MAZDA AND AHRIMAN
The creator Ahura Mazda and his evil brother, Ahriman, forever fight each other for power in the myths of Ancient Persia.

▲ LAV AND KUSH
These twin brothers are the sons of Rama and Sita in Hindu mythology. Both went on to become rulers and establish new cities.

Kush

Lav

◀ FREY AND FREYJA
Freyja, the goddess of love, and her brother Frey, the god of prosperity and weather, are leading members of the Vanir, a group of Norse gods associated with fertility.

▲ AMATERASU AND SUSANO-O
Susano-O, the Japanese storm god, often troubles his sister, the sun goddess Amaterasu. After he destroys her crops, Amaterasu hides in a cave, leaving the world in darkness.

CASTOR AND POLLUX ▶
In Greek myth, the stepbrothers Castor and Pollux took part in the hero Jason's quest for the Golden Fleece. In a later adventure, after Castor is fatally wounded, Zeus turns the brothers into the stars of the constellation Gemini.

◀ VALI AND SUGREEVA
In the Hindu epic Ramayana, the ape brothers Vali and Sugreeva fight over the kingdom of Kishkindha. Sugreeva defeats the mighty Vali with Rama's help.

The Wawilak Sisters

The Aboriginal story about the Wawilak (or Wagilak) Sisters is from Arnhem Land in northern Australia. These sisters are sacred beings, who form the land as they walk across it. On their journey, they have a deadly encounter with a creature called Wititj, the Olive Python. The Wawilak tribe consider the sisters to be their ancestors.

There were once two sisters who walked out of the sea in southeast Arnhem Land and began their journey north, carrying their woven pandanus baskets (dilly bags). The elder sister carried a young child, while the younger of the two was expecting a baby. As they walked, the sisters called out names of various land features—hills, valleys, lakes, and rivers—giving them their form as they did so. After some time they stopped beside a water hole to rest, tired from the work of creation. What they did not realize was that they had settled by the home of the sacred Olive Python called Wititj.

The elder sister went to hunt for creatures so they could have a meal, while the younger sister sat down, feeling that her child might soon be born. Sure enough, the young woman gave birth and was cradling her baby in her arms when her elder sister returned. The birth of the baby had disturbed Wititj, alerting the python to the presence of the women and children.

A SURPRISE ATTACK

The women then set about preparing a fire. When they placed their food on the coals of the fire, what happened next took them by surprise. The creatures came back to life,

◀ THE SISTERS
These statues represent the two Wawilak Sisters as they journeyed across the land.

Aboriginal oral stories were first depicted in rock art and later in paintings on tree barks.

jumped out of the heat, and into the sacred water hole. This intrusion into his domain enraged Wititj so much that the python emerged from the water and swallowed the women and children whole.

A TIMELY RESCUE

The sisters' cries and the sounds made by the snake as he swallowed them attracted the attention of all the other snakes. When they asked Wititj what was going on, the python lied and said that he had caught a large kangaroo, which had made a lot of noise as it was being eaten. The other snakes found this hard to believe because the noises they had heard were not those of a kangaroo. When they questioned Wititj further, the Olive Python finally admitted to eating the sisters and their children. The other snakes were so appalled by this that they made strong winds blow and torrential rains fall from the sky. The Olive Python was

This intrusion **enraged Wititj** so much that the python **emerged from the water** and **swallowed the women and children**.

▲ **ANT BITES**
Green weaver ants, common in northern Australia, bite instead of sting, releasing a painful liquid. The Wawilak Sisters and their children are brought back to life by the irritation of ant bites.

tossed around by the winds and rain, and the movement made the snake vomit up the sisters and their children. As they emerged, the women and children fell on an ant nest. The ants bit these intruders furiously for falling on their home, and the pain and irritation caused by the ant bites brought the four back to life.

The massive python wraps his body around the women and their children before swallowing them.

▲ **TRADITIONAL PAINTING**
This bark painting by the artist Samuel Lipundja from the Gupapuyngu people of Arnhem Land depicts the Wawilak Sisters surrounded by a snake. In Aboriginal art from Arnhem Land, reptiles are shown using a style of fine crosshatching.

KUNAPIPI

In some Aboriginal stories, the goddess Kunapipi plays a role in the creation of the world. Believed to be the mother goddess of the Aboriginal tribes of northern Australia, she gives birth to human beings and animals. Tales of Kunapipi creating animals describe her asking galah parrots to paint their feathers with certain colors.

Galah parrot

Maori deities

The gods and goddesses of the Maori people of New Zealand are shared with other Polynesian islands in the Pacific Ocean, though their names (and sometimes roles) vary depending on the region. Many of these gods and goddesses are involved in creation, while others represent forces of nature, survival skills, or crafts.

Rangi and Papa

- **Also known as:** Ranginui, Langi (Rangi); Papatuanuku (Papa)
- **Shown with:** Usually with each other

Rangi, the sky god, was the husband of the goddess Papa, who represented Earth. At the beginning of time, the pair held each other closely, until their son Tane (see opposite), the god of trees and forests, pushed them apart, separating the sky from Earth. After Rangi was parted from his wife, he sobbed so hard that his tears fell from the sky as rain.

In Maori rituals, people carve wooden sticks called *taumata atua* ("god sticks") to call upon the deities.

Tangaroa

- **Also known as:** Kanaloa, Tagaloa
- **Shown with:** Other gods crawling over his body, zigzag stick

On several Polynesian islands, Tangaroa is the primal creator god. He lived inside a great shell, which he forced open, and the two halves made Earth and the sky. Tangaroa created soil with his own flesh, mountains with his bones, and clouds from his internal organs.

Tane

- **Also known as:** Tanemahuta
- **Shown with:** Sometimes with Rangi and Papa

Known as the god of trees and forests, Tane created the first trees, which were humanlike. He thought the branches of the trees were legs and the roots were hair, and planted them upside down. When the trees did not grow, Tane turned them around. The god also produced wood and plant fibers, helping people make things.

Tawhiri

- **Also known as:** Tawhirimatea
- **Shown with:** Rising sun, corkscrew-shaped stick

The god of the weather, Tawhiri was one of the sons of Rangi and Papa. When Tane forced his parents apart, Tawhiri could sense their pain. He fought Tane and his other brothers, bringing many storms that flooded large parts of Earth, creating the oceans.

Rongo and Haumia

- **Also known as:** Rongomaraeroa (Rongo); Haumiaroa (Haumia)
- **Shown with:** Unknown

Rongo was the god of peace and took care of farmed plants, while Haumia was the god of wild food. When their parents Rangi and Papa separated, the rage of their brother Tawhiri forced Rongo and Haumia to hide themselves in their mother's body for protection.

Tu

- **Also known as:** Tumatauenga, Ku
- **Shown with:** Straight staff

The Maori worshipped the god of war, Tu, before a battle. Many baby boys were dedicated to him in traditional ceremonies in the hope that they would become great warriors. The god showed the people how to hunt animals for food using snares, nets, and digging sticks.

Hine-nui-i-te-pō

- **Also known as:** Hinetitama
- **Shown with:** Unknown

Hine-nui-i-te-pō (see p.229) was the daughter of Tane and Hineahuone ("Earth-formed Maiden"). She was known as Hinetitama ("Dawn Maiden") in the living world, but after moving to the Underworld she became the "Ancestress of the Night." She ruled the Underworld and protected the dead after they entered the dark realm.

Maui's feats

The trickster called Maui is a major mythological figure throughout the islands of Polynesia, a large area of the Pacific Ocean stretching from New Zealand to Hawaii. In some myths Maui is a god, while in others he is mortal. While mischief-making features in many of the stories about him, Maui is also a hero, using his skills to improve the lives of humankind.

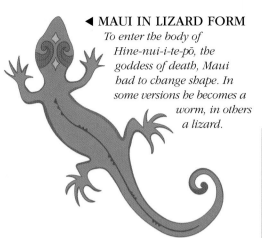

◄ **MAUI IN LIZARD FORM**
To enter the body of Hine-nui-i-te-pō, the goddess of death, Maui had to change shape. In some versions he becomes a worm, in others a lizard.

OCEANIA

Maui was the son of the god Ru and Buataranga, a woman who guarded the path to the Underworld. Although he was quite frail as a baby, Maui grew up to be strong and clever. He would play practical jokes on the other gods and made mischief everywhere he went.

POLYNESIA IS CREATED

Among Maui's first actions was the creation of the Polynesian islands. His mother gave him a magic fishhook, which he took straight to the ocean to try out. Maui put the hook on the end of a line and cast it out far into the water. Soon there was a powerful tug on the line and Maui knew he had caught something enormous. He pulled on the line with all his strength, which slowly raised up a piece of land from under the sea. This land was the first of many Polynesian islands.

Maui is one of the main characters in the 2016 Disney film Moana.

◄ HELPING THE PEOPLE
The sky was only 6½ ft (2 m) above the ground and did not give people enough space to move around. Maui helped the people by lifting the sky with his great power.

RAISING THE SKY

As new islands arose, the people spread out across them. However, the sky was so close to the ground that people were barely able to stand upright. Maui's father Ru had planted wooden poles in the ground to raise the sky a little, but Maui decided to help the people by doing more. He took the form of a giant human and as he stood up to his full height, he pushed the sky far away from Earth.

QUEST FOR IMMORTALITY

Maui's adventures brought him fame, but this was not important to Maui. He wanted to live forever and expressed this wish to his mother. She told him that his only chance of becoming immortal was to kill the goddess of death, Hine-nui-i-te-pō (see p.227), by crushing her heart. Maui's mother also told him that if he was able to do this, he would win immortality not just for himself but for all humankind. Maui sought out the goddess of death and found her sleeping in a garden. He took the form of a lizard and quietly climbed inside the deity. At this some of the birds and animals watching began to laugh loudly,

and the noise woke Hine-nui-i-te-pō up. The goddess immediately realized that there was something crawling around in her body, and so she contracted her muscles, crushing Maui inside her. This was the end of the trickster-hero Maui and it also sealed the fate of every living being in the world, by preventing them from becoming immortal.

FISHHOOKS

The islands of Polynesia depend mainly on fishing for food. The early rituals and practices of these cultures, including the making of fishhooks, reflected the significance of fishing. Hooks were carved from wood, bone, or pearl shell, and their appearance was important, as it showed respect for the fish.

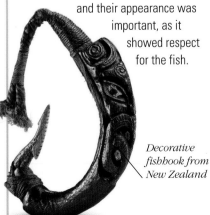

Decorative fishhook from New Zealand

HAWAIIAN PAINTING
This artwork shows Maui raising the Polynesian islands with his mother's magical fishhook. He uses the Hawaiian mud hen, the sacred bird of the Hawaiian goddess Hina, as bait.

Glossary

Afterlife The continued existence of the soul after the death of the body.

Alchemy A mixture of science and magic that involved combining ingredients such as herbs and minerals to try to turn things into gold.

Amulet An object, such as a piece of jewelry or a gemstone, that is said to protect its owner from evil spirits, curses, or illness.

Ancestor A person from whom someone is descended.

Avatar In Hindu mythology, a form taken by a god or goddess to appear on Earth. Some gods and goddesses have many different avatars.

▲ NARASIMHA, THE FOURTH AVATAR OF THE GOD VISHNU

Chaos A vast, disorganized void that existed before the world was created.

Clay tablet A block of clay on which stories and events have been written and depicted.

Cosmic Something that is vast and spreads throughout the cosmos.

Cosmos The ordered universe.

Creation story/myth A story that describes how the world was created by forces, supernatural beings, gods, or goddesses.

Curse A magical spell intended to cause harm to other beings.

Deity *See God/Goddess.*

Demigod/Demigoddess A being that is part god or goddess and part human; one parent is a god or goddess, and the other is human.

Demon/Demoness An evil creature that torments others and causes pain and suffering.

Divine Connected with Heaven, a god, or a goddess.

Dragon A mythical creature that can breathe fire and often guards treasure.

Dwarf A short, humanlike being.

Elixir A magical potion that can cure illness or make someone immortal.

Enchantress A woman who practices magic.

Epic Long poems or stories that describe an event of great historical and cultural significance.

Fate Future events outside a being's control that they cannot avoid. Some gods and goddesses can change the fate of other beings, especially if they feel that it is deserved.

Folk tale A local story passed down from generation to generation, initially by word of mouth.

Fortune A force that determines whether events are good or bad. A being or an object can naturally possess, or be granted or cursed with, good fortune or misfortune.

Funeral games Ancient athletic competitions held in the honor of a person who had recently died.

God/Goddess An immortal, powerful being that is worshipped by others. Creator gods and goddesses created the world.

Heaven A peaceful realm where an afterlife can be experienced. Heaven can have different names, and is usually ruled by a god or goddess.

Hero/Heroine A being who is courageous and triumphs against evil.

Immortal A being that can live forever.

Incarnation The physical form of a god or goddess.

Luck A random force linked to a being or an object that determines whether events are good or bad.

Magic A mysterious, supernatural force. Magic can be naturally possessed by beings or objects, or used to cast spells or curses.

Mortal A being who will die.

Nymph A magical being resembling a woman, usually possessing remarkable beauty. Most nymphs live in natural environments such as rivers, lakes, woodlands, or meadows.

Omen A prophecy or a sign that foretells events, such as a catastrophic flood or a heroic victory.

Oracle A person who can predict the future for those seeking advice.

Origin story A story that describes how people came to be.

Otherworld A world in which magical beings exist.

Patron A being, god, or goddess that protects a particular group of people or a place. A patron may also simply be a supporter of creative arts, crafts, or sciences.

Primal/Primordial The first to be created; the most important.

Prophecy A prediction of the future.

Prophet *See Oracle.*

Purify The act of cleansing oneself of something undesirable.

Quest A long journey or a difficult task, typically carried out for a prize or treasure.

Realm One area or part of the universe. Some myths feature many different realms.

Revenge An act of punishment carried out in return for a wrong or injury.

Revere To admire and respect heroes or rulers, and also worship deities.

▲ PEOPLE CONSULTING THE ORACLE AT DELPHI FOR ADVICE

Ritual A series of actions performed in a certain way to please a god or goddess, or to summon an event such as rain for a plentiful harvest.

Sacred Connected with a god or goddess and worthy of respect.

Sacrifice To kill a person or animal during a ritual, believing that it will please a god or goddess.

Shaman A person who is believed to have magical powers, such as the ability to communicate with spirits, heal wounds, or predict the future.

Shape-shift The ability to change form. Some shape-shifters can change from humanlike forms to animals or other creatures at will.

Shrine A building, object, or place that is considered sacred, and where people may pray to the god or goddess the shrine is associated with.

Sibyl A female prophet or priestess associated with a certain holy site. Some sibyls can also talk to the dead.

Soul The spiritual, nonphysical part of a human or animal. Some

cultures believe that souls continue to exist after the body has died.

Spirit A supernatural being. A nature spirit lives inside natural objects or places, such as a tree or in the ocean. A spirit can also refer to a being's soul.

Supernatural Powers that are beyond what is normal, such as great strength or shape-shifting.

Supreme A god, goddess, or being who holds the highest position of authority. They possess unlimited power.

Talisman Something that is believed to bring good fortune or magical abilities to its owner.

Temple A building where people worship gods or goddesses.

Tragedy A terrible event that causes pain and suffering. Myths or heroes that are associated with tragedy are described as tragic.

Trickster A mischievous being that upsets the gods and goddesses and the normal order of things. Some tricksters may be gods or goddesses themselves.

Underworld The realm to which people go after death. It is also home to evil spirits and demons. It has different names in different cultures, appears in many myths, and is usually ruled by a god or goddess.

Universe All the different realms of the created world make up the universe. *See also Cosmos.*

Void A place where nothing exists. Beings can be banished to the void.

Witch/Wizard A being who has magical powers, which can be used to help or harm others.

Index

Acknowledgments

Dorling Kindersley would like to thank:
Sam Atkinson, Kelsie Besaw, Virien Chopra, Ankona Das, Manan Kapoor, Sukriti Kapoor, and Francesco Piscitelli for editorial assistance; Anthony Wallis of the Aboriginal Artists Agency Ltd, Rona Glynn-McDonald of Common Ground First Nations, and Catherine O'Loughlin for their help on the Oceania chapter; Baibhav Parida for illustrations; Deepak Negi and Nishwan Rasool for picture research; Mohd Rizwan for color work; Harish Aggarwal, Emma Dawson, Priyanka Sharma, and Saloni Singh for the jacket; Helen Peters for indexing; and Caroline Stamps for proofreading

The publisher would like to thank the following for their kind permission to reproduce their photographs:

(Key: a-above; b-below/bottom; c-center; f-far; l-left; r-right; t-top)

1 Meenakshi Madan. 2–3 Bridgeman Images: Private Collection / Christie's Images. **4 Alamy Stock Photo:** Louis Atherton (1); Vincent Lowe (3); geogphotos (6); Granger Historical Picture Archive (7). **Getty Images:** Ann Ronan Pictures / Print Collector (2); Killer Stock Inc / Jim Zuckerman / Corbis (4); DEA / Bardazzi (5); Leemage / Universal Images Group (8). **5 123RF.com:** yukoogurafan (6). **age fotostock:** Steve Vidler (14). **Alamy Stock Photo:** Adam Eastland (9); Roman Nerud (1); Vintage Archives (3); Science History Images (4); Lanmas (7); Universal Art Archive (13). **Bridgeman Images:** Free Library of Philadelphia / Children's Literature Research Collection (2). **Getty Images:** Klaus Lang (10); Photo 12 / Universal Images Group (5); The Print Collector (11). **Nicholas Kinney:** (8). **Perlmutter Gallery:** Artist: Jenness Cortez (12). **Photo Courtesy of Kenji Nagai & Spirit Wrestler Gallery, Vancouver, Canada:** June Northcroft Grant ONZM / Māori -Te Arawa, Tūwharetoa, Tuhourangi-Ngāti Wahiao (16). **The Magic Mo:** Artist: Dietrich Varez (15). **6 akg-images:** Roland and Sabrina Michaud (bl). **Alamy Stock Photo:** Peter Horree (tr). **7 Alamy Stock Photo:** Science History Images (tl). **The Metropolitan Museum of Art, New York:** Rogers Fund, 1928 / Acc No: 28.3.35 (cr). **Museum of Contemporary Art Australia:** Gift of Arnott's Biscuits Ltd, 1993 / Acc No: 1993.27 / Artist: Yirawala / Work: Luma Luma and the sacred power Mardayi / © estate of the artist licensed by Aboriginal

Artists Agency Ltd (bl). **8–9 Getty Images:** DEA / G. Dagli Orti / De Agostini. **10 Alamy Stock Photo:** Lanmas (bl). **11 Alamy Stock Photo:** Science History Images (tl). **12 Alamy Stock Photo:** Zoonar GmbH (bc). **Los Angeles County Museum of Art:** (cl). **13 Alamy Stock Photo:** Interfoto (tr); Adrian Sherratt (tl); Prisma Archivo (b). **14–15 Getty Images:** Mondadori Portfolio. **15 Alamy Stock Photo:** Louis Atherton (br). **16–17 The Walters Art Museum, Baltimore. 17 Alamy Stock Photo:** Hemis (tr). **18 Getty Images:** DEA / G. Cigolini (bl). **18–19 Alamy Stock Photo:** Lebrecht Music & Arts. **19 Bridgeman Images:** Vatican Museums and Galleries, Vatican City (br). **20 Getty Images:** DEA / A. Dagli Orti / De Agostini (bl). **21 Alamy Stock Photo:** Charles Walker Collection (tl). **Bridgeman Images:** Trustees of the Royal Watercolour Society, London, UK (br). **22 Alamy Stock Photo:** Dimitris K. (bl); World History Archive (c). **23 akg-images:** Erich Lessing (br). **Getty Images:** Ann Ronan Pictures / Print Collector (tl). **24 Art Resource, NY:** The New York Public Library. **25 Bridgeman Images:** Private Collection / The Stapleton Collection (cr). **Getty Images:** Greek School (tr). **26 Bridgeman Images:** AISA (t). **27 Bridgeman Images:** De Morgan Collection, courtesy of the De Morgan Foundation (cl); Leeds Museums and Galleries (Leeds Art Gallery) UK (br). **28 Bridgeman Images:** Galleria degli Uffizi, Florence, Tuscany, Italy / Mondadori Portfolio / Electa (c); Philadelphia Museum of Art, Pennsylvania, PA, USA / Gift of Stella Kramrisch, 1987 (bl). **Joe Mabel:** Crow Collection of Asian Art, Dallas, Texas, United States (tl). **Photo Scala, Florence:** The Metropolitan Museum of Art / Art Resource (bc). **28–29 Alamy Stock Photo:** Henry Westheim Photography. **29 Alamy Stock Photo:** Visual Arts Resource (bl); Vincent Lowe (br). **Getty Images:** Hulton Archive (tr). **Photo Courtesy of Kenji Nagai & Spirit Wrestler Gallery, Vancouver, Canada:** June Northcroft Grant ONZM / Māori -Te Arawa, Tūwharetoa, Tuhourangi-Ngāti Wahiao (bc). **Photo Scala, Florence:** bpk, Bildagentur fuer Kunst, Kultur und Geschichte, Berlin (tl). **30 © Marie-Lan Nguyen / Wikimedia Commons:** Louvre Museum, Paris (tl). **31 Alamy Stock Photo:** Angelina Stoykova (tr). **32 Getty Images:** Mustafacan (tc). **33 Bridgeman Images:** Tokyo Fuji Art Museum, Tokyo, Japan (tr). **34 akg-images:** Album / Oronoz (tr). **Getty Images:** Fine Art Images / Heritage Images (bl). **35 Bridgeman Images:** Private Collection / By

courtesy of Julian Hartnoll (b). **36–37 Getty Images:** Fine Art / VCG Wilson / Corbis. **36 Barnes & Noble Booksellers, Inc.:** (bl). **37 Alamy Stock Photo:** Azoor Photo (br). **38 Getty Images:** DEA / Bardazzi (bl). **39 Getty Images:** Ashmolean Museum / Heritage Images (b); Killer Stock Inc / Jim Zuckerman / Corbis (tr). **Photo Scala, Florence:** bpk, Picture Agency for Art, Culture and History, Berlin (tl). **40 Bridgeman Images:** Lebrecht History (bl). **Getty Images:** Fine Art Images / Heritage Images (tr). **41 Bridgeman Images:** Fitzwilliam Museum, University of Cambridge, UK. **42 Getty Images:** Leemage / Universal Images Group (br); The Print Collector (cl). **43 Image © James Gurney, BDSP, 2016. 44 Bridgeman Images:** Musee du Bardo, Tunis, Tunisia (c); National Archaeological Museum, Athens, Greece / Ancient Art and Architecture Collection Ltd (bl). **44–45 Alamy Stock Photo:** Chronicle. **45 Alamy Stock Photo:** Peter Horree (br). **Rijksmuseum, Amsterdam:** (cr). **46 Alamy Stock Photo:** Granger Historical Picture Archive (bl). **47 Alamy Stock Photo:** Lebrecht Music & Arts (bl). **Bridgeman Images:** (t); Musee des Beaux-Arts, Marseille, France (br). **48 Alamy Stock Photo:** Prisma Archivo (bl). **49 Alamy Stock Photo:** www.BibleLandPictures.com (tc). **Bridgeman Images:** Musee Massey, Tarbes, France (b). **50 Bridgeman Images:** Musee de Picardie, Amiens, France (tr). **50–51 Getty Images:** Mladn61. **52 Getty Images:** De Agostini / S. Vannini (cl). **The Metropolitan Museum of Art, New York:** Gift of Mrs. Myron C. Taylor, 1938 / Acc No: 38.5 (tl). **Reprinted with permission of the Second Face Museum of Cultural Masks. © 2017. All rights reserved.:** (bl). **52–53 Bridgeman Images:** The Stapleton Collection. **53 Alamy Stock Photo:** Interfoto (c); Mireille Vautier (tc). **Bridgeman Images:** Museum of Fine Arts, Boston, Massachusetts, USA / Gift of L. Aaron Lebowich (tl). **Getty Images:** DEA / G. Dagli Orti / De Agostini (bl). **Myriam Nader Haitian Art Gallery:** (br). **54–55 Alamy Stock Photo:** Vintage Archives (b). **55 Bridgeman Images:** Isadora (tr). **56 Alamy Stock Photo:** Chronicle (tc); Granger Historical Picture Archive (bl). **57 The Metropolitan Museum of Art, New York:** Fletcher Fund, 1930 / Acc No: 30.11.9 (br). **58–59 Aberdeen City Council (Art Gallery & Museums Collections):** (t). **59 RMN:** Hervé Lewandowski (br). **60 Mondadori Portfolio:** (b). **61 Alamy Stock Photo:** Ian G Dagnall (cr); Granger Historical Picture Archive (tc). **62 Getty**

Images: Alessandro Vasari / Archivio Vasari / Mondadori Portfolio (tl); Werner Forman / Universal Images Group (bc). **63 Bridgeman Images:** Whitworth Art Gallery, The University of Manchester, UK (bl). **Getty Images:** The Print Collector (tr). **64–65 Alamy Stock Photo:** Lebrecht Music & Arts (b). **65 Elisabeth Fillet:** (tr). **66 Alamy Stock Photo:** Visual Arts Resource (bl). **66–67 Jemma Westing**. **67 Alamy Stock Photo:** Chronicle (tr). **68 Alamy Stock Photo:** Ivy Close Images (t). **Getty Images:** Josef F. Stuefer (br). **69 Getty Images:** Fine Art Images / Heritage Images (br). **70 Alamy Stock Photo:** History and Art Collection (tr). **Getty Images:** Marilyna (br). **71 Astound US Inc:** Ashley Stewart (br). **72 Alamy Stock Photo:** Prisma Archivo (tl). **73 Alamy Stock Photo:** AF Fotografie (bl); Janzig / Europe (r). **Getty Images:** De Agostini (tl). **74 Getty Images:** Fine Art Images / Heritage Images (bl). **75 Getty Images:** Fine Art Images / Heritage Images (tr). **76–77 Getty Images:** Fine Art Images / Heritage Images. **77 Getty Images:** ahavelaar (br). **78 Alamy Stock Photo:** Hemis (bc). **Bridgeman Images:** PVDE (c). **79 Bridgeman Images:** Look and Learn. **80 Bridgeman Images:** Look and Learn (cr). **Pagan Studio "Yarinka":** (l). **81 Getty Images:** MNStudio (tr). **Ted Nasmith:** (b). **82 Alamy Stock Photo:** Visual Arts Resource. **83 Alamy Stock Photo:** Radharc Images (tr). **Bridgeman Images:** The Stapleton Collection (bl). **84–85 Enrico Martino:** Artist: Desmond Kinney. **86 123RF.com:** jvdwolf (br). **Getty Images:** Historica Graphica Collection / Heritage Images (tl). **87 Bridgeman Images:** Free Library of Philadelphia / Children's Literature Research Collection (b). **88 Bridgeman Images:** Private Collection (b); © SZ Photo / Scherl (c). **89 AF Fotografie:** (bl). **Roland Smithies / luped.com:** Artist: Roger Garland / Lakeside Gallery (tr). **90 Dorling Kindersley:** Mark Hamblin (cr). **91 Alamy Stock Photo:** Ivy Close Images. **92 Bridgeman Images:** Look and Learn (br); National Museum Wales (tl). **93 Alamy Stock Photo:** Holmes Garden Photos (br). **Getty Images:** Fine Art Images / Heritage Images (t). **94 Alamy Stock Photo:** geogphotos (bl). **95 Alamy Stock Photo:** Beryl Peters Collection (br). **Bridgeman Images:** Private Collection (tl). **96 Bridgeman Images:** Look and Learn. **97 Alamy Stock Photo:** Ian Gunning (tr); LH Images (bl). **98–99 Ксения Бубаня :** (bc). **98 Photo Scala, Florence:** Photo Josse / Musee Guimet, Paris (cl). **Thijs Kinkhorst:** CC-BY2.5 (bl). **Wiener Museum of Decorative Arts:** (ca). **99 Alamy Stock Photo:** Science History Images (bc). **Bridgeman Images:** Museum of Fine Arts, Boston, Massachusetts, USA / Gift of Prof. and Mrs. Otto Oksala, Dr. Sauli Hakkinen, and Mr. Niilo Lehtonen (c). **Getty Images:**

DEA / A. Dagli Orti / De Agostini (tc); Historical Picture Archive / Corbis (br). **100 Getty Images:** Fine Art Images / Heritage Images (bl). **101 Alamy Stock Photo:** Chronicle (bl); Roman Nerud (tr). **102 AF Fotografie:** © DACS 2019. **103 Getty Images:** Fine Art Images / Heritage Images (br). **104 TopFoto.co.uk:** Sputnik (br). **105 Bridgeman Images:** Private Collection (bl). **Анна Виноградова:** (tr). **106–107 Bridgeman Images:** British Library Board. All Rights Reserved. **108 Getty Images:** CM Dixon / Print Collector (tl). **109 Alamy Stock Photo:** Classic Image / Artist: Ernest Charles Wallcousins. **110 Alamy Stock Photo:** Heritage Image Partnership Ltd (bl). **110–111 The Metropolitan Museum of Art, New York:** Dodge Fund, 1933 / Acc No: 33.35.3 (t). **111 RMN:** - Grand Palais (musée du Louvre) / Franck Raux (bl). **112 Alamy Stock Photo:** Lanmas (r). **113 The Trustees of the British Museum:** (tr, tl). **Getty Images:** Nik Wheeler (bl). **114 Getty Images:** DEA / A. Dagli Orti / De Agostini (br); DEA / G. Dagli Orti / De Agostini (l). **115 The Trustees of the British Museum:** (t). **Getty Images:** De Agostini / G. Dagli Orti (br). **116 Alamy Stock Photo:** Interfoto (ca); Gary E Perkin (tl); Joshua Morphies (br). **B.G. Sharma:** (bl). **117 akg-images:** Roland & Sabrina Michaud (br). **Alamy Stock Photo:** Science History Images (tl). **Goran Gecovski:** (cb). **Getty Images:** Werner Forman / Universal Images Group (ca). **Napier Museum:** (tr). **118 akg-images:** Erich Lessing. **119 Getty Images:** DEA / Ara Guler / De Agostini (bl). **120–121 Alamy Stock Photo:** Eric Lafforgue. **120 Bridgeman Images:** Cincinnati Art Museum, Ohio, USA / Museum Purchase from A.V. Pope (bl). **121 Alamy Stock Photo:** Heritage Image Partnership Ltd (bc). **122 Bridgeman Images:** British Library Board. All Rights Reserved (bl). **123 Getty Images:** Leemage (tl); Photo 12 / Universal Images Group (b). **124 National Museum of Mongolia:** (bl). **126 Getty Images:** Historical Picture Archive / Corbis / Artist: Leyendecker (bl). **The Metropolitan Museum of Art, New York:** Rogers Fund, 1930 / Acc No: 30.4.142 (ca); Rogers Fund, 1919 / Acc No: 19.192.81.1, .7, .42, .46, .55 (cb). **Photo Scala, Florence:** The British Library Board (cl). **126–127 Alamy Stock Photo:** North Wind Picture Archives (c). **127 Alamy Stock Photo:** age fotostock (cl); Chronicle (tr); The Picture Art Collection / The San Diego Museum of Art / Edwin Binney 3rd Collection Acc No: 1990.77 (cb); Dinodia Photos (br). **Getty Images:** DEA / G. Dagli Orti/ De Agostini (tl). **128 akg-images:** Pictures from History (br). **Alamy Stock Photo:** John Astor (tl). **129 Bridgeman Images:** Pictures from History (tr). **130 Getty Images:** iStock / Phawat Topaisan (bl). **Mary Evans Picture Library:** Library of Congress (cr). **RMN:** Grand Palais

(MNAAG, Paris) / Thierry Ollivier (tl). **131 akg-images:** Pictures from History. **132 Alamy Stock Photo:** B Christopher (bc). **The Cleveland Museum Of Art:** Severance and Greta Millikin Collection / (CC0 1.0) (cl). **132–133 Alamy Stock Photo:** Louise Batalla Duran. **133 akg-images:** Interfoto (c). **RMN:** Thierry Ollivier (br). **The Walters Art Museum, Baltimore:** (bl). **134 Nicholas Kinney. 135 Getty Images:** Imagemore Co, Ltd (tr). **136–137 Liu Nan:** Artist: Liu Ji You. **136 123RF.com:** yukoogurafan (bl). **137 akg-images:** Fotoe (tr). **Getty Images:** Culture Club (br). **138–139 Bridgeman Images:** Pictures from History / David Henley. **140 Getty Images:** The Print Collector (b). **141 Alamy Stock Photo:** Coward_lion (t). **Los Angeles County Museum of Art:** (br). **142 Alamy Stock Photo:** John Steele (c). **The Trustees of the British Museum:** (tl). **143 Getty Images:** John Stevenson / Asian Art & Archaeology, Inc. / Corbis. **144 Alamy Stock Photo:** imageBROKER (bl). **RMN:** Thierry Ollivier (br). **145 Alamy Stock Photo:** Tibor Bognar (tr). **Bridgeman Images:** Museum of Fine Arts, Boston, Massachusetts, USA / William S. and John T. Spaulding Collection (bl). **146 Bridgeman Images:** Museum of Fine Arts, Boston, Massachusetts, USA / Gift of the Anne Gordon Keidel Trust of June 2016. **147 Alamy Stock Photo:** Sourcenext (tr). **Atomi University:** (br). **148 Alamy Stock Photo:** Charles Walker Collection (bl); Science History Images (cr). **Asadal / (주)아사:** (cb). **Bridgeman Images:** CCI (cl). **The Trustees of the British Museum:** (br). **148–149 Alamy Stock Photo:** Pongphan Ruengchai. **149 Alamy Stock Photo:** History and Art Collection (cr). **Los Angeles County Museum of Art:** Indian Art Special Purpose Fund (M.74.102.4) (cb). **Photo Scala, Florence:** Courtesy of the Ministero Beni e Att. Culturali e del Turismo (bl). **150 akg-images:** Roland and Sabrina Michaud (bl). **151 Alamy Stock Photo:** Dinodia Photos. **152 Bridgeman Images:** The Stapleton Collection (cl). **152–153 The Trustees of the British Museum. 153 Exotic India:** (tr). **154–155 Alamy Stock Photo:** Aaron Alex. **154 Getty Images:** Perspectives / Alex Adam (bl). **155 Alamy Stock Photo:** Edwin Binney 3rd Collection / The San Diego Museum of Art / The Picture Art Collection (cl). **The Trustees of the British Museum:** (tr). **Exotic India:** (br). **156 Alamy Stock Photo:** V&A Images (tr). Exotic India: (bl). **157 Alamy Stock Photo:** Vintage Archives. **158 Alamy Stock Photo:** Indiascapes (b). **159 akg-images:** (tr). **160 Alamy Stock Photo:** Dinodia Photos (bl); MCLA Collection (t). **161 Alamy Stock Photo:** Universal Images Group North America LLC (tr). **Bridgeman Images:** British Library Board. All Rights Reserved (b). **162 akg-images:** Erich Lessing (cr). **Alamy**